The
EVERYTHING
Koran Book

Dear Reader:

When I opened up the Koran to pick a list of subjec.. ior this book, I felt as though I was lost at sea. I'd grown up with the Koran in my school backpack. I'd studied it with as much attention as I'd studied English. So why was I suddenly overwhelmed? I realized that no matter how much I studied this text, I'd always discover new things. Problem was, how to get all that into one book.

Regardless, I jotted down some fifty topics and narrowed them down to what I thought readers would probably like to learn about. I kept the hot topics on my list: Heaven and Hell, the jinn, marriage, terrorism, and so forth. The more I wrote, the more I learned. For each subject, I eagerly flipped back and forth through the pages of the Koran to extract what I needed. By the time I had finished writing this book, I sat back, thinking, *Now where's my Ph.D.?*

The Everything® Koran Book says something about nearly everything in the Koran. I learned a great deal writing it and my hope is that you will learn much from it, too. Now turn the page and indulge.

Sincerely,

Duaa Anwar

The EVERYTHING® Series

Editorial

Publishing Director	Gary M. Krebs
Managing Editor	Kate McBride
Copy Chief	Laura MacLaughlin
Acquisitions Editor	Eric M. Hall
Development Editor	Christina MacDonald
Production Editor	Jamie Wielgus

Production

Production Director	Susan Beale
Production Manager	Michelle Roy Kelly
Series Designers	Daria Perreault
	Colleen Cunningham
	John Paulhus
Cover Design	Paul Beatrice
	Matt LeBlanc
Layout and Graphics	Colleen Cunningham
	Rachael Eiben
	Michelle Roy Kelly
	John Paulhus
	Daria Perreault
	Erin Ring
Series Cover Artist	Barry Littmann
Technical Reviewer	Amanda Roraback

Visit the entire Everything® Series at www.everything.com

THE
EVERYTHING
KORAN
BOOK

Understand the origins and influence
of the Muslim Holy Book
and the teachings of Allah

Duaa Anwar

Adams Media
Avon, Massachusetts

For Mom and Dad; you teach well.

An Everything® Series Book.
Everything® and everything.com® are registered trademarks of F+W Publications, Inc.

Published by Adams Media, an F+W Publications Company
57 Littlefield Street, Avon, MA 02322 U.S.A.
www.adamsmedia.com

ISBN: 1-59337-139-X
Printed in the United States of America.

J I H G F E D C B A

Library of Congress Cataloging-in-Publication Data
Anwar, Duaa.
The everything Koran book / Duaa Anwar.
          p.   cm.
(An everything series book)
ISBN 1-59337-139-X
1. Koran--Theology. 2. Koran--Criticism, interpretation, etc.
3. Islam--Doctrines. I. Title. II. Series: Everything series.
          BP132.A67   2005
     297.1'2261--dc22   2004013265

This book is available at quantity discounts for bulk purchases.
For information, call 1-800-872-5627.

Contents

Acknowledgments

This book, like most others, came together not by the efforts of the author alone, but with the cumulative support, inspiration, and hard work of many people. Although my family was a little concerned about the seriousness of the project at hand, they quickly switched mode and shared their knowledge, digging for facts while I was busy writing—thank you, Mom, Dad, and brother Karim. My ever-constructive critic, little sister Lamia, thank you for your honest opinion. Aunt Salwa and husband, thank you for expertly answering my never-ending questions. I'm especially thankful to W.A.K.—who wishes to remain anonymous—for giving me the confidence to take on this project, and for believing in me.

My eternal thanks to Barb Doyen, my agent, for launching my writing career and putting me in touch with Adams Media. Editors Eric Hall and Christina MacDonald, your patience and dedication have been invaluable.

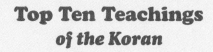

Top Ten Teachings
of the Koran

1. God is one, neither begets nor begotten, and His name is Allah. He is the Supreme Being.

2. The Koran is the literal word of Allah revealed to Prophet Muhammad to be delivered to mankind.

3. Following and trusting Muhammad's Sunnah is mandatory. Together with the Koran, they are the teachings that constitute Islam.

4. Allah Himself protects the Koran from alteration or corruption.

5. The universe and all that live in it are Allah's creation. He is aware of everything that goes on within it.

6. Adam, the first human, was created out of mud, and Eve was created out of Adam. Humans are Allah's vicegerents on Earth.

7. The world will come to an end at a time only Allah knows of. On the Last Day, life will perish, then will be resurrected for judgment.

8. People's deeds (both good and bad) are constantly recorded. These deeds, along with the people's beliefs about God, will count toward reward in Heaven or punishment in Hell.

9. The Koran demands belief in the prophets before Muhammad, such as Abraham, Moses, and Jesus.

10. Initiating hostilities is condemned in the Koran, but defending one's property, family, faith, or land is required.

Introduction

▶ The Koran is one of the three surviving Holy Books, revealed after the Torah and the Gospel. Its message is quite different from the others, calling for belief in the one God, Allah. Believed by Muslims to be entirely the word of God, the Koran was the beginning of Islam more than 1,400 years ago. Today, statistics say that Islam is spreading faster than any other religion across the globe. Yet, as Islam grows, so does a storm of opposing ideas.

Islam started suffering from common misconceptions in the past few decades. Somehow, a web of rumors managed to enclose it. Many Muslims tried tearing the web by spreading awareness about the truth of the Koran, but their efforts proved weak against the tide of accusations against Islam. Islam was thought of as a violent, barbaric, bloodthirsty, backward, and oppressive religion.

False accusations, every Muslim thought. All one has to do to find out about Islam is read its Holy Book, the Koran. The truth is right in it, and, according to Muslims, it's a beautiful, peaceful truth. After examining the Koran, Islam takes on a very different shape from that commonly imagined. That snarling, fiery dragon of Islam turns into an image of peace and tranquility. Interestingly, the Koran knows it is attacked, and knows it contains sufficient proof to defend itself. In it, you'll find a few hundred challenging questions directed at you, such as, "You've seen the perfect orbiting of planets, doesn't that make you wonder?" The Koran utilizes material evidence to defend its divine origin, then presents a system of behavior that is far from violence or hatred.

Some people think that because the Koran is a holy book, it might be long and boring. What's interesting about the Koran is that it jumps from one subject to another so smoothly that you hardly feel the transition, and it holds your interest. Most chapters of the Koran discuss a few dozen topics; yet the words flow from topic to topic, making them all seem like one big woven tapestry. In this book, you will find information on a variety of subjects in the Koran. Although this book is in no way exhaustive of the entire Koran, it has taken the essence of the Koran and put together a guide suited for a curious observer or an intermediate learner.

You will find supportive quotes from the Koran throughout, so having a copy of the Holy Book handy is not necessary, but it may be an advantage for further study. All quotes are taken from Mohammed Pickthall's *The Meaning of the Glorious Quran*. There are several other English translations, so choose whichever you are comfortable with. Pickthall's translation is very literal, while others focus on the implied meanings of the words. Remember that the Koran is originally in Arabic, which is the only accepted version for Muslims to use in worship or when reading or reciting the Koran aloud. For the purpose of understanding the text, however, the English translation can be used.

A few goals of the Koran are to instill morals in society, prevent crime, establish stability, protect the family, maintain equality between men and women, create a conscience, promote knowledge, and, of course, preach Islam. The Koran specifically discusses all these topics. The religion of Islam is taken wholly from the Koran and the teachings of Prophet Muhammad, to whom the book was revealed. Therefore, understanding the Koran is understanding Islam.

Chapter 1

The Koran: Exactly What Is It?

Millions of people take the Koran as a guidebook to life. The ancient text discusses hundreds of topics on all aspects of life, including science, ethics, justice, history, social order, faith, and the afterlife. Along with the teachings of Prophet Muhammad, the Koran provides everything a Muslim needs to know about Islamic faith. It is true that it is ancient, but the Scripture clearly states that it was sent down as a guide for all humankind until the end of time.

An Entire Faith Based on the Book

Islam is a deep and extensive religion. It derives its thoroughness from the Koran, the Holy Book upon which it is based. The Koran contains teachings on everything one needs to know to be a faithful believer of Allah. Since some certain details, like how to perform Islamic prayer, are not thoroughly described in the Holy Book, Prophet Muhammad filled in the gaps according to instructions he received from Allah. In other words, the Koran provided the solid base and general guidelines, while the Prophet preached the specifics.

Dimensions of the Text

Muslims teach that the ancient text of the Koran was revealed about 1,400 years ago to Prophet Muhammad. The original language of the Koran is Arabic. It is the last of all Holy Books, reaching humanity after the Gospel and the Torah. Revelation of the Koran did not happen all at once, but occurred over the course of about twenty-three years.

The Koran is made up of 114 *Surahs* (or Suras)—the Arabic term for Koranic chapter—of varying lengths. A Surah is composed of numbered verses, with the longest Surah containing 286 verses. The Surahs were revealed in parts to the Prophet on certain occasions, and not in the order they are placed in the Koran. Muslims believe that Muhammad completed the final organization of the Koran according to divine instruction. Koranic verses are referenced by Surah and verse, for example 33:36 means Surah 33, verse 36. The verses are referenced like this throughout this book.

A Way of Life

The Koran is the beating heart of Islam. Islam emerged from the Koran . . . without it there would be no Islam. Scholars say that if the Koran were any shorter, Islam would be a frail religion, as people's knowledge of it would be incomplete and there would be holes gaping at scholars. However, as it is, the Koran provides everything Muslims need to know about their religion, defining Islam to an extent that leaves no questions unanswered. Although the Koran is fairly straightforward and logical, because of its extensiveness, it can seem inaccessible for people who don't understand it well.

God gave Himself ninety-nine names, all listed at various places in the Koran. The one primary name for God is Allah. His other names (all in Arabic) are attributes, such as the Most Merciful, the Most Gracious, the Greatest, and the All-Knowing. Muslims may use any of these ninety-nine names when they speak of God.

The Koran talks about an abundance of subjects. Apart from awing readers with its beautiful prose, it also awes scientists with surprisingly accurate information about microbiology, physiology, astronomy, and many other fields. Additionally, it is a book of historic recollections, telling stories about the prophets that came before Muhammad, such as Solomon, Abraham, and Moses.

Another important aspect of the Koran is that much of its text preaches high moral standards, urging people to abide by a strict code of ethics. This is where the Koran is taken as a guidebook to life. For example, the Koran strongly condemns hypocrisy, fraud, and gossip, and encourages good qualities such as modesty, truthfulness, and kindness. Numerous parts of the Holy Book advocate good qualities, while other parts remind violators of the eternal Hell that awaits them.

Above all, though, the Koran's most significant objective is to allow humankind to learn about the Creator. As Allah speaks to humankind through the Koran, He tells them that He is the sole Supreme Being and the one and only Creator. He has no partners or family. He has full control of the universe and all that He created, and He is the only one to be worshipped. This idea is repeated throughout the Koran; for example, Surah 112 reads: "[S]ay He is Allah, the One! Allah, the eternally Besought of all! He begets not nor was he begotten, and there is none comparable unto Him."

The Breadth of Islam

The Koran is one of the most widely read books in the world. Today, there are approximately 1 billion Muslims—a good number of them new converts. Statistics say that Islam is the fastest-spreading religion. The Koran plays the key role in converting non-Muslims to Islam. Yet, sometimes the Koran is not read with a keen interest in Islam, but merely with a curiosity or desire to learn something, or simply for inspiration.

You may have noticed that Islam is concentrated in Arab countries. This is a result of two factors: the first is that the Koran was revealed in Arabic, and the second that it was revealed in Arabia. As Arabs traveled to regions that are now Syria and Jordan, and also to North Africa, the word about Islam spread with them. Eventually, many non-Arab countries embraced the Arabic language and Islam as well.

FACT

You can find the Koran sold in every corner of the globe, translated into most of the world's languages. However, Muslims stress the importance of reading the Koran in its original language, Arabic, believing that translations dilute the message and take away from its natural beauty.

The Relationship Between Koran and Sunnah

According to the Koran, Prophet Muhammad was chosen by Allah to be His messenger to the world. Allah revealed the Koran to him, and also supplied him with additional information to convey to the people. As Islam is derived from the Koran, the smaller details are derived from the teachings of the Prophet. Those teachings are called *Sunnah* (or Sunna). For example, Allah asks Muslims for five prayers a day, but the Prophet used to add more prayers in between the five compulsory ones. Following the Prophet's examples, or Sunnah, leads to great rewards from Allah and allowance for sins to be forgiven on Judgment Day.

Some Sunnah have to do with the way the Prophet carried out his daily life. Others give the Prophet's explanation of Koranic text. These clarifications are found in the *Hadith*—quotes and anecdotes of Muhammad. There are thousands of Hadith that Muslims use to understand the Koran and Allah's instructions thoroughly. A simple example would be as follows: The Koran states in reference to ablution, or ritual cleansing, that a person must wash his arms to the elbows, and his face, head, and feet. Prophet Muhammad complements the Koran by teaching his followers exactly how to wash, what other body parts to include, and the number of repetitions.

It is important to emphasize that the Prophet's Sunnah and Hadith are believed to be of divine source, like the Koran itself. Any other rituals of worship innovated by people that are not in accordance with the Koran or the Sunnah are variations of the original Islamic teachings. The Koran comments on this as follows: "It is not fitting for a Believer, man or woman, when a matter has been decided by Allah and His Messenger to have any option about their decision: if any one disobeys Allah and His Messenger, he is indeed on a clearly wrong path" (33:36).

From a general perspective, the Koran and the Sunnah are the two sources of Islam. The Koran comes first, then the Sunnah complements it, explaining and clarifying what is difficult for the people to understand. Prophet Muhammad provided guidance through his Hadith and gave the people an example to follow. Muslims consider him the role model for Islam, and his teachings cannot be separated from the teachings of the Koran.

ALERT!

According to Islamic teachings, ablution is a standard requirement before most acts of worship. The Koran and the Sunnah teach that the hands, mouth, nostrils, arms, face, head, ears, and feet must be washed or wiped with clean water in that particular order to qualify as proper ablution.

The Role of the Sunnah

When scholars debate over a certain Islamic topic, they use quotes from the Koran and Sunnah to support their arguments. If a supporting statement they want is not available in the Koran, they quote a Hadith. The Hadith are integral for the survival of Islam. There are a few thousand of them that are available to answer common questions and interpret many verses in the Koran. They address specific Islamic situations or problems and propose solutions.

Traditions of the Prophet

The Koran asks people to observe, learn, and follow the traditions of Prophet Muhammad. Such traditions include how he prayed, ate, slept, walked, spoke, worshipped, and generally went about his life. Muslims learn about these traditions from the Hadith, which give the Prophet's quotes and anecdotes as well as eyewitness accounts by his companions.

Because the Koran urges the true believer to live as the Prophet lived, many Muslims try to emulate him as much as possible. The Koran says that Prophet Muhammad is guided onto the right path, so Muslims believe it is in their best interest to follow the Prophet. Adding extra prayers between the main prayers is an example of a tradition learned from Muhammad and replicated by millions of Muslims.

The Sunnah refers to the entire package of traditions, anecdotes, quotes, and Hadith left by Prophet Muhammad. A Hadith is part of the Sunnah, but specifically a quote from the Prophet.

The Hadith

A Hadith is almost always a quote of Prophet Muhammad from someone who was present with the Prophet at the moment he said it. Usually, a Hadith is preceded by the name of the person who transmitted the information, such as, "According to Aisha, Prophet Muhammad said so and so." There are thousands of Hadith that are referenced this way.

The Hadith is the word of Muhammad, not Allah. The Hadith were not preserved as well as the Koran, and scholars say that a few Hadith underwent slight distortion as they were transmitted from reference to reference. Therefore, Hadith have three classifications: authenticated Hadith, valid Hadith, and weak Hadith. An authenticated Hadith is a real and accurate quote of Muhammad. A valid Hadith is less established and its integrity suffers from a minor degree of doubt. A weak Hadith is just what the name implies—the Prophet may or may not have said it.

The Qudsi Hadith

A Qudsi Hadith, also known as Hadith Qudsi (holy), is very different from the ordinary Hadith. A Qudsi Hadith is Allah's words narrated through the Prophet; for example, Prophet Muhammad said, "On Judgment Day, Allah will speak to the people of heaven, telling them . . ." A Qudsi Hadith quotes Allah Himself, but in a manner and style different from the Koran.

There are, however, some scholars who doubt that such a Hadith is entirely the word of Allah. Qudsi Hadith can be used for reference, but they are not considered equal to the Koran. For one thing, a Muslim cannot recite a Qudsi Hadith in prayer, even though it is the word of Allah. The Koran does not mention the Hadith, but Muslims are delighted to have them as an additional source of information about their faith. In the years following the Prophet's death, scholars collected both Qudsi and normal Hadith and preserved them in books that are still in print to this day. Examples of these books are *Sahih Al Bukhari* and *Sahih Muslim*, among many others, all readily available in Islamic book sections.

ALERT!

When Muslims say or hear Prophet Muhammad's name, they always follow it with (in Arabic) "Peace and blessings be upon him." When the name of one of his close friends is mentioned, they follow it with "May Allah be pleased with him." Muslims also follow the name of Allah with "the Supreme, the Almighty."

Straight from the Heavens

Muslims believe Prophet Muhammad was the last of the prophets, as the Koran clearly states. Prophet Muhammad didn't know he was a messenger of Allah until his unexpected encounter with Angel Gabriel. Muhammad was in his forties at the time of the encounter, which marked the first revelation of the Koran.

According to the Koran, Allah gave direct instructions to Angel Gabriel, assigning him as the carrier of the words sent down to Prophet Muhammad. Angel Gabriel flew down from the Heavens to Muhammad on various occasions, delivering divine instructions that shaped the Sunnah, and divine words composing the Holy Book. Muslims completely believe that the words that make up the Koran were bestowed upon Muhammad and that they are the actual, literal spoken words of Allah.

Yet, what was revealed that first night was merely a flash—nothing more than a few words. The remainder of the Koran was revealed to Muhammad over the following twenty-three years. Before his death, Prophet Muhammad presented his people with the complete text in the same form that it is in today. (More on this story is found in Chapters 2 and 3.)

The Language of the Koran

The Koran is a sacred, protected text. Every true Muslim can quote from it. Memorizing parts of it is an honored tradition among all Muslims. However, memorization only counts when it is in original form: Arabic. Translations of the Holy Book are to help non-Arabs understand the text, but they in no way reveal the power of the original Arabic Koran.

The Koran can be read in English or in any other language for the purpose of studying or understanding it, but when a recital is required, such as in a prayer, it is only acceptable to Allah in the original form. Recitals must also be impeccable.

QUESTION?

How many letters are there in the Arabic alphabet?
Arabic contains twenty-seven letters, whereas English contains twenty-six. However, many Arabic letters have no close correspondent in English and vice versa. Non-Arabs find pronunciation of some Arabic letters very challenging, while Arabs find it fairly easy to pronounce English letters.

Translations and Interpretations

When Allah spoke the words of the Koran to Angel Gabriel, He spoke in Arabic. When Angel Gabriel flew down to Prophet Muhammad, he bestowed the words of the Koran exactly as Allah spoke them. Muhammad diligently memorized them, then had them recorded in writing. Through faithful preservation, what we have today in the Koran is believed by Muslims to be Allah's words exactly as they were revealed to the Prophet.

It is a common sight to see Muslims moved to tears as they read the Koran, whether on pilgrimage in Mecca at the Kaaba, or sitting in their own home. Often, the awareness that what is being read is the Creator's actual words gives a Muslim the chills. The might and mercy of Allah are crystal clear in the Koran, sometimes leading a believer to feel very insignificant in the scheme of the universe.

Formal Arabic differs from the Arabic dialect spoken in Arab countries. Every region has a dialect of its own, but people of all regions understand each other well. Formal Arabic is used in all publications, speeches, TV and radio, and all situations in which a degree of formality is required.

To truly capture these emotions, the Koran needs to be read in its original form. As previously mentioned, translations of the Koran only translate the meaning, not the actual words. Not only do translations of the Koran lose their power as the literal words of Allah, but because Arabic is an immensely rich language that cannot be translated word for word to any other language, translations of the Koran lose much of the intensity and radiance of the original Arabic.

Arabic is a language that has not changed since the time of Muhammad. English, for instance, has changed dramatically. If you look at the language in early medieval England and compare it to modern English, you will see that it has evolved dramatically; Old English, as it is termed, is impossible to understand without considerable study of the language. Arabic underwent no such evolutionary process; formal Arabic, like that of the Koran, is a standard subject taught in Arab schools to this day.

The Meaning of "We"

Due to the complexity of Arabic vocabulary, translators often end up choosing the closest counterpart in the language of translation. When literary compromises are made in the course of translation, sometimes the text strays off the intended meaning, or causes confusion. The Koran wisely addresses this issue: "And verily We have displayed for mankind in this Koran all manner of similitudes, but man is more than anything contentious" (18:54).

A common issue of debate, and one that can be pointed out in the previous verse, is the use of the pronoun *we* in the Koran. In the Arabic language, the pronoun *we* is commonly used to signify respect. A person may speak about himself in this plural form when he is a figure of authority, saying, for example, "We have decided to accept this proposal," even if he is really referring only to himself and not to a group. This use of the pronoun is rare in English but is sometimes used among royalty when they speak of themselves.

Since Allah is the Creator and the greatest authority, He refers to Himself as "We" in the Koran for the purposes of respect and glorification. Confusion arises when someone reading an English translation understands the pronoun as reference to a group. The Koran leaves no doubts in this matter: "Your God is one God, there is no God but Him, the Beneficent, the Merciful" (2:163).

Reading and Memorizing

The Koran and the Sunnah set rules Muslims must follow when attempting to read the Koran. Before even touching the Holy Book, the body must be cleansed through ablution. Allah specifies this in the Koran: "That (this) is indeed a noble Koran. In a book kept hidden. Which none touches but the purified. A revelation from the Lord of the Worlds" (56:77–80).

Scholars add that the mind must be clear and ready for the task, not lingering on other thoughts or distracted by other matters. The reader should be decently dressed, too—breezy summer wear is not appropriate! The objective is to treat and approach the Koran with utmost respect.

When reading the Koran it is also important to take a reasonably respectful posture. According to Islam, sitting at your desk, in an armchair, or on a ground cushion with your legs crossed are all acceptable positions, but leaning back in your seat and throwing your legs over your desk is not!

Muslims regularly pick up and read the Koran, even if they have already read it many times before. They say that the Koran, especially in the original Arabic, brings peace and tranquility to the mind and soul, and Muslims often read it for that purpose. Moreover, no matter how many times it is read, there is always a new discovery or enlightenment, or a lesson learned. Muslims take it as a guide for life that takes the effort out of deciding where one belongs, and why one exists. They believe it sets down a path to be followed.

Reading is one thing, however, and memorizing is another. The Koran's rich dynamic prose makes memorization a daunting task, even for the fluent Arabic speaker. All memorization is done in Arabic, and there is never room for mistakes when reciting—every word must be correctly pronounced, no word may be omitted, no letter forgotten. Memorizing the entire Holy Book is quite an achievement! Despite that, you will find thousands of Muslims who have memorized all 600 pages of the Koran and can recite any verse almost at the press of a button.

Chapter 2

The Messenger: Prophet Muhammad

Prophet Muhammad lived forty years as an ordinary citizen, followed by twenty-three years as a messenger of Allah. His life both before and after the first revelation is compelling; the man was well known in his tribe and possessed many qualities rare to the people of that period. He traveled the lands of Arabia, flew up to the Heavens and back, fought in battles, and still managed to preach and to become a living, breathing example of the Koran.

Prophet Muhammad Before the Revelation

Muhammad was born in A.D. 526 in a tribe called Quraish. After he was orphaned, he was raised by a kind and loving grandfather named Abdul Muttalib, then by his uncle, Abu Talib, after his grandfather's death. The Quraish tribe lived in Mecca (pronounced Makka), which is now a major city in Saudi Arabia. The tribe was chaotic, unruly, rash, vulgar, hostile, yet very eloquent and poetic. They provided a rough environment for the messenger of Allah, but many of its people were in desperate need of guidance.

QUESTION?

What is the Kaaba?
The Kaaba was built by Prophet Abraham and his son, Prophet Ishmael, 2,000 years before Muhammad was born. Abraham was ordered by Allah to build the cube-shaped structure as a house of Allah and a place for worship. It is said that Allah's throne in the Heavens is directly aligned with the Kaaba on Earth. The Kaaba is located inside the Sacred Mosque (Masjid Al Haram) in Mecca.

Society and Culture of the Era

By the time Muhammad was born, it had been centuries since Jesus lived, and the people of Arabia had again turned away from God and His Scriptures. The majority of them had reverted to idolatry, the worship of physical objects as gods, building their stone idols around the Kaaba. While they regarded these stones as gods, a small minority known as the Hunafa (seekers of the truth) was repulsed by this behavior. Although the Hunafa did not condone the worship of stone statues, they knew no other faith to believe in. They had heard of Abraham and his preaching, but that had been such a long time in the past that his teachings had been lost.

There was a general lack of rules at the time. Slavery was at its peak, women were oppressed, babies buried alive, among other barbaric patterns of behavior. Vengeance was a common thing—if one person was murdered in a family or clan, that family would seek the killers and murder them and/or their families. Gambling and alcoholism were widespread.

Yet despite their disorder, the people of Quraish were generous and hospitable. They accommodated guests and travelers with great care and mercy. Their comprehensive knowledge of Arabic served them well as poets and writers. The tribe was well respected in Arabia.

The Birth of the Last Prophet

Muhammad's father died while Amina, his wife, was pregnant with Muhammad. Amina had an idea her child would be special. Her pregnancy was a peaceful and comfortable one, during which she experienced many visions concerning her unborn child. On one occasion, she heard a voice telling her, "You are carrying in your womb the master of this nation. When he is born say, 'I place him under the protection of the One from the evil of every envier.' Call him Muhammad."

The birth happened at nighttime with the help of a midwife. It is said that a sweet scent of musk emanated from a birthmark on the infant's back between his shoulders. He was named Muhammad, a name never previously used. The infant was cradled with delight by his grandfather, Abdul Muttalib. The news of the birth traveled fast due to Abdul Muttalib's high status in the tribe.

Muhammad's lineage goes back 3,500 years to the time of Prophet Abraham. He is a descendant of Prophet Ishmael, Abraham's son. Just as Abraham preached for one God, his family and descendants carried forth his message all the way down to Abdul Muttalib, who always believed in the one God, Allah.

Soon, however, Amina and Abdul Muttalib decided to find a foster mother for the baby in order to have him raised in the desert. It was common for families to send their children to Bedouin foster parents for many reasons, such as to teach them Arabic in the purest form (for which the Bedouins were well known), and to protect them from diseases that sometimes were prevalent in the cities. Muhammad was then given to Halima, a poor Bedouin mother who traveled with her husband, and who lovingly nurtured the boy until he reached the age of six.

Muhammad returned to Mecca to live with his mother, but it wasn't long before she was stricken with an illness that took her life. The grieving grandfather gave the little boy a loving home, raising him with more devotion and care than he did his own children. However, Abdul Muttalib was already in his eighties, and passed away when Muhammad was ten. Muhammad's uncle, Abu Talib, then became his guardian.

The Early Years

As Muhammad reached his teens, he learned the arts of self-defense and archery, as well as skills of trade. Trade was common practice and a steady source of income. Muhammad accompanied his uncle's trade caravan trips to the north, and soon the word about his honesty and dependability in carrying out business transactions reached far, making him a frequently sought-after agent for conducting trade affairs.

One person who heard of the young man people trusted so fervently was a wealthy widow named Khadija. She held high status in the tribe and regularly dispatched trade caravans to different regions of Arabia. Muhammad's reputation dazzled her, and she requested that he take her caravans on a trading journey, promising to double his fees. She was duly impressed when he returned with higher profits than usual.

Eventually, Muhammad's fondness for Khadija grew and they married. He was twenty-five, and she was nearing forty but still held a great deal of beauty. The age difference apparently proved irrelevant, as the couple shared twenty-six years of marriage. Even though their wealth increased, Muhammad maintained a humble lifestyle, choosing to distribute portions of his income to the needy.

FACT

Prophet Muhammad married twelve times, mostly for humane purposes, such as offering physical and financial security to women who needed it. He always admired and respected each wife, never once mistreating them. Likewise, his wives loved him.

The successful marriage elevated Muhammad to an important and trusted figure in Mecca. Together, Muhammad and Khadija had six children—two boys who sadly died very young, and four cherished girls, Fatima, Ruqaiya, Umm Kulthoom, and Zainab. The couple was extremely devoted to each other, offering unlimited support to each other as living conditions deteriorated during Muhammad's preaching in Mecca. Khadija was the first convert to Islam after the revelation of prophecy to Muhammad. When she died in A.D. 576, her death left him distraught, and although he remarried later on, he always talked of Khadija with the greatest love and respect.

Angel Gabriel Reveals Himself

Muhammad was never among those who worshipped the stone idols. He followed his grandfather's example, believing that the real Creator must be out there somewhere. He spent time in nature and frequently meditated. When revelation came to him, he reacted as any human would: with fear and confusion. The encounter with an apparition not from our world left him shaken, but the Prophet soon got back on his feet, recognizing the mission that had been divinely assigned to him.

The Cave Refuge

In the far outskirts of Mecca stands a mountain called Mount Hira. In his attempts to escape the corruption of Quraish, Muhammad often retreated to one of Mount Hira's caves. He was appalled at his tribe's religious rituals. The stone idols were scattered in and around the Kaaba, which was supposed to be the house of the Creator alone. Unable to endure such contempt, he sought the peace and tranquility of the cave to think and wonder about the Creator.

FACT

Muhammad made it a custom to retreat to the cave at Mount Hira, particularly during the month of Ramadan. He spent hours meditating—his chosen way of worshipping the Creator. His retreats would last so long that he sometimes carried food to keep him from starving. Khadija supported her husband, sending him extra supplies when she suspected that his provisions had run out.

A Light from the Heavens

On the twenty-seventh day of Ramadan in the year that he turned forty, Muhammad sat meditating in the cave of Mount Hira. Night had fallen and he sat consumed in his thoughts, when he heard a voice that shook him to the core. The apparition that appeared took his breath away with its size and brightness that filled the sky. When it spoke, it said to him, "Read!"

Muhammad was eloquent, having been educated in spoken language and poetry in his younger years, but he never learned to read or write. Anxiously but respectfully, he answered, "I cannot read." Again, the apparition ordered him to read. Muhammad's answer was the same. Then the apparition said, "Read: In the name of your Lord who created; created man from a clot. Read: And your Lord is the Most Bounteous; Who taught by the pen; taught man that which he knew not" (96:1–5).

The words found their way directly to Muhammad's mind and heart. The apparition departed, and Muhammad set off down the mountainside in haste. Khadija, who was climbing up with fresh provisions, met him halfway. He ran to her, frantically calling out, "Cover me! Cover me!" And he told her what he had just experienced.

His First Night as Prophet

Muhammad feared that the apparition he saw was an evil spirit or *jinn*. Khadija managed to calm him down and took him to a relative of hers who was well versed with the Jewish and Christian Scriptures. The man, named Waraqah, had lost his sight with advancing age, but his memory and studies of the ancient Scriptures were clear.

Muhammad and Khadija consulted Waraqah, asking his expert opinion on the encounter. Enthusiastically, Waraqah replied that the time had come for the last prophet of Allah to be sent to the people. He reminded them that all previous prophets, including Adam, Noah, Moses, Abraham, Joseph, and Jesus, were visited by the same apparition that had visited Muhammad that night. Waraqah told them that the apparition was the angel of highest stature in the Heavens, Angel Gabriel.

To further explain himself to the confused couple, Waraqah quoted verses from the Gospel and Torah that indicate there will be a prophet to come who will restore order and guide the people once again to Allah. Waraqah told Muhammad he must be that prophet. Dazed by the ordeal, Muhammad and Khadija returned home. By then, Muhammad's faith and belief in Allah had solidified and he embraced his duty as His messenger.

Islamic records state that Angel Gabriel visited Prophet Adam 12 times, Prophet Noah 50 times, Prophet Moses 400 times, Prophet Jesus 10 times, and Prophet Muhammad at least 23,000 times. It was during these visits to Muhammad that he delivered the 6,236 verses of the Koran.

Clashes Against the Prophet

For the first three years after he was visited by Angel Gabriel, Muhammad limited his preaching to his close family and friends. Apart from his wife, only a few cousins and friends converted to Islam. Muhammad was afraid of Quraish's reaction if they heard of his preaching; they were hostile and unpredictable. To avoid bringing trouble upon himself and his followers, he conducted his prayers and preaching in secrecy.

Allah, however, intended for Muhammad to preach to the whole world. But Muhammad still feared the people of Quraish, so Allah sent to him the following verses: "[S]o proclaim that which you are commanded, and withdraw from the idolaters. Lo! We are Sufficient for you against the scoffers, who set some other god along with Allah. But they will come to know. Well know We that your bosom is at time oppressed by what they say" (15:94–97).

Encouraged by Allah's assurance, Muhammad slowly but surely made his message public. He began by preaching to his extended family. Eventually, he worked up the courage to face the tribe of Quraish. One day, he stood on a hill and called upon them. When they gathered, he told them about Allah, but didn't get far, as they quickly turned their backs and walked away, mocking and ridiculing him. Although

Muhammad was highly respected and renowned for his truthfulness, when it came to his preaching, Quraish rejected him.

Hostility Toward Muslims

Eventually, however, some of the tribe's members listened to Muhammad. As more people converted to Islam, the concern of the Quraish leaders grew, and hostility toward new converts increased. The large and mighty tribesmen seized the new converts, particularly weaker ones, like slaves, and locked them into torture chambers. Their creative methods of torture included suffocating converts by placing massive rocks on their chests, abandoning them on the scorching desert sand, forcing them to lie flat on hot coals, and severely beating them. Yet none of the converts surrendered the belief in Allah.

Hostility was not limited to new converts, but extended to include the Prophet himself. Although they would have loved to kill him, the Quraish leaders couldn't simply do it because they were afraid it would cause feuds, which were common at the time. Therefore, Muhammad's enemies reverted to mockery and verbal abuse. His enemies' aggression was never fruitful, however, as divine intervention always protected the Prophet.

FACT

Mecca and Medina are the two holy cities of Islam, located in Saudi Arabia. The original name of Medina, Yathrib, was changed after Prophet Muhammad migrated there. The word *medina* means city; the city's name refers to it being the "City of Muhammad."

One interesting account tells of what happened near the Kaaba as Muhammad was consumed in prayer. A hateful enemy of Islam with the nickname Abu Jahl (meaning Father of Ignorance) schemed to knock the Prophet dead with a massive rock. Abu Jahl staggered toward the praying Prophet before the anticipating eyes of the tribe, lifted the rock, and was prepared to strike when suddenly his eyes widened with fear; he dropped the rock and ran away, terrified. Abu Jahl later told the crowd that he had seen an enormous creature with a huge head and a terrifying set of teeth glowering at him, ready to shred him if he thought to proceed. Later, Prophet Muhammad told his companions that the creature Abu Jahl had seen was Angel Gabriel in disguise.

The Hijrah (Migration)

When conditions became too difficult to tolerate, Muhammad advised the Muslims of Quraish to migrate to Medina (a city in Saudi Arabia that still exists today). When the rest of Quraish heard of the migration, they became outraged that Islam would now spread to farther regions, and all their efforts in seizing and restraining the spread of Islam would have been in vain.

The tribe gathered to discuss this critical issue. They decided that they would put an end to it once and for all by killing Muhammad. Because they feared the vengeance of his family, they selected random men who would all strike simultaneously and kill the Prophet, so that the blame would fall on the entire tribe rather than on a single individual. That way, they could protect their families from feuds.

The tribe plotted to hide in the bushes around Muhammad's house, and strike him when he left at dawn for prayer. That night, Allah sent Angel Gabriel down to warn Muhammad of the danger and to grant him permission to migrate to Medina. Muhammad's cousin, Ali, offered to help by wearing the Prophet's cloak and sleeping in his bed. If one of the enemies came to check, he would think the Prophet was still sleeping soundly.

Muhammad walked out of his house before the eyes of the enemies, but not one person saw him. He picked up a handful of sand and cast it upon them, and they fell asleep one after the other. Muhammad made his way to the house of his loyal friend, Abu Bakr, and they set out on their way to Medina. When morning came, the enemies awoke to discover that the Prophet had slipped through their fingers; the Koran comments, "We have set a barrier before them and a barrier behind them, and thus have covered them so that they see not" (36:9).

The Islamic calendar was established from the year of the Hijrah (or Hegira). Before that, the Arabs had been aware of passing months but had not been counting years. The Hijrah took place on the year A.D. 579. Based on this starting date, the year A.D. 2000 corresponds with the year 1421 in the Islamic calendar.

Life in Medina

The numbers of Muslims increased greatly in Medina, but the original dwellers of the city were Jews. Before similar conflicts to those in Mecca could arise between the two groups, they decided to draw up a treaty to protect the rights of everyone. This settled disputes, but resentment still sizzled under the surface. Nevertheless, Muhammad quickly gained public support and became a trusted and respected leader.

As Islam flourished in Medina, the Prophet's mosque was constructed. Muhammad, already married to his second wife, Sawda, married his third wife, Aisha, who was yet at a tender age. (Khadijah had passed away three years before the Hijrah.) Although the situation appeared stable, threats of hostility from Mecca disturbed the Prophet. It appeared that the people of Quraish were still bitter about the escape of Muslims from Mecca, and that they were determined to fight them.

Wars and Battles

With the passage of time, the air between Muslims and the other groups thickened. The spark that caused the explosion was a dispute over a trade caravan. Immediately, Quraish gathered 950 soldiers and 700 camels and marched toward Medina to fight Muhammad. Learning of their advance, Muhammad called upon Muslims and prepared an army of just over 300 soldiers and a meager 70 camels. They had limited supplies and provisions, and their armor was sparse and weak.

The two armies battled away from the city in a region called Badr, and later the battle became known as the Battle of Badr. The Muslims knew they were outnumbered, but their faith in Allah strengthened their will. Muhammad prayed to Allah for support, and in response, Allah sent thousands of angel soldiers to the battlefield. The Koran says, "And when you did say unto the believers: Is it not sufficient for you that your Lord should support you with three thousand angels sent down (to your help)?" (3:124). One Muslim soldier reported to the Prophet seeing an angel fighting at his side, riding a horse whose hooves never touched the ground. Victory was declared to the Muslims. They had only fourteen casualties, while the enemies' dead totaled seventy, with an additional seventy taken as prisoners.

Wars continued between the Muslims in Medina and the pagan tribes of Mecca and other parts of Arabia. Alliances were formed between the Jews and pagans against the Muslims. Yet, after many years and many battles, the Muslim community gained more power, and Muhammad's influence strengthened. After many years, Mecca was peacefully reopened for Muslim inhabitants, idolatry was banished, laws were set, women regained equality to men, thousands embraced Islam, and it was a time of enlightenment and knowledge.

FACT

Islamic teachings urge Muslims to remember Allah in their speech. Four common phrases that Muslims might repeat numerous times a day in their conversations with others are "Allahu Akbar," meaning Allah the Greatest; "Al Hamdu Lillah," meaning praise be to Allah; "Insha Allah," meaning Allah willing; and "Subhan Allah," meaning exalted is Allah.

Characteristics and Traits of Muhammad

Muhammad's life is chronicled down to minor details in Islamic books. He led the people by way of example. His habits and manners were beyond compare, and his companions tried to imitate him. He was always known as the Honest, the Truthful. He often went to bed on an empty stomach because he'd given his food to someone more in need. Interestingly, he emphasized the nutritious value of foods such as honey, dates, milk, and olive oil. He ate with his right hand (throughout the Koran, the right hand is held in higher esteem than the left) and always pronounced *Bismillah*—meaning "In the name of Allah"—before eating.

Muhammad immersed himself in worship of Allah, spending lengthy portions of the nights praying. Despite being promised Paradise, Muhammad was a humble person. He never looked down upon the poor or slaves, and he even accepted their invitations to meals, although he knew they would only serve him bread dipped in fat. He always made himself available for questions or guidance to anyone who sought it. He maintained a calm demeanor and never lost his temper or struck at anyone except in battle.

The Prophet's virtues are too numerous to mention. The man was a role model for Muslims, setting standards that Muslims spend their lives trying to achieve. He was loved by Allah, as is said in the Koran: "Lo! Allah and His angels shower blessings on the Prophet. O you who believe! Ask blessings on him and salute him with a worthy salutation" (33:56).

ALERT!

It is prohibited in Islam to depict the face of Allah or any of the prophets. Any attempt to graphically illustrate or impersonate their voices or characters is extremely unacceptable to Muslims. That includes paintings, pictures, cartoons, and live-action films. The reason for this is that the glory and might of Allah is beyond human imagination, and that his prophets must retain their honor and respect.

The Prophet's Miracles

Like the prophets that preceded him, Muhammad was blessed with enough miracles to fill an entire book. His greatest miracle was, of course, delivering the Koran itself. Apart from that, Islamic records state he also healed wounds, foretold the future, raised water to the surface of dry land, and satisfied the hunger of his armies in battle with minimal amounts of food.

One night, Muhammad was confronted by a group of pagans who challenged him to split the moon if he was truly a prophet of Allah. Muhammad raised his hand to the moon, and miraculously, the moon split in half, one side moving to the right of a mountain, and the other to its left. Although a few of the men submitted instantly to Allah, the others sneered and jeered, claiming it was nothing but witchcraft. With the help of Allah, Muhammad performed many other miracles; two of the most famous associated with him are detailed in the following sections.

Touching the Heavens

In Muhammad's early years of prophethood, the most phenomenal of all miracles took place, the Isra Wal Miraj (Night Journey). It happened on a night when Muhammad rose from sleep and walked to the Kaaba. The peace of the night overcame him and he fell asleep near the Kaaba, only to awaken to Angel Gabriel's voice. When Muhammad looked up, he found that Gabriel had brought along a winged white creature about the size and shape of a mule, which Gabriel introduced as the Buraq. Muhammad mounted the Buraq along with Angel Gabriel and Angel Mikail.

The length of the Buraq's strides spanned horizon to horizon. Soon, Muhammad reached the Aqsa Mosque (meaning "farthest mosque") in Jerusalem, where he met previous prophets; among them were Abraham, Moses, and Jesus. Muhammad led them in a prayer at the Aqsa Mosque. Afterward, Muhammad again mounted the Buraq, which carried him and the angels to the Heavens.

Prophet Muhammad's miraculous visit to Jerusalem followed by a trip to the Heavens and back with Angel Gabriel is known as Al-Isra Wal Miraj. To this date, Muslims celebrate the memory of that glorious night, and in many countries it is considered a public holiday.

Muhammad ascended through seven Heavens, and each had a gate with angels standing guard. He met the prophets in the Heavens: Adam in the first, Jesus in the second, Moses in the sixth, and Abraham in the seventh. In the seventh Heaven, Muhammad glimpsed Paradise and conversed with the Creator.

He returned home that same night onboard the Buraq in the company of Angel Gabriel and in time for the dawn prayer. The purpose of this miracle is explained in the Koran: "Glorified be He Who carried His servant by night from the Inviolable Place of Worship to the Far Distant Place of Worship in the neighborhood where We have blessed, that We might show him of Our tokens!" (17:1).

The Hideout

When Muhammad escaped Mecca with his dear friend, Abu Bakr, the rage of the Quraish was such that they would not let the two migrate to Medina in peace. They set out search parties across the desert led by expert trackers to find the escapees and kill them. Aware they were being pursued, Muhammad and Abu Bakr slipped into a cave in which they decided to hide.

As the search party drew near the mouth of the cave, the agitated Abu Bakr whispered to the Prophet, "If they look under their feet they will see us!" Muhammad replied, "What do you think of two people who Allah is their third?" Allah had indeed protected them, sending them a spider that wove a web across the mouth of the cave, and a pair of pigeons who built a nest near the cave's entry and settled in it. When the searchers arrived at the cave, they quickly dismissed it as being deserted, as evident from the spider's web and the nest in which the female pigeon nestled. The Prophet and Abu Bakr survived and continued the migration to Medina.

The Death of the Last Prophet

In the tenth year after the Hijrah, Prophet Muhammad announced that he would lead that year's pilgrimage to Mecca (for more about pilgrimage, see Chapter 4). More than 30,000 men, women, and children congregated in Medina to join the Prophet on the pilgrimage. In Mecca, they performed the rites, then they gathered on Mount Arafat, thirteen miles from Mecca—a standard part of a pilgrimage—where Prophet Muhammad gave his last sermon. He spoke about morality, family, respect, and the greatness and oneness of Allah. The journey became known as the Farewell Pilgrimage.

In the months following the Farewell Pilgrimage and in the approach of the eleventh year after the Hijrah, Muhammad's health deteriorated. He was no longer able to lead prayers and was forced to stay in bed. On the last day of Muhammad's life, Allah blessed him with a surge of strength, and he was able to lead the dawn prayer one last time.

Muhammad's family was stricken with grief, knowing that he was living his last hours. His daughter Fatima was at his side when he whispered something that made her weep, followed by a whisper that made her laugh. Later, she said that she wept when her father told her he was about to die, and laughed when he told her she would be the first of his family to follow him to Heaven.

The angel of death descended upon Muhammad and asked permission to take his soul, something that he had never before done. The Prophet accepted, then his soul departed. Prophet Muhammad completed his message of Islam from Allah before he died at the age of sixty-three.

Chapter 3

 Compilation
and Preservation
of the Koran

The entire volume of the Koran was released from the Heavens in one night, but it was revealed to the Prophet in segments. It took years for the revelation to be completed, and when it was finally over, he faced the task of compiling the Scripture and preserving it from corruption. Thanks to the caliphs who ruled after the Prophet, the Koran was protected for centuries and was handed down from one generation to the next.

The Revelation of the Koran

Muhammad received the Koran over the course of twenty-three years. Sometime around the first night of revelation, Allah sent down the entire Koran as one complete text from the Preserved Tablet to the first and lowest of the Heavens. The tablet remained there, and Gabriel carried the Scripture to the Prophet a few verses at a time. It is believed that the Preserved Tablet is a board on which the past, present, and future of the universe, from galaxies to the tiniest microorganism, is inscribed. The Koran mentions the Preserved Tablet in the following verses: "Nay, but those who disbelieve live in denial. And Allah surrounds them on all sides. Nay, but it is a glorious Koran, on a Preserved Tablet" (85:19–22).

The Night of Power

The night the Koran descended down to the lowest Heaven was somewhere around the twenty-seventh day of Ramadan. It became known as Lailatu Al Qadr—the Night of Power. Muslim scholars differ as to the exact date, although they agree that it was an odd-numbered day. The Shiahs believe that the twenty-first is the correct date. The Night of Power is the most sacred, highly esteemed night of the year. The Koran promises abundant rewards to those who spend that night in worship and prayer.

Both the Koran and Hadith speak about the Night of Power. The Koran speaks to the importance of the night:

> Lo! We revealed it on the Night of Power. Ah, what will convey unto you what the Night of Power is! The Night of Power is better than a thousand months. The angels and the Spirit (Angel Gabriel) descend therein, by the permission of their Lord, with all decrees. (That night is) Peace until the rising of dawn. (97:1–5)

After the first revelation of the Koran, Muhammad lived thirteen years in Mecca before he was driven away to Medina. The revelations continued while the Prophet lived in Medina and never ceased until very shortly before his death.

FACT

Although many believe that the first revelation of the Koran occurred on the twenty-seventh of Ramadan, Prophet Muhammad urges Muslims to spend the last *ten* nights of the holy month of Ramadan indulged in prayer, as the exact moment that the Koran descended down from the Heavens is not known.

Means of Revelation

Angel Gabriel carried down the revelations as ordered by Allah when Muhammad needed guidance or when conflicts arose among the people. Sometimes revelations came to resolve a conflict, sometimes to comment on a situation, and sometimes as a reminder to the people.

Muslim scholars believe the Koran could have been sent down all at once in one thick volume, but for the sake of protecting and preserving the Koran, Allah knew to send it down in segments. The reasons for sending it in segments are believed to be as follows:

- To strengthen the heart and will of the Prophet with a steady flow of revelations
- To gradually reveal the laws of society so the people could adapt at a comfortable pace after centuries of corruption
- To ease the Prophet's task of memorizing, studying, and recording
- To accommodate the Prophet's human capacity that can only deliver the message a portion at a time

Many Muslims believe it was a mercy from Allah that the Koran came down in portions. It allowed the Prophet ample time between revelations to thoroughly memorize, understand, and teach it to his companions, who eventually became teachers for others as well. The Koran says, "And those who disbelieve say: Why is the Koran not revealed unto him all at once? (It is revealed) thus that We may strengthen your heart therewith; and We have arranged it in right order" (25:32). Of course, others argue, if Allah had willed, He could have endowed Muhammad with supernatural abilities to memorize the Koran all at one time.

ALERT!

Muhammad was illiterate at the time of the first revelation. It's not known whether he learned to write later in his lifetime, but a verse in the Koran states that Muhammad had never read any of the other Holy Books revealed before the Koran nor had he recorded the Koran in writing himself.

Early Revelations

In the previous chapter, Muhammad's encounter with Angel Gabriel in the cave of Mount Hira is described in detail. The words Gabriel spoke on that occasion were the first words ever revealed from the Koran. However, those few verses were only the first five out of nineteen that make up Surah 96, entitled Al Alaq—meaning "The Blood Clot." The remaining verses of this Surah were revealed at a later time, but before Muhammad began his public preaching, when he was being harassed for his unfamiliar prayers in front of the Kaaba. The revelation was sent to him to comment on the situation and comfort and reassure the Prophet, and to instruct him to continue praying in the same place and manner.

Following the first revelation was a period in which no revelations came to the Prophet. This intermission worried him, until one day he heard a voice from above. When he glanced at the sky, he saw Angel Gabriel. Frightened, he rushed to his house and wrapped himself up in a blanket. The following verses were the second revelation: "O you enveloped in your cloak, arise and warn! Your Lord magnify. Your raiment purify, and shun pollution. And show not favor, seeking worldly gain! For the sake of your Lord, be patient" (74:1–7).

The third revelation came from Surah Al Muzzamil, but the fourth was more prominent. It came down to Muhammad as a complete Surah, Al Fatiha (The Opener). This Surah is formally considered the first and opening chapter to the Koran as it carries the very essence of the Holy Book:

In the name of Allah, the Beneficent, the Merciful. Praise be to Allah, the Lord of the worlds; the Beneficent, the Merciful. Owner of the Day of Judgment. You alone we worship, You alone we ask for help. Show us the straight path; The path of those whom You have favored, not (the path) of those who earn Your anger nor of those who go astray.

The Final Revelation

Most of the Koran was revealed during the first thirteen years of Muhammad's life as the Prophet, while he was in Mecca. The Surahs revealed in Mecca are classified as Meccan Surahs, and mostly deal with the concepts of Heaven and Hell, and the belief and worship of one God. The remaining Surahs that were revealed in Medina are classified as Medinan Surahs, and mostly deal with laws of society and specifics of Islamic faith.

There is a slight disagreement between scholars as to which was the last verse revealed to the Prophet before his death. Some scholars believe the last revelation was Surah 5, verse 3, which Muhammad recited in his last sermon at the Farewell Pilgrimage: "This day I have perfected your religion for you and completed My favor unto you, and have chosen for you as religion Al-Islam . . ." However, others believe that the revelations continued until the death of the Prophet, making it unlikely that this verse was the last.

The majority declare that the very end of revelation was as follows: "And guard yourselves against a day in which you will be brought back to Allah, Then every soul will be paid in full that which it has earned, and they will not be wronged" (2:281). There is some further disagreement here between scholars, but it is a relatively minor issue because the two other verses in question are numbers 278 and 282 of the same Surah, and basically refer to the same subject of verse 281.

FACT

You will notice that all the Surah titles in the Koran begin with "Al." In Arabic, the word *Al* means "the," so a title like Al Alaq means "The Alaq"— or "The Blood Clot."

The Organization of the Koran

Thousands of visits (it may have been 23,000, 24,000, or 27,000, according to different scholars) from Angel Gabriel left Muhammad with hundreds of pieces of the Koran revealed over the twenty-three-year period of his prophethood. Some of the shorter Surahs came down as one piece, but some others took months—if not years—to compile.

Of course, piecing together so many little revelations to form complete Surahs was beyond Muhammad's capabilities. Alone, he wouldn't have known where to place each new revelation. That was where Angel Gabriel came in, relaying Allah's instruction about the exact positioning of each verse. Muhammad learned the teachings from the Angel, then had the revelations recorded in written form precisely where he was told. After the course of more than two decades, the Koran was delivered to humankind in the order and arrangement in which it still exists today.

Special Surahs in the Koran

Muslims often recite certain verses in specific situations. To protect oneself from evil, for example, Muslims sometimes recite Surah Al Nass (The People) and Surah Al Falaq (The Dawn). Other Surahs serve as important references, such as Surah Al Talaq (The Divorce), which appropriately deals with matters of divorce.

Muslims believe that the Koran is complete the way it is, with every word and every verse containing depth of meaning. Although all Surahs are equally important and cannot be left out, some Surahs hold a special status due to their meaning, purpose, or occasion of revelation.

Al Fatiha (The Opener)

Al Fatiha was among the earliest revelations to the Prophet. In most copies of the Koran, you will find this Surah on the very first page in a graphically decorated and ornamented frame, as opposed to the other Surahs that are printed on plain paper. As the first and opening Surah to the Holy Koran, Al Fatiha is held in very high regard.

Allah sent the words of Al Fatiha to be recited by people in the form of a prayer. If you notice, the words speak directly to the Lord, such as "Owner of the Day of Judgment," "You alone we worship," "You alone we ask for help," "Show us the straight path." The words summarize the very reason the Koran came into existence.

Al Fatiha is the most commonly read or recited Surah in the Koran. It is read in each of the five daily compulsory prayers from two to four times, depending on the prayer, and in all voluntary prayers. It is read at times of fear to comfort the soul and repel evil. It is also read as an opener to certain acts or missions, such as at the engagement of couples, at the start of a journey, at the opening of a new business, and many other occasions. Reading this Surah blesses the occasion, protecting and supporting it with the divine help of Allah.

Al Baqara (The Cow)

Containing 286 verses, Surah Al Baqara is by far the longest Surah in the Holy Book. It is the second Surah in the Koran, just after Al Fatiha. While Al Fatiha speaks the prayer, "[S]how us the straight path," Al Baqara's very first verses answer this prayer:

> This is the Scripture whereof there is no doubt, a guidance unto those who ward off (evil). Who believe in the unseen, and establish worship, and spend of that We have bestowed upon them; and who believe in that which is revealed unto you (Muhammad) and that which was revealed before you, and are certain of the hereafter. These depend on guidance from their Lord. These are the successful. (2:2–5)

The name "The Cow" derives from a story about Moses that is told in verses 67 to 73—only seven out of the 286 verses. Allah had instructed Moses to ask his people to find a certain cow to slaughter, and in their search for it, they become puzzled as to which cow was the right one. Allah describes the cow, and they eventually find it.

A small part of Al Baqara was revealed in Mecca, but the greater part was revealed in Medina, so Muslims have classified it as Medinan. The main theme of the Surah is guidance. Almost one-third of it addresses the Jewish people, describing in great detail their reaction to Islam. Allah invites them and all humankind to read the signs of the Creator and follow the straight path to Heaven.

The story of Adam, Eve, and Satan is covered in nine verses of Al Baqara. Allah forbids Adam from eating from a certain tree, but, seduced by Satan, Adam disobeys Allah, is banished from Heaven, and sent down to Earth.

ALERT!

Surah titles in the Koran are often composed of one or two words. With some Surahs reaching fifty pages long, such a short title hardly describes all the subjects discussed within it. Therefore, many of these titles refer to merely one of the many subjects in the Surah, which may or may not be the most prominent subject.

The last 120 verses or so confirm the concepts of life after death and the existence of Heaven and Hell. They also mention the importance of the Pillars of Faith and Islam, such as prayer, fasting, and pilgrimage. Moreover, the last part of this Surah introduces the laws of business and financial transaction. Finally, the Surah ends with a prayer similar to that in Al Fatiha, in which believers seek forgiveness and assistance of Allah. Not only is Al Baqara the longest Surah, it is the most comprehensive, broad-based Surah in the Holy Koran.

Other Significant Surahs

Without exception, all Surahs in the Koran discuss an important subject matter that people could not do without; therefore each holds an equal amount of significance. However, there are certain verses or Surahs that are frequently recited for a specific purpose, such as Al Fatiha, as described previously. By using the Sunnah for reference, we discover the occasions that caused the Prophet to recite certain verses.

In times of fear, sadness, agitation, or confusion, it is appropriate to recite the last three Surahs in the Koran three times in succession. Surah 114, which is also the last in the Koran, is "say: I seek refuge with the Lord of mankind, the King of mankind, the God of Mankind, from the evil of the sneaking whisperer, who whispers in the hearts of mankind, of the jinn and of mankind." The first of the three Surahs addresses the oneness of the Creator (Surah 112), and the second (Surah 113) is similar in context to the one just quoted. These Surahs are believed to repel evil and calm the soul, so many Muslims will recite them just before bed to prevent nightmares and to have a good night's sleep.

In addition to the three Surahs mentioned, it is advisable to recite on the same occasions the verse of Al Kurssi (meaning "The Throne," verse 255 from Surah Al Baqara). The verse is well learned by most Muslims:

Allah! There is no God but Him, the Alive, the Eternal. Neither slumber nor sleep overtakes Him. Unto Him belongs whatsoever is in the heavens and whatsoever is in the earth. Who is he that intercedes with Him but by His leave? He knows that which is in front of them and that which is behind, while they encompass nothing of His knowledge except what He will. His throne includes the heavens and the earth, and He is never weary of preserving them. He is the Sublime, the Tremendous.

There are other Surahs to be read or recited at times of illness to speed up recovery by the will of Allah, some at the death of a person, some on the sacred day of Friday, and some before bedtime. These Surahs or verses are read as prayers to Allah, seeking His protection or asking His blessings. Although used for different occasions, one Surah does not possess greater value over another, as the whole Koran is to be taken as one entity.

Preserving the Holy Book

The last revelation of the Koran came to Muhammad about nine days before he passed away. Historical evidence dictates that the Koran was collected into one written volume before Muhammad's death. It was his companions who took over the responsibility of ensuring that the Koran was preserved.

FACT

Muhammad's companions are very highly respected in Islam. During his years of preaching, his companions who followed his example had become examples themselves to the ideals of Islam. As a reward for their dedication to the faith, Allah inspired Muhammad to announce to ten of them that they had been promised Paradise. Abu Bakr, Umar, and Uthman were three of the ten.

In the Days of Muhammad

With each new revelation, Muhammad called upon his scribes to record the verses in writing. Verses were inscribed on boards or scraps of leather, using ink and animal bones. He would tell the scribe exactly where to place each verse, thereby making sure the Koran was in proper order.

Prophet Muhammad regularly recited the Koran to his companions, who memorized the verses and went to inscribe it on their own materials. Many of his close friends memorized all 114 Surahs of the Koran before Muhammad's death. The Prophet wanted to be sure their memorization of the Koran was impeccable, and he had them recite it to him on many occasions to check and recheck that their recitation was clean and absolutely free of errors.

Angel Gabriel played an important role as well. Every year in the holy month of Ramadan, Muhammad would retreat to the mosque, where he would spend the last ten days of the month in prayer and worship. Angel Gabriel would descend upon him, and together they would learn the Koran as far as the revelations had taken it. Muhammad would recite to the angel all that had been revealed to that point. Shortly before his death, Muhammad recited the complete Koran to Gabriel, not once, but twice.

There is evidence that the text was presented to many people in book form before the Prophet's death. Such evidence is derived from the Hadith as well as biographies of the people close to the Prophet. For example, Muhammad once said, "Do not take the Koran on a journey with you, for I am afraid lest it should fall into the hands of the enemy." He also said on the day of the Farewell Pilgrimage, "I have left with you something which if you will hold fast to it, you will never fall into error: a plain indication, the book of Allah, and the practice of his prophet." Both of these Hadith and many others indicate that the Koran existed as a book in the time of Muhammad.

Before Muhammad died in A.D. 632, he declared that Abu Bakr would rule as caliph. Abu Bakr ruled for a mere two years, then Umar, another of the Prophet's trusted companions, ruled until the year A.D. 644. The caliph to whom credit is owed for preparing and printing the Koran as it is known today is Uthman, who ruled from A.D. 644 to 656.

Collecting the Scripts

It is not entirely clear whether the last copies of the Koran left behind by Muhammad were complete. What is known, though, is that it had been completely memorized by many of his close companions. His closest companion and the man who accompanied him on the Hijrah, Abu Bakr, took over as caliph after he passed away. During Abu Bakr's reign, in the year of A.D. 633, a battle ensued and took the lives of many who had memorized the Koran. Fearing the Koran might be lost, Abu Bakr decided to collect the revelations into one volume.

Muhammad's reliable scribe, Zaid, was appointed by Abu Bakr to find and gather all the scripts of the Koran from every available source, including the memories of those who had known it by heart. The inscribed scraps of leaves, leather, and boards were collected from many homes, including that of the Prophet. Then Abu Bakr had it copied onto loose sheets, which he bound together and preserved.

One Copy for All

Twelve years after the death of the Prophet, Uthman came to hold the caliphate. Uthman was one of the Prophet's closest companions and was thoroughly versed with the Koran. In A.D. 653, during the spread of Islam in Asia, word reached Uthman that the Muslims in battle had different recitations of the Koran due to changing dialects. Alarmed, Uthman decided to settle the issue once and for all.

Uthman sent for Abu Bakr's copy of the Koran and appointed Zaid again, along with three Muslim men of Quraish, to duplicate it into bound volumes. The Quraishi men's purpose was to make sure that the dialect in the copies remained the original Quraishi dialect in which the Koran was revealed. After several copies were made, Uthman ordered every other copy, fragment, scrap, or sheet of Scripture to be burned. These actions were necessary to ensure that the Koran remained preserved in its original form, and safe from alteration.

All Muslims of the era approved the burning of the fragments. Uthman duplicated many copies, but the exact number is not known. He sent one copy each to Mecca, Medina, Basra (in Iraq), Kufa (in Iraq), and Damascus (in Syria), and retained one for himself, which makes it safe to assume that at least six standard volumes were copied in his reign.

FACT

It wasn't until the seventeenth century that the Koran was printed with the new technology of movable type. Until then, every copy of the Koran had to be handwritten, which resulted in variations in its appearance. When the Koran went into print, it was finally standardized with a single appropriate type.

Ancient Copies of the Koran

The very oldest copies of the Koran were normally made of parchment. Printing machinery had not yet been invented and all books had to be written by hand. The calligraphy used in the ancient times evolved as the centuries passed, making it easy to approximate the date to which a certain manuscript belongs.

Chronologically speaking, the oldest complete copies of the Koran are those that the Caliph Uthman prepared in the seventh century A.D. These were written on parchment made of gazelle skin, were very large and beautiful, and their characteristics match no other copy made at a later date. Several of Uthman's copies were traced until the twentieth century, but vanished after the two World Wars.

A very old copy of the Koran, said to be Uthman's own, is currently in Uzbekistan. It is said to have found its way from Morocco to Uzbekistan in 1485, then it was taken to Russia in 1869, and returned only in 1917. Although age had taken a toll on it, about fifty facsimile copies were made of the book and sent to some Muslim leaders. One copy was sent to Columbia University Library, where it was studied and authenticated, and where it remains today. Based on the dates of Uthman's reign, this Koran is about 1,350 years old.

The Egyptian National Library in Egypt keeps a copy of the Koran that dates back to A.D. 688, fifty-eight years after the Prophet's death. It is also written on parchment made of gazelle skin. There are other ancient copies as well; however, Uthman's copy remains the oldest existing copy of the Koran in the world today.

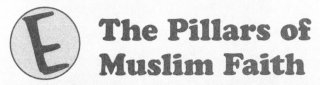

Chapter 4

The Pillars of Muslim Faith

A Muslim is not a Muslim unless he or she understands, believes, and abides by the Eleven Pillars that make up Islamic faith. These pillars are so important that at least one of them is mentioned on almost every page of the Koran. If one of these pillars is not established in a Muslim's heart, his faith would be incomplete. While these pillars form the basics of Islam, they are just the beginning—they would not guarantee Heaven to someone who believed in them but lived a life full of sins.

The Nonbeliever, the Believer, and the Muslim

Ultimate Islamic faith comes down to believing in one Creator. Islam's very essence is in believing with your heart, mind, and soul that the Creator of the worlds is one and that He is the Supreme Being.

Believers and Nonbelievers

Some people don't believe in a Creator. They believe that the formation of the universe is not of divine origin and that life began by coincidence. Consequently, they don't believe in life after death, or Heaven and Hell. Islam calls these people "nonbelievers" due to their rejection of a Creator and the creation concept.

The next classification of people is "believers." These people believe in the existence of a Creator, but may not necessarily share all the beliefs of Muslims. When the Koran refers to believers, it addresses only the group that abides by strict criteria called the Six Pillars of Faith. To fit the Koran's definition of a believer, you must:

1. Believe in Allah
2. Believe in His angels
3. Believe in His Holy Books
4. Believe in His messengers
5. Believe in fate and destiny
6. Believe in the afterlife and the Last Day

"Believing" means understanding each of these points and implicitly trusting that they are real. If a person does not embrace even just one of these beliefs, it makes that person a nonbeliever. In other words, it's all or nothing.

The Muslim

The third classification of people in the Koran is the Muslim. A brief definition of a Muslim is "a practicing believer." According to the Koran, believing in the Six Pillars of Faith leads a person to about halfway along the correct path, but to become truly dedicated and reach for Paradise, one must perform or practice the actions prescribed by Allah in the manner prescribed by His teachings. These final five requirements are the Five Pillars of Islam. They require Muslims to:

1. Declare faith in Allah and in His Prophet Muhammad
2. Perform five prayers a day
3. Spend toward charity
4. Perform pilgrimage to the Kaaba
5. Fast the month of Ramadan

Just as a believer is not a believer if he or she misses one Pillar of Faith, a Muslim's religion is incomplete if he or she misses one Pillar of Islam. Believing without practicing may not grant quick access to Heaven (see Chapter 15 for more about Heaven). Allah repeatedly stresses in the Koran that all believers must follow the pillars of Islam and perform many good acts if they want to be rewarded. However, a prerequisite to being Muslim is to be a believer in the first place.

FACT

There are many Muslims who neglect practicing their faith. They may skip prayer, ignore giving out the annual alms, or feel too fatigued to fast the entire month of Ramadan. According to the Koran and Sunnah, such are major faults that make their religion incomplete. As such, they are not true Muslims according to Allah.

Belief in the Koran

Allah has given humankind six foundations of faith to keep them on the right path. Perhaps the most critical of those beliefs is the belief in the Koran. Why? Because, quite plainly, if you lose your faith in the Koran, your faith in any or all of the other pillars will be shaken. It is the Koran that states what the other pillars are, and it is the Koran that presents their existence as a matter of fact. In other words, if you don't believe in the

Koran, how can you believe what it says about the Creator, the angels, or the afterlife?

According to the Koran, a Muslim must believe the entire Koran, not just parts of it. Doubting any part of it is like doubting the whole volume. The same rule applies: all or none at all. Once a Muslim embraces the Six Pillars of Faith, he or she can begin practicing the faith that Allah teaches in His Holy Book.

Belief in Allah and the Angels

The first and foremost belief is the belief in Allah, followed closely by belief in the angels. But what is Allah? He is God, but the Islamic perception of God is different from that of any other religion. From the Koran, Muslims learn He is the Creator and everything else is His creation. He created the angels without a will of their own to serve him. Since all this is in the Koran, a Muslim must believe it.

Belief in Allah

In both the Six Pillars of Faith and the Five Pillars of Islam, the first subject is the belief in Allah and his oneness. This short Surah accurately sums it up: "[S]ay: He is Allah, the One! Allah, the eternally Besought of all. He begets not nor was begotten. And there is none comparable unto Him" (Surah 112). Allah reinforces this fact over and over again in the Koran, sometimes addressing those who refuse to believe, and sometimes those who believe the Creator has children, advocates, or "parts."

Apart from believing in His existence, it is also important for a Muslim to understand and respect Allah's virtues. Allah has given Himself ninety-nine names in the Koran that describe His virtues. For example, He tells us He's the Most Merciful. Notice, He doesn't say He is merciful, but specifically says "*the Most* Merciful," conveying that His mercy is above all.

Muslims believe from the Koran that Allah is called the Supreme Being because He rules the entire universe. Many of His other ninety-nine names explain his supremacy. He is the All-Knowing, the All-Hearing, and the All-Seeing. He explains in the Koran that not a grain of sand escapes His knowledge. So, in order for the belief in Allah to be complete, one must acknowledge that Allah is not only the Creator, but also that He is superior to all of His creation in every way, knowing the thoughts of all of humankind and what's in their hearts.

FACT

Muslims pronounce the name of Allah at the start of everything. In the Koran, at the beginning of every Surah just under the title, you will find the phrase "In the name of Allah, the Merciful, the Compassionate." Muslims also pronounce this phrase before any action that needs blessing, such as before eating, driving a car, or taking an exam.

Belief in the Angels

Most people who believe in the angels are inspired and soothed by their existence. The common popular view of angels—that they are heavenly creatures whose job is to serve God, helping and protecting His other creatures on Earth—is similar to what is taught in the Koran. Actually, Muslims believe that angels are Allah's soldiers, workers, and worshippers.

Scholars say that Allah created angels from light. Allah mentions angels in many places in the Koran, and in many verses, He converses with them. Muslims believe that unlike humans, angels were created as believers in Allah and cannot deviate to atheism or other beliefs. Angels worship and obey Allah's every word, as on the day He created Adam; He asked them to bow before Adam and they did. Angels are repelled by places where corruption is prevalent, and they gather in places of worship.

There are probably thousands of duties performed by angels, but the Koran only explains a few. Each person on Earth has one angel assigned to record her good deeds, and another to record her bad deeds. The Koran also says that there are other angels surrounding each person to protect him from harm. Angels hear people's prayers for help and carry the messages to Allah. It is also said that angels are always there to protect children from harm. There are two angels who interrogate the dead in their graves, there are angels guarding Heaven and Hell, and there are angels who are in charge of running the Last Day.

Do angels ever appear to people?
Common Muslim belief is that only the prophets have seen angels and recognized them as such, while prophet Muhammad saw Angel Gabriel in his true form. However, Islam does not claim that it is impossible for angels to appear to normal people.

The most famous, most highly regarded of angels is Angel Gabriel, who brought down Allah's message to all the prophets. The Angel of Death, or Azrael as he is known to Muslims, is another well-known angel, who takes people's souls when they die.

From Holy Books to the Last Day

Without messengers to bring messages from God, humankind wouldn't have known about the Creator. The Koran says that Allah sends a prophet to every community to ensure that everyone gets the message. Although the Koran mentions only a few of the prophets, scholars estimate their total number in the thousands. The Koran also demands belief in the Holy Books sent to the prophets, and it mentions five books specifically.

Belief in the Holy Books

The Koran was the last divine revelation sent to mankind, but not the only one. Allah states very clearly in the Koran that he sent revelations to the prophets before Muhammad. Muslims cannot deny the existence of such Scripture according to the following verse: "O you who believe! Believe in Allah and His messenger and the Scripture that He has revealed unto His messenger and the Scripture which He has revealed aforetime. Whoso disbelieves in Allah and His angels and His scriptures and His messengers and the Last Day, he verily has wandered far astray" (4:136).

Muslims understand from the Koran that Allah revealed the Scrolls to Abraham, the Psalms to David, the Torah to Moses, the Gospel to Jesus, and finally the Koran to Muhammad. Although the Koran says Muslims must believe in those Scriptures, it also warns them to be aware that due to poor preservation, the original message from Allah has been distorted over the years. On the other hand, Allah promises in the Koran that it will always be protected from distortion. (For more on this, see Chapter 19.)

ALERT!

Usually when one Pillar of Faith is mentioned in the Koran, you will find others listed, confirming the necessity to believe in all of them together. Surah 4, verse 136, declares five of the Pillars of Faith.

Belief in the Prophets

The first prophet on earth was the first man created. According to the Koran, that man was Adam. Although he originally stayed in Heaven, his seduction by Satan resulted in his descent to this world. In Islam, Adam's repentance to Allah was accepted, but his duty was to adopt this planet, serve it well, and guide the people who would come after him to Allah. From then on, prophets came and went, until the last of them, who was Prophet Muhammad.

The Koran requires belief in the twenty-five prophets of Allah mentioned in the text. These were not the only prophets, though, as Allah says He has sent a prophet to every community, many of whom are not mentioned in the Koran. Muslims are required to believe in all the prophets, whether or not the Koran mentions them by name. These prophets include Moses of Judaism and Jesus of Christianity. Muslims are also required to believe in the prophets' message, which the Koran states as being the same as Muhammad's: faith in Allah.

FACT

Scholars say that Allah's prophets were the best of their people. They represented the highest moral standards and possessed likable character. It was necessary for them to be pleasant in order to attract people to their preaching.

Belief in Destiny

The concept of fate puzzles many people. In a whim of pride, a person may claim that he is master of his own destiny. That may be true to a certain extent, but according to the Koran, fate interferes everywhere, changing realities, influencing the way events unfold. The Arabic word for fate or destiny is *qadar*. All qadar is in the hands of Allah; in the Koran, He says He knows your whole life story from the day of your conception to the day you are judged before Him.

Some believe that if Allah knows your life before you live it, then He created you predestined for Heaven or Hell. That is a misunderstanding, because the Koran makes it clear that Allah created every person with great freedom of choice. For example, a teenager chooses to take drugs and drop out of school rather than study and get into college, and later on leads a miserable street life. Is that fate? No, that's personal choice. Allah just knows the decisions you're about to make before you make them.

The Koran explains that even though we make our own decisions, fate throws certain challenges to test how we react. Imagine you're driving on your way to the most important business presentation of your life and you're running late. Suddenly a car crashes into yours and you're forced to miss the presentation as you wait for the police to arrive. As a result, you lose a definite chance to get promoted. So far, that's fate. But whether you practice patience and have faith in Allah or start cursing your luck and quit your job altogether is personal choice.

Regardless of the situation, the Koran advises Muslims to be patient and remain trusting in Allah and that He will eventually bless the righteous, be it in life or the afterlife. That is belief in destiny.

Belief in the Last Day

Based on the Koran, Muslims believe that just as every living thing dies eventually, this world that we know will inevitably end, too. That will be the Last Day described in the Koran.

The Koran says that on the Last Day, the dead will be resurrected and every person will be judged. Generally speaking, believing worshippers (including Christians and Jews who believe in Allah and the Last Day and live righteous lives) will go to Heaven and nonbelievers will go to Hell.

That doesn't mean that today's dead have to wait in their graves until then—their souls move on to the afterlife, a place where reward and punishment also exist (see Chapter 14 for information about the soul). The afterlife, the Last Day, and Judgment Day all refer to the same basic belief that life after death is the end of life's tests, and the beginning of eternal reward or punishment.

Allah has a very solid reward system. Good deeds and acts of worship are rewarded by *Hasanat*—positive points added to your score. Allah says that each Hasana (singular form) is multiplied by ten. If you do a good deed worth five Hasanat, you actually earn fifty. Some verses say certain Hasanat are multiplied by 700. Sins, however, are counted in singles.

The Five Pillars of Islam

Allah says in the Koran that Islam is His chosen religion for the people. To believe in Him makes one a good person, but may or may not satisfy requirements for Heaven. A Muslim who is familiar with the Koran knows that she can't live her life simply believing without doing anything about it. In fact, a Muslim is expected by Allah to fulfill all of the Five Pillars of Islam. Those five obligations may seem like a lot of worship, but true Muslims perform them diligently with a wholehearted love of Allah.

Declaration of Faith

The very first step a new convert takes is a Declaration of Faith. The English translation of the declaration is "I testify that there is no god but Allah, and that Muhammad is His slave and messenger." After the convert utters these words from the heart, Allah embraces the new convert into Islam.

The declaration is not limited to new converts, however. Prophet Muhammad stressed that Muslims must repeat the declaration regularly throughout their life. Muslims repeat it in prayers by obligation, and voluntarily throughout the day to affirm their submission to Allah. Every time a Muslim utters the declaration, he or she gains reward. According to the Koran, it is also essential that a dying person utter those words before his soul departs (unless he dies suddenly, of course).

FACT

The word *Islam* comes from "salam," which means peace and submission. Allah gave the religion this name to imply that the people submit to His will, respectfully worshipping Him as the only Lord. "Islam" also describes the essence of the faith as being very much based on peace rather than violence.

The Hajj (Pilgrimage)

The Hajj to Mecca is an exhausting and expensive mission done at the end of every Ramadan by a few million pilgrims. Approximately a week or two is needed to complete the physically strenuous rituals. Because of its tremendous difficulty, Allah mercifully accepts it if performed once in a lifetime. According to Islam, people who can't perform it due to serious restrictions, such as financial or health problems, are excused and will not be punished in the afterlife.

Pilgrims at the Hajj are similar to monks at a monastery. Pilgrims cleanse their hearts and free their minds of worldly concerns in the rituals of Hajj, devoting themselves entirely to Allah. Muslims recall never feeling as close to Allah as they do at the Kaaba. At that sacred place, even amidst the chaos of millions of pilgrims, not a foul word is spoken, not a sin committed, and not even a creature as small as an insect is killed, as these actions offend the holy sanctity of the Kaaba and its surrounding land. This is in compliance to the instruction of the Koran.

Before arriving within the boundaries of Mecca, men must be wearing only an *Ihram*—two white cloths wrapped around their bodies to symbolize their birth into a towel. Women wear traditional Islamic dress in modest colors, revealing only their hands and faces. The Hajj begins with seven laps walked around the Kaaba and concludes with a visit to Prophet Muhammad's tomb in Medina (which is not obligatory but performed as a sign of respect to the Prophet). The Koran describes most of the rituals of the Hajj.

Obligatory Charity

From the beginning of time, the distribution of wealth throughout the world has never been even. Poverty is widespread and people die of hunger every day. To counter this, Allah demands in the Koran that people give a certain amount of their savings to charity. Muslims believe that if this duty is neglected, their wealth will be condemned to remain of little value, as money will disappear as quickly as it is gained.

Of course, the amount of obligatory charity—known as *Zakat* in the Koran—is not at the discretion of the individual. Very specifically, the Sunnah defines the amount as 2.5 percent of a person's total savings accumulated during a one-year period. Every year a person must calculate the exact amount and give it to charity if he or she is to be a righteous Muslim.

ALERT!

It is very inappropriate for a person to publicize his or her generosity in giving to charity. Islam advises people to be as discreet as possible when giving to charity, as their goal should be reward from Allah, not praise from other people.

Five Prayers a Day

Islamic prayer is discussed numerous times throughout the Koran to stress its importance. Muslims are required to pray five times a day. Each prayer typically lasts five minutes, leading to twenty-five minutes of prayer *every day*. The Koran makes it clear that neglecting prayer is a grievous sin that will be punished in Hell, making prayer compulsory for every Muslim.

Praying is probably the most important, and unfortunately most neglected, form of worship prescribed for Muslims. Prayer is mentioned often in the Koran; for example, "And they are ordered naught else than to serve Allah, keeping religion pure for Him, as men by nature upright, and to establish prayer and to pay the poor-due. That is true religion" (98:5). Muslims agree that regular prayer purifies the mind and soul and serves as a constant reminder of Allah, deterring people from committing sin.

Allah asks Muslims to pray five times a day at specific times according to the sun: dawn, midday, afternoon, sunset, and nightfall. No guesswork determines prayer times; mosques announce the exact time for each prayer through microphones by an announcement called the *Adhan*. People can perform the designated prayer at any time before the next Adhan, meaning that when the midday Adhan is announced, a Muslim technically has until the afternoon Adhan to perform the midday prayer. However, Islam strongly urges that every prayer take place as close as possible to its Adhan. If one prayer is missed, it is excusable to complete it along with the next prayer as long as it wasn't missed due to mere negligence.

Prayer is performed in accordance with a strict set of rules set by the Koran and Sunnah. First, one must cleanse his or her body and soul through ablution. Each prayer is composed of several *Rakaas*—a prescribed set of rites. In each Rakaa, Surah Al Fatiha is read as well as some verses of the Koran, then the person bows and prostrates while uttering specific words of devotion. Wishing peace upon the two angels recording the deeds concludes prayer: one *Salam* (an uttered greeting) to the left, and one to the right.

FACT

Every Friday, Muslims gather in mosques to perform the midday prayer together. The Friday group prayer is compulsory in Islam, while group prayers in general are highly rewarded. In a group prayer, one person called the Imam stands in front of the other worshippers and leads the prayer.

Angel Gabriel taught Muhammad how to pray, and the Prophet relayed the instruction to the people. Muhammad was so dedicated that he always offered voluntary prayers before and after compulsory ones, and he taught additional types of prayers that a Muslim can offer. Prayers that are outside the standard form do not include any reciting of the Koran; these are the kinds of prayers that speak directly to Allah, seeking His guidance and assistance, such as, "Allah, please help me get through this."

Fasting the Month of Ramadan

Ramadan may be known as the month of the Islamic calendar during which Muslims don't eat, but there is much more to it than fasting. The holy month of Ramadan presents thirty days of intensive worship in addition to fasting, such as an increase in the number of prayers, reading the Koran, or spending time in solitude at the mosque. Additionally, Muslims have to avoid committing sins and must stay away from certain worldly pleasures. All this happens in Ramadan because it is the month the Koran descended to the lowest Heaven, and when the first few words were revealed to Muhammad.

According to Islamic teaching, Muslims begin their fast after a meal called *Suhoor* just before dawn, and break it at the sunset Adhan with a meal called *Iftar*. In those approximately thirteen hours between dawn and sunset, they may not eat or drink, smoke, or even swallow anything but their own saliva. According to Islamic law based on the Koran and Sunnah, swallowing blood from a bleeding gum or even licking a postage stamp may result in breaking the fast. Other things that break a fast are inhaling strong odors that reach the throat, menstruation, foul speech, and any form of courtship between unmarried men and women.

Missing a day's fasting in Ramadan is a major sin according to the Koran, unless it is excusable for reasons such as illness, travel, or menstruation. Every day missed with a suitable excuse must be made up for outside the month of Ramadan. Days missed with no excuse have different rulings.

Menstruation prevents women from fasting or praying because blood is considered unclean, and a state of purity is a prerequisite to being involved in worship. Once menstruation is over, a woman showers and performs ablution to enter the state of purity once more.

Based on the teachings of the Koran and Sunnah, Muslims understand that the wisdom of fasting is to learn patience, engage in worship, avoid sin, and remind oneself of the people less fortunate in the world. Also, serving Iftar meals to the poor is dearly appreciated by Allah and earns a person tremendous reward.

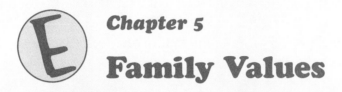

Chapter 5

Family Values

In Islam, maintaining family bonds is a sacred duty. Family is not limited to parents and children, but also includes uncles, aunts, cousins, nephews, grandparents, and in-laws. Each member has a duty to fulfill toward one another. The concept of the family as the nucleus of society is so important that it is nearly a Pillar of Faith. The Koran and Muhammad have both discussed family matters extensively, covering issues from smooth running of the household to distributing an inheritance.

The Nucleus of Society

The Koran and Sunnah provide solid rules for a family to follow. They do not underestimate the importance of keeping this unit healthy. Both offer the guidance necessary to keep it on the right track. Unlike in other societies, the basic family nucleus in Islam doesn't survive on its own, but is tied to an interconnected web of nuclei that includes relatives and their families, too. Given the right conditions and environment defined by the Koran, each nucleus will prosper and in turn affect other nuclei within the interconnected web.

FACT

The Koran reminds Muslims that they are all brothers and sisters from a spiritual point of view. The reminder serves to confirm their duties toward one another in terms of providing protection, education, and other assistance. It implies that the Muslim society is all one big family in which all members must support one another.

Value of the Family

In Islam, families are required by the Koran to maintain strong bonds and never, ever cut blood ties. Islam places such importance on the family because, quite briefly, its responsibility and influence spans generations. For example, Muslims believe if two parents neglect the moral upbringing of their children, it is likely that their children's lack of morality will reflect upon their grandchildren, and so on. The more families of this type there are, the more immorality will spread in society. On the other hand, if two parents agree as to the importance of high morality and raise their children accordingly, future generations will more likely carry the same high standards. A parent's responsibility doesn't end when the child reaches the age of eighteen—it continues until Allah takes the soul of one of them.

Structure of the Family

The family in Islam can roughly be divided into three parts. The first part is the main, or core, family; the second includes aunts, uncles, cousins, nephews, and nieces; and the third part includes non–blood relatives like stepparents, brothers- and sisters-in-law, uncle's wife, etc. These divisions make prioritization easy for individual family members, and play an important role when it comes time to distribute an inheritance. The greatest emphasis is placed on the core family: husband, wife, children, and the children's grandparents.

The Koran states that the core family owes the biggest responsibility toward one another. The mother and father work toward providing the best for their children because they are their number one priority. Closely matched in priority are grandparents (parents of the mother and father) who, due to their age, will need a portion of their children's attention. The second part of the extended family demands a little less attention, while the third demands the least.

To paint a clearer picture, let's assume you are an unmarried child living with your parents. Your parents, siblings, and grandparents are your core family. When you get married, your spouse, children, and parents become your core family, while your siblings join the second part, demanding less of your attention. Your siblings' spouses will join the third part, to which you owe the least responsibility. (Parents-in-law are to be held in high regard and treated in the same manner as your own parents.) This is the proper Islamic family structure as preached by the Koran and Sunnah.

In Islamic tradition, any servants in the household are considered part of the family in a metaphorical sense. This means that they should be treated with the same dignity and respect as the blood-members, dress similarly, dine at the same table, and be entitled to the same basic rights except in regard to certain legal matters.

The Ideal Environment

The family is expected to provide the proper environment for the children, both physical and nonphysical. The nonphysical environment describes what the child is exposed to, such as the general mood of the household, the parent's example, the media, peer pressure, etc. The physical environment describes the actual house and neighborhood in which the child lives. Both have significant influence on children's development, and the Koran and the Sunnah stress both.

According to Islamic teaching, parents should strive to provide the best possible environment for their children. For example, parents should not provoke sibling rivalry by discriminating between their children. They should provide access to books and experiences that will help the children develop a better mind. A good environment exposes children to ideals in every aspect and leaves a positive imprint on them. This concept is at the heart of Islam.

The Man: Husband and Father

A man with the intention of starting a family first becomes a husband, then a father, then a father-in-law, and finally a grandfather. At each of these stages, he has to follow certain responsibilities assigned to him by the Koran. It's his job to provide for his family. He is also the head of the family, protector of the wife, teacher of the children. If he neglects any of these sacred duties, an angel records these sins.

Main Provider

There is no leniency described in the Koran or the Sunnah toward a man who refuses to spend his money on his wife and children. The assignment is clear and concise: "Men are in charge of women" (4:34). Then, still on the issue of family, the Koran adds, "Let him who has abundance spend of his abundance, and he whose provision is measured, let him spend of that which Allah has given him. Allah asks naught of any soul except that which He has given it" (65:7).

So the Koran obligates the man to spend his money on his family's food, shelter, clothing, education, and so on, but it also explains that he is expected to spend only what he can afford. In order to spend, he needs a source of income, which makes him the main provider—the one who struggles to maintain a living standard for his family. For as long as he is capable of doing this, no one else is obligated to provide for the family. In Middle Eastern societies, the man's responsibilities as provider elevate him to be the head of the family.

FACT

An interesting Hadith of Muhammad encourages expenditure in many directions while still confirming the duty of the man toward his home: "A Dinar you spend in Allah's way, or to free a slave, or as a charity you give to a needy person, or to support your family, the one yielding the greatest reward is that which you spend on your family."

Life with the Wife

Just as he looks after his children, the father must not forget his role as a husband. Islam defines the treatment of wives in the Koran and the Sunnah and concentrates on getting this message across, instructing men to "consort with them in kindness" (4:19). The Koran asks husbands to treat their wives with kindness, understanding, and respect. The husband is as obliged to provide his wife's food and clothing as he is for his children; he will be condemned if he ignores her needs, just as he would be if he ignored the needs of his children. To summarize, Prophet Muhammad said, "The believers who show the most perfect faith are those who have the best behavior, and the best of you are those who are the best to their wives."

The Woman: Wife and Mother

The Koran gave the good wife and mother very high status. The work and effort a woman exerts in the running of her household, spending time with her husband, and raising her children involves enormous commitment and is not underestimated in Islam. Like the husband, the wife has been given a set of instructions and a warning to keep her from neglecting her duties. According to the Koran, it is a major sin if a woman ignores her husband's needs or neglects her children (unless she is not capable due to health reasons).

Duties Toward the Household

Unlike her husband, the wife is not obligated to spend money on her family. She may or may not work for pay, and if she does, the money she earns is hers to keep. The Koran specifically tells men not to take their wives' money by force. Muslim authorities say that if the family is in need of extra financing, it is favorable for the wife to share in meeting the expenses, for which Allah will reward her. Whether she chooses to spend or to save her earnings is entirely her decision.

As for the living environment, there is no specific law in the Koran that obliges women to take over the cleaning and maintaining of the house. A woman's direct responsibility is satisfying the needs of her husband and children. However, Muslims view the responsibility of maintaining the household environment as an inherent part of satisfying the family's needs. Therefore, a Muslim career woman would neither be exempt from nor required to perform her household duties, but in a matter of good manners, the husband's willingness to help her will be rewarded.

Not all husbands and wives follow the rules set to them by the Koran and the Sunnah; some men beat their wives and some wives neglect their children. According to Islam, even a mistreated member of the family must abide by the rules, as it is up to Allah to punish the one who strays from the right path.

Life with the Husband

Women in modern times struggle to achieve equality with men and as they do, they sometimes struggle for the upper hand in the running of the family and household. While men are asked to treat their wives with utmost consideration, their assigned role as the head of the family is a position that is indisputable in Islam. Even if a woman equally provides for the family, she is to remain deferential to her husband. Islam requires her to make him comfortable and respect his wishes.

Allah says in the Koran, "Men are the protectors and maintainers of women, because Allah has given the one more (strength) than the other, and because they support them from their means. Therefore the righteous women are devoutly obedient, guarding in secret that which Allah has guarded" (4:34). Allah does not intend for the husband and wife to compete for domination over each other. He states in the Koran that He created them to complement each other according to their best natural abilities. The previous verse explains that men are head of the family because they protect and provide. In turn, women must respectfully satisfy their wishes.

Scholars explain that the requirement of wives to fulfill their husbands' requests is not to be taken as oppression of women. If the husband treats his wife in the manner outlined previously, the wife's requests will consequently be fulfilled, too. And of course, the husband's requests of his wife must be reasonable, as mentioned in the Koran. Scholars describe a righteous wife as patient with her husband even in his outbursts, just as a righteous husband is kind and respectful to her. According to the Koran and Sunnah, tyranny should never rule the household and all matters of the family should be decided in consultation with its members.

Pregnancy and Abortion

To protect the sanctity of the family, the Koran forbids premarital sex. Children must be conceived within marriage in order to be legitimate. Because the family is sacred, Allah protects it by forbidding pre- or extramarital affairs. This way, children are raised with both real parents who complement each other's duties in taking care of the kids, lineage is defined and protected, and no child somewhere down the line will end up marrying a half-sister he never knew about.

Most Muslim scholars agree that birth control is acceptable for couples who are not ready for a child, or whose means cannot support more than a certain number of children. However, scholars state that using birth control with an intention to never have children is undesirable in Islam.

Islam teaches that the woman can conceive only through her husband. The law of the Koran strictly prohibits modern inventions like artificial insemination by men other than the husband. Other practices such as surrogate mothering are also unlawful. The mixing of blood outside the marriage bond is akin to adultery. Scholars conclude from the teachings of the Koran and Muhammad that conception and childbearing is only permitted between husband and wife. Any children created through external donors or surrogate mothers would not be 100 percent the husband's and wife's blood, and—according to adoption laws—cannot be given the family name and are exempt from receiving inheritance. The objective is to have each child conceived within wedlock with the intent that the child will grow up in a secure and legitimate environment.

The issue of abortion has caused some debate among Islamic scholars. The Koran forbids parents from killing their children but does not refer specifically to abortion. Most scholars conclude from the Koran and the Sunnah that abortion is forbidden because it is the killing of a child. Others say that abortion is allowed in the first few weeks after conception, while the embryo is more or less unformed. Islamic teachings do not entirely confirm either side of the argument. Abortion due to a health risk for the mother is another issue, and Islamic law allows it.

QUESTION?

What does the Koran say about circumcision?
Circumcision of baby boys is not compulsory in Islam but Prophet Muhammad advises it for hygienic purposes. A qualified doctor performs the small surgical operation, which involves removal of part of the foreskin of the penis, at a hospital.

Raising the Children

Muslims view the birth of a child as a small miracle and a blessing from Allah. Children are valuable gems not only to their parents, but to Allah as well. The Koran provides guidelines to help people raise their children correctly with regard to their health, education, and virtues. Both mother and father have separate and shared roles in the upbringing of their kids.

The Mother's Role

The Koran leaves no doubt that a newborn should be looked after by his or her mother. Only if the baby is an orphan or the child's mother is unavailable due to serious circumstances can someone else take over. Allah says that mothers should breastfeed their babies, preferably until they reach the age of two. Modern scientific evidence that mother's milk boosts a baby's health and builds a strong immune system shows the wisdom of this advice to mothers.

Discriminating between your children is a sin in Islam. The Koran and the Sunnah urge parents to love and treat their children equally without giving preference to any one of them. Such behavior plants resentment in children and leads to instability in the family bond.

The Father's Role

Fathers should spend quality time with their children, strengthening the bonds they share. Father-child relationships should be based on love, cooperation, communication, and respect, and the children should always feel they can confide in their father. Prophet Muhammad once heard of a father who admitted to never kissing his children. Muhammad scolded him for lack of mercy and compassion toward his children.

The Koran emphasizes the father's responsibility as a role model in practicing his faith. Men are asked to plant the seed of faith in their children from an early age and to teach them about the Koran. Since the child is 100 percent the responsibility of the parents, they will be held accountable for his or her upbringing on Judgment Day.

Children's Duties Toward Parents

The Koran states that children should obey their parents and carefully choose their words when speaking to them. Shouting or using profanity against parents is not allowed under any circumstances. These rules require children to recognize the immeasurable efforts that parents exert in raising and providing for them. By obeying them, they return some of the favors that their parents bestow upon them.

Mothers in particular have a very high status in Islam. Prophet Muhammad said that Paradise is at the feet of mothers. By "mothers" he meant righteous mothers who have done their job to the fullest. The Prophet also emphasizes that sons and daughters must honor their mother, and that the biggest debt they owe is the one to their mother for raising them.

Once children eventually grow up and start families of their own, the roles are reversed, and the children have to look after their parents in their old age. There is a beautiful verse in the Koran on this subject:

Your Lord has decreed, that you worship none but Him, and (that you show) kindness to parents. If one of them or both of them attain old age with you, say not "Fie" unto them nor repulse them, but speak unto them a gracious word. And lower unto them the wing of submission through mercy, and say: My Lord! Have mercy on them both as they did care for me when I was little. (17:23–24)

These words address children directly, ordering them to respect and fully accept the caretaking of their aging parents without considering it a burden.

The children's duty toward their parents doesn't end with the death of the parents. One common and very encouraged Islamic practice based on several of Muhammad's Hadith is to perform good deeds in the name of the parents, so that the reward goes to the soul of the dead parent.

For example, a son may perform pilgrimage in his dead father's name, and the reward will go to the father, perhaps earning him more luxury in Heaven, or rescuing him from Hell. The son gets rewarded too for his devotion to his father.

Islamic Views on Adoption

Pre-Islamic Arabia practiced adoption more than today's modern societies. It was commonplace for a stranger to join a family, be given its name, and be treated like a member, even given rights to an inheritance. When Islam came, it defined the practice within a strict set of rules. Adopting a child and giving him or her rights equal to that of a natural child, such as the family name and a portion of inheritance, became forbidden. This is because the adopted child's lineage must not get mixed up with another lineage. In Islam, lineage is not just names—it's a blood relation. Scholars explain that because marriage is prohibited to blood relatives (except to cousins), getting lineage mixed up can cause confusions in the future as to whether someone is a real blood relative, and whether or not they can be married. Additionally, since the adoptee is not a blood relative, Islam forbids that child from having any right to the inheritance. If the child had such rights, it could lead to distress among the real family when it came to distributing the inheritance.

Also, an adoptee is considered a stranger, and as such cannot be allowed to intermingle with boys and girls (particularly after puberty) who he or she could technically marry. In other words, because the adopted child is not a blood relative, he or she is legally allowed to marry a son or daughter of the adopter, which makes it improper by Koranic standards to have the two living together on casual basis.

All this is not to say that Islam is against adoption. On the contrary, taking in an orphan for raising, sheltering, feeding, and educating is one of the most honorable deeds one can do. Prophet Muhammad said, "I, and the one who raises an orphan, will be like these two in Heaven . . ." and he held up his middle and index finger with a slight gap in between, indicating the closeness the two will share. Islamic adoption is done within a set of rules: the child's lineage must be preserved, and he must be separated from other "marriage-able" members of the family if he has reached puberty.

ALERT!

Islam specifies that lineage can only come through the natural father. Unlike many other societies, a Muslim woman's family name remains unaltered even after marriage; she cannot be called or referred to by her husband's lineage. Only the children carry the father's name. (Although, in some Muslim countries the woman will take her husband's name due to governmental laws.)

Distribution of an Inheritance

The Koran dedicates about two pages that explain in detail the fair distribution of an inheritance, clearly stating that the system is from the wisdom of Allah and that all Muslims must follow it. It leaves almost no one out. Eligible heirs of the deceased are children, parents, spouse, and brothers and sisters. A person has the right to control only a portion of his wealth, choosing to whom it would go; the rest is divided by the laws of the Koran.

The laws of inheritance are thorough and complex. Before anything goes to any heir, all debts owed by the deceased must be paid and settled from the inheritance. The Koran specifies the portion each member receives. The Holy Book addresses every situation, whether the deceased has a full family of parents, children, and siblings, or if he has none at all. The specified portions prevent disputes from arising within the family, and ensure fair division of the inheritance, with priority given to the deceased's children.

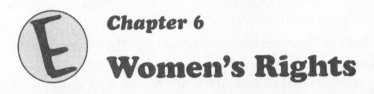

Chapter 6

Women's Rights

Oppression of women reached its heights in ancient Arabia before Muhammad came to be a prophet. When the Koran was revealed, the practices that oppressed women were abolished, and women were granted rights equal to men's. Contrary to common belief, the Koran is not disrespectful of women. Rather, it elevates their status, protects them, and earns them respect. The Koran gives women equal rights in education, career, marriage, and divorce. It is the misapplication of the Koran that sometimes leads to inequality.

Gender Equality in the Koran

The equality of men and women was established in the Koran fourteen centuries ago. The Koran came down at a time when women desperately needed rights, and it contained a timeless message to men and women. The message was that men are not better or superior to women, and that women have rights and deserve equal respect. In the Koran, women's rights are different from men's, but not less. For example, women have freedom with their possessions, but inherit less than male heirs who have to spend and provide for their families.

Some religions and faiths claim that a man is a superior creation to a woman. The Koran states otherwise: "He it is who did create you from a single soul, and therefrom did make his mate that he might take rest in her. And when he covered her she bore a light burden (baby), and she passed (unnoticed) with it, but when it became heavy they cried unto Allah, their Lord, saying: If You give unto us aright we shall be of the thankful" (7:189). This verse clearly shows that Allah created men and women from the same being and split it in two, which shows that the two are equal creations. It also mentions that the two were created to find harmony with each other, fall in love, live together, and have children: "And of His signs is this: He created for you helpmeets from yourselves that you might find rest in them, and He ordained between you love and mercy" (30:21).

The Koran does not blame Eve for the "fall" of Adam to Earth, nor does it deem childbirth and labor a punishment to women for disobeying Allah. It addresses Adam and Eve equally; they were both guilty, and they were both forgiven.

The fact that Allah created man and woman from the same being gives them equal importance, although they have different responsibilities. A woman bears children, so Muslims believe her duty as mother would be sacrificed if she was also ordered by Allah to work and provide for the family. A man is free from the responsibilities of pregnancy and nursing, so Allah leaves it up to him to go out and earn a living for the family, a position that, in Islam, also gives him the opportunity to protect and maintain order within the family. The point is that the Koran granted men and women equal importance, but assigned them different duties that *do not* make one superior to the other.

According to the Koran, men and women are equal vicegerents on Earth and both will be rewarded or punished equally: "And whoso does good works, whether male or female, and he (or she) is a believer, such will enter paradise and they will not be wronged in the dint in a date-stone" (4:124). Similar punishment is not only reserved for the afterlife, but applies to this world as well. For example, the punishment for adultery is the same for men as it is for women, indicating that both genders possess the same reasoning ability.

Modest Islamic Dress

The Koran did not leave it up to people to decide how to cover or display their bodies. For a set of reasons, Allah instructed men and women to dress in a certain way in public. It is common knowledge that women are assigned a certain dressing style, but what many people don't know is that men also have modesty requirements. They must cover their bodies from navel to knee. Skimpy swim shorts are *haram* (forbidden) for men to wear, as they display what should be covered.

What is the Hijab?

The Arabic word *hijab* derives from a root word that means "cover." There are many interpretations of women's Islamic hijab around the world, among both Muslim and non-Muslim communities. Perhaps the obvious interpretation to most people is that it's a covering of the hair. Many Muslim women wear hijab in their own invented way—which is not always appropriate. Some wear a colorful sheer scarf, some may free their bangs from underneath, some wear it loose so that it keeps falling, and some cover their heads but wear excessive makeup and tight, body-defining clothing.

There should be no reason for this confusion, because the Koran is straight to the point regarding hijab: "And tell the believing women to lower their gaze and be modest, and to display of their adornment only that which is apparent, and to draw their veils over their bosoms, and not to reveal their adornment except to their husbands or father or . . ." (24:31). The Koran is saying that women can only show "that which is apparent," indicating the face and hands. Women may reveal their adornment (interpreted as "hair") to husbands, fathers, and close family, which is also explained later in the same verse.

Another verse states: "O Prophet, tell your wives and your daughters and the women of the believers to draw their cloaks close round them (when they go abroad). That will be better, so that they may be recognized and not annoyed. Allah is ever Forgiving, Merciful" (33:59). By combining this with teachings from the Sunnah, Muslims conclude that the lawful hijab is the covering of a woman's body except for her face, hands, and feet. The cover should not be brightly colored, sheer, or tight fitting, as such things would attract attention.

ALERT!

It is true that the hijab must not attract attention, but it doesn't mean it must be ugly. Modern versions of the hijab can be very chic, such as a dark blue suit consisting of a long skirt, a jacket, and a flared scarf that covers the head and drapes loosely over the chest, making a woman look decent, pleasant, and modern.

Reasons for Hijab

Muslims believe that Allah created men to be attracted and aroused by women to ensure the continuation of life. This applies to both humans and to male and female animals. It is common in nature to see males chasing females, fighting each other for mating rights, and displaying their strength, skill, or beauty to impress the females. Men are not animals, of course, and can control themselves. That's why Allah commands them to lower their gazes, too, as He instructs women.

Of course, women cannot take all of the blame for the stares of men, but if they follow the instruction of the Koran, they can help control it. Allah's intention is to control both sides, commanding men not to ogle, and women not to make a temptation out of themselves. Scholars like to imagine a society in which women do not display their beauty publicly, temptation is low, and men will be less likely to harass women and less inclined to think they can approach any woman. Then scholars contrast this with a society in which women freely bare themselves publicly, temptation is high, and men will be more inclined to approach them sexually. Muslims believe that marriages in the first type of society will more likely remain intact, as neither husband nor wife will be tempted or seduced by others.

Islam explains that the hijab also protects a woman's respect and dignity. It does not limit her freedom in her home, at social events, in her job performance, or even in attracting a potential husband. Muslim women who wear the hijab say that this modest dress allows others to see and appreciate their character rather than their looks.

FACT

Some Muslim women choose to cover themselves completely from head to toe, wearing veils over their faces and even gloves to cover their hands. There is no specific reference in the Koran to this type of hijab being compulsory, although one Hadith says that it is a good deed to do so.

Various Rights

Since the Koran deems a woman an equal creation to a man, her rights are more or less the same as his. Prophet Muhammad's children were all girls (except for a couple of boys who died before maturity), and he provided an example to Muslims on how women should be treated. In no way is a woman rendered inferior or less deserving than a man in the Koran. In fact, you may be surprised at how much attention the Koran devotes to keeping women happy.

Right to Education

Islam recognizes the woman as the mother and bearer of children who constitute future generations. Neglecting female children's education is neglecting the education of future generations, boys and girls alike. Only an intelligent, educated, and ethical woman can be a good mother who is able to raise healthy, productive individuals who will benefit society.

Based on the Koran and Sunnah, Islam teaches that parents should not discriminate between their boys and girls when it comes to their education. Both should be able to go to school with an equal desire to learn and succeed. Education should not be limited to schools, but also extends to the parents, who teach them about their religion and train them in practicing their faith early on in their lives. Religious education and upbringing is extremely important to Muslims because they believe it plants moral seeds that will later grow and become an integral part of the individual.

Knowledge and science hold very high precedence in Islam. The Koran commands people to seek knowledge even if they have to travel the Earth to find it. Prophet Muhammad also said, "Seeking knowledge is mandatory for every Muslim." His wives and daughters were thoroughly educated and well versed in some sciences.

There is no ideal Islamic society in the world today. Everywhere there are Muslims who don't understand Islamic faith or misapply it to their lives. Many think girls are inferior to boys and end up discriminating between the two, neglecting the girls' proper education.

Financial Liberty

The Koran gives a woman great liberty with her money and assets. She is free from the obligation to provide for anyone. She doesn't even have to sustain herself unless she has no family. At every stage in her life there is a man in her family required by Koranic law to sustain her. If she's single, her father or brother is responsible for her, and if she's married, then her husband is responsible.

Of course, it would be selfish of her to abuse this right by saving all her money and letting her sustainer work himself to death. There are exceptions to every rule. If, for example, a wealthy widow can provide for herself, it would be kind of her to refuse provisions from her less-fortunate brother who has a family of his own to look after. This is where morals and ethics come into play, and where the absence of ethical choices would be judged by the wisdom of Allah.

By the law of the Koran, women generally inherit less than men. But again, their inheritance is theirs to save or invest, while men have to spend their share on their families. A woman would be rewarded, though, if she used her assets or inheritance to improve her family's life-style. In brief, a woman can keep her money or do whatever she wants with it, but if she participates in household expenses, Allah would be pleased with her.

Right to Pursue a Career

Islam left the choice to work open for a woman, on the condition that she does not neglect her duties toward her husband and children. According to the Koran, women have no financial responsibilities like men, so they are not pressured to find jobs and earn a living. However, scholars say if women can ensure that their duties toward their families will not suffer, they can establish a career. Women can also invest their money and start their own businesses. Prophet Muhammad's first wife, Khadija, was a businesswoman herself and a trader, which indicates by example the freedom of women in Islam to regulate income.

It's important to note that whatever job a woman chooses, it must be within the limits of modesty. In other words, the job must not violate Islamic regulations. She should not be obligated to dress in a way that's not modest, or mingle on a deep and personal level with strange men.

ALERT!

A "strange" man to a woman is anyone who is outside her close family. If he is not her husband, son, brother, father, grandfather, father-in-law, uncle, or nephew, then she must wear the hijab and observe her modesty in his presence.

Marriage and Divorce

No woman can ever be forced into a marriage according to Islamic law. She has the right to accept or refuse a marriage proposal. Forced marriages are less common nowadays than they used to be, as people are starting to break free from tradition and open their eyes to the real teachings of the Koran and Sunnah. The consent of the bride is a legal Islamic requirement before the marriage contract is drawn. If the bride is against the marriage and the contract is sealed anyway, the marriage would be deemed invalid according to Islamic rules.

Wedding Bliss

Islamic tradition dictates that a man should ask for woman's hand in marriage from her male guardian, who could be her father, brother, uncle, or even son. If she has no male relatives alive, then her mother, elder sister, aunt, or any other guardian would do. A prospective husband carries the burden of having to visit a bride's home, undergo a stressful (but appropriately kind and respectful) interrogation by her guardians, and subject himself to acceptance or rejection. Normally, reasonable parents do not pass a judgment on the man before consulting their daughter.

For a man to propose to a woman's family in her home is an act of respect and honor toward her as he becomes bound to keep his word before the family. The presence of the family also serves as protection of the bride's dignity. But that's not the end of it for the groom . . . the law of Allah commands him to present his bride with a gift called *mahr*: "And give unto the women (whom you marry) free gift of their marriage portions; but if they of their own accord remit unto you a part thereof, then you are welcome to absorb it (in your wealth)" (4:4).

This gift could take the form of anything the groom can afford: a sum of cash, jewelry, a piece of property, etc. If he is completely broke, Islam allows him to marry her if he can teach her some of the Koran as a gift. The gift goes to the bride and is left entirely at her disposal even if divorce occurs. In case the marriage is dissolved before consummation, the woman keeps half the amount or value of the gift.

The groom is responsible for setting up the home as his means would allow. In reality, however, the bride's family often helps out financially because the burden is usually too great for the groom to handle alone. Allah rewards families that work in harmony to ease the pressure on the bride and groom. Once married, apart from the financial duties of the newlywed husband, he is required by the Koran to fulfill his wife's emotional and physical needs, just as she is required to fulfill his. (More on this in Chapter 11.)

A couple can divorce twice and reconcile, but the third divorce is final. After that, they cannot remarry unless the woman marries another man and *he* divorces her. Only then can she remarry her first husband. This is Allah's law that prevents people from taking marriage and divorce lightly.

Before and after Divorce

Divorce is Allah's most despised *halal* (meaning legal or permitted). It cannot be made illegal because some marriages lack compatibility and simply must be broken. Allah allowed divorce in the Koran, but supplied it with a list of conditions. If the couple fails to make a private reconciliation, Allah advises that before the decision to divorce is made, a trusted arbiter from the wife's family and another from the husband's family get together to try to sort things out for the couple. If they still don't reach an agreement and divorce is inevitable, then all that is required is for the husband to say, "I divorce you," in a calm and functioning state of mind, and the divorce would be valid.

A woman cannot divorce her husband the same way, but she can get her divorce in court. After the verbal divorce, the wife can continue living in her house for a set period of three months: "Women who are divorced shall wait, keeping themselves apart, three (monthly) courses. And it is not lawful for them that they should conceal that which Allah has created in their wombs if they are believers in Allah and the Last Day" (2:228). In other words, during this period the woman will be able to find out if she is pregnant, which may serve as a reason for the couple to get back together. The couple can be divorced twice verbally and get back together without the need of renewing the marriage contract.

By Koranic law, a divorced woman is entitled to be treated kindly and fairly by her ex-husband. He is responsible for her provisions for some time, but certainly not for life. He is not allowed to take any of her possessions, assets, money, or even the gifts he had given her. Allah protected the rights of divorced women in an entire two-page Surah as well as all throughout the Koran, warning that a breach of those rights is a major sin for the violator.

Domestic Violence

Wife battering is a common problem in all the world's societies. Islam has a unique view of this issue; beating, battering, and abuse are not allowed, but Islam does allow using physical force against wives, within set limits.

This quote from the Koran addresses the issue directly: "As for those (women) from whom you fear rebellion, admonish them, then banish them to beds apart, then scourge them. But if they obey you, seek not a way against them. Lo! Allah is ever High Exalted, Great" (4:34). For the unknowing observer, it appears as if the Koran isn't against wife beating, but a thorough explanation may reveal a few surprises.

First and foremost, preservation of the family is paramount in the Koran. The previous verse presents a system that's supposed to help keep the family together. The very first words in the quote refer to a wife who deliberately displays rebellious ill conduct toward her husband, home, or family. Instead of the husband jumping to divorce, Allah advises him to first "admonish" her—telling him to talk to her in a gentle manner and ask her to change her ways.

FACT

Opting for the last resort of physical force against a wife should be the exception, not the norm. Prophet Muhammad preached to men that they should be kind and gentle to women. Men who violate the rule and take to beating their wives on a regular basis are sinning.

If she does not change her attitude, the next step is to "banish them to beds apart"—telling the husband not to share a bed with her and keep his distance for some time until she comes to her senses. If after a long time she still insists on her behavior and the marriage is at risk, the last resort for the husband would be what scholars interpret as a "whisk" against her—one that would not cause pain or leave a bruise (according to Prophet Muhammad) but would merely serve to stir them both emotionally. Muslims believe the wisdom is in the emotional aftermath, which leaves the couple apologetic and more willing to work together toward holding on to the marriage.

Of course, this applies to the couple who are still in love and do not wish to break up their marriage. If they cannot tolerate living with each other, they can simply get a divorce before going through any of these stages. The Koran's advice to "beat" does not mean batter or abuse. It means, by the Prophet's definition, a quick and painless strike that avoids the face or head that serves to shake them both out of the cold that has frozen their relationship. That way, a marriage can be mended and the family remains protected.

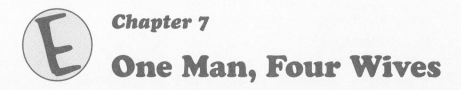

Chapter 7

One Man, Four Wives

There is no question that the Koran allows a man to take more than one wife. Polygamy in Islam has become a subject for criticism by non-Muslims who consider it immoral and a disgrace. Islam defends itself, saying it is a logical religion that wouldn't have permitted polygamy if it weren't for solid reasons. It is true that a man can marry up to four women, but strict conditions apply. Allowing polygamy is not meant to dishonor women. By contrast, it is a social necessity with a primary goal of protecting women.

Polygamy in the Past and Present

In many cultures throughout history it has been common for men to have several wives. The concept of a man marrying more than one wife was widely accepted and never frowned upon. Many considered it a way of life. Polygamy was familiar in the days of the Pharaohs of ancient Egypt when kings like Ramses II had eight wives. Men took multiple wives for themselves before and after the time of ancient Egypt and in different lands across the globe.

In pre-Islamic Arabia, the norm was to marry women in multiples. It was a very common occurrence for a man to have ten wives at his disposal at any given time. To them, women were inferior, so it was no wonder they took the issue of polygamy lightly. There were no laws to protect these women, and in many cases they'd be neglected and ignored by their husbands for younger, prettier wives. The children of the less-favored wives also suffered from negligence, often going inappropriately fed, clothed, or sheltered.

FACT

The term *polygamy* refers to marriage to more than one partner. There are two types of polygamy: polyandry, in which a woman has several husbands, and polygyny, in which a man has several wives. Islam forbids polyandry but allows polygyny of up to four wives.

Polygamy was not limited to irresponsible men; Allah's pure and obedient prophets had many wives, too. Prophet Abraham had two wives, who gave birth to the prophets Ishmael and Isaac. Prophet Jacob had his son Prophet Joseph from one of his four wives. Prophets Solomon and David had even many more. And, of course, the last of the prophets, Muhammad, had several wives as well. In each case of marriage with each of the prophets, there was wisdom and sufficient cause. (Muhammad's various marriages will be discussed later in this chapter.)

Today, only Islamic countries allow a man to have more than one wife. The majority of countries in the world hold polygamy to be illegal, although some men in these countries still practice it secretly. While men in Islamic countries openly practice lawful polygamy, today's polygamy among Muslims is sometimes far from the ideal the Koran described, and many men abuse this right in ways that are counter to the rights of women.

Polygamy in Islam

Polygamy is not an Islamic invention. The Koran permits it, but does nothing to encourage it (the Koran actually does more to *discourage* it). Experts say that permitting polygamy never had anything to do with sating men's desire for women; its objective had always been purely social. Islam recognizes the woman as an equal creation to the man, and therefore, Islam does not allow polygamy based on a disrespect for women. When polygamy is viewed from a female perspective, it is often seen as unjust and downright outrageous, but when viewed from a social perspective, polygamy becomes a cure for many social diseases.

Before exploring the issue of polygamy further, note that the Koran strictly prohibits sex outside the marriage bond. There are no excuses and the punishment is severe, unless the convicted chooses to repent. No husband or wife is allowed to have extramarital affairs. No one is allowed to get intimate with another if they are not married. Polygamy has nothing to do with sexual promiscuity or multiple unmarried partners.

The verse that permits polygamy in the Koran is as follows: "And if you fear that you will not deal fairly by the orphans, marry of the women, who seem good to you, two or three or four; and if you fear that you cannot do justice (to so many) then one (only)" (4:3). Through this verse, we understand that a man is allowed to marry up to four wives.

Polygamy may be allowed, but very few people practice it nowadays even in countries where it is allowed. The greatest majority of men choose monogamy where they find that sharing a life with one woman and their children is more fulfilling than maintaining a family circle of several wives and ten or more children.

Varying Opinions

The general belief is that verse 3 of Surah 4 (quoted in the previous section) permits polygamy, but some people claim otherwise. By dissecting the verse, they conclude that Allah tells people they can marry up to four wives, but—hold on—if they fear doing injustice to their wives, then they must marry only *one*. Based on that, they conclude that since a man could never be entirely fair to all wives, polygamy is illegal.

Scholars disagree with this, of course. Their argument is that the Koran would not permit something, and then disallow it. If Allah wanted to forbid polygamy, He would state that very clearly in the Koran. He would not give the permission with one hand, then take it with the other. Further evidence of the legality of polygamy is found in the Hadith and Sunnah, where Prophet Muhammad allowed new Muslim converts to keep four wives, and other Muslims to marry more than one wife if they wanted. Therefore, the argument against the legality of polygamy is weak.

Caution Against Polygamy

Every word in verse 3 of Surah 4 should be studied carefully. Upon closer observation, you'll notice that there are social reasons for polygamy, conditions that apply, as well as a limit on the number of wives. Each of these aspects will be discussed in detail in the next few pages, but the primary point to note here is that a man can have a maximum of four wives at the same time. If he thinks he can't be fair to two or more wives, then *only one* is allowed.

Later in the same Surah, Allah says, "You will not be able to deal equally between (your) wives, however much you wish (to do so): But turn not altogether away (from one), leaving her as in suspense. If you do good and keep from evil, lo! Allah is ever Forgiving, Merciful" (4:129). Here Allah is telling people that it is difficult for men to be completely fair between several wives, which in a way discourages polygamy. Roughly, the previous verses translate to: "Do it if you want, but you know you won't be fair. And because you won't be fair, marry just one—that's better for you in life and afterlife."

FACT

The Koran permits polygamy to allow flexibility with the ever-changing conditions of society, but does not in any way recommend or encourage it. In the Koran, Allah tells people that polygamy is difficult for them, and that one wife is most suited to their natural abilities.

Justification of Polygamy

At the time that polygamy was pronounced legal in Islam, men of the Arab desert tribes already had multiple wives. As they converted to Islam one after the other, Prophet Muhammad told them they could keep a maximum of four of their wives. Those who had fifteen wives suddenly had to be content with four, which was a radical change for most men. However, as the revelations came down, people learned more about morals and values, and above all, the treatment of women. Young single men who married as Muslims learned that one wife was more than enough if they were to grant her the rights defined by the Koran.

With the passing of time, the norm of polygamy became the exception. Realizing their responsibilities toward their wives and children, many men rejected the extra burden of a second wife. Muslims believe the Koran is a book that can be applied to any time and place, and as a result, it could not have permitted polygamy for the circumstances of A.D. 600 with a disregard for social changes in the future. They believe Allah permitted polygamy for all times because there would always be a need for it.

The Social Perspective

In justification of polygamy, scholars point to today's society in the United States or Europe, where polygamy is not practiced. They observe the cycles of marriage and divorce among those who have only one wife at a time, but who often have more than one wife in succession. Infidelity rates are soaring. Many men cheat on their wives, and they can easily discard their mistresses, as these women have no rights. Scholars point out that neither party is satisfied in such situations.

In addition, the number of illegitimate children is on the increase, leading to the problems of undetermined paternity, unwanted children, unpaid child support, and other such complications. These are the inevitable consequences of pre- or extramarital affairs.

The Koran presents polygamy as a solution to this problem. Instead of having a society full of infidelity, broken marriages, illegitimate children, and lost rights, a man is allowed to marry up to four women and grant each one her full rights as a wife. All his children are sheltered, clothed, fed, educated, and raised in a family environment. When he passes away, the inheritance is divided among all his wives and children. The end result is seen in the eyes of a Muslim as the protection of all women within the sanctity of the family, where a woman would not be used, exploited, cheated on, or discarded for another.

ALERT!

Some wealthy men abuse the right to marry several women. They keep their wives for a certain time and "replace" them with others when they've had enough. This practice does not conform to Islamic teachings because it rejects the whole objective of marriage. Allah condemns men who repeatedly marry and divorce.

The Individual Perspective

Righteous Muslim women avoid engaging in sexual activities with anyone other than their husbands. Would these women choose a lonely, loveless life or a life with a shared husband and a chance at motherhood? It may not be the ideal situation of one husband and one wife sharing a life together, but it may still be better than spinsterhood for some women.

A widow whose husband dies and leaves her with three children to raise and no money to support them may find the idea of a shared husband appealing. A husband would support her and her children in every way possible and provide a loving home for them. Another example would be a menopausal woman who hasn't been fortunate in finding her soul mate, and is now too old to conceive; she may find refuge with a husband who would treat her kindly, sustain her, and share her life, even if he had another wife. It may sound like charity, but according to scholars, Islamic polygamy's true goal is to protect the less fortunate women and save society from falling into promiscuity and its consequences.

Conditions Apply

If all the Koran did was let men know they can have up to four wives, things would quickly get out of hand. The Koran provides a solid system of guidelines for any man thinking of marrying at all. Getting married to a first wife—never mind a second—should never be a miscalculated decision. The Koran holds every man responsible for every marital decision he makes, and every step or action he takes in protecting and satisfying his wife. If, despite the warning in the Koran, a man insists on marrying a second wife, he increases his risk of falling into error by unjustly dealing with his wives.

FACT

If a man chooses to marry a widow with children from another man, the teachings in the Koran obligate him to treat, protect, educate, and spend on all her children as if they were his own, regardless of whether the woman is his first or second wife.

Before taking the plunge into marriage, the Koran and the Sunnah advise people to be adequately prepared in terms of finances, psychology, emotions, and physical health. These conditions help to ensure that a woman will be well taken care of once married. For a second, third, or fourth wife, the strain multiplies because the husband must be fair and just in dividing his care, attention, and finances among them.

Financial Capability

Being the supporter of the family according to the Koran, a man works very hard to provide them with the best he can afford. But before he forms a family, he should be sure that he can afford a wife. If he is seriously stricken with poverty, scholars advise it is better to wait until his situation improves so that he doesn't cause any suffering to his wife.

However, assuming he is an average person with a job that pays sufficiently, a decent place to live, enough food to keep him full, and a little excess money in the end, it is safe for him to marry and fulfill his Islamic duties toward his wife.

If then he feels tempted to marry another, he *must* first be sure that he can afford it because the Koran obliges him to sustain all wives equally. This means that he should have enough to pay her matrimonial gift, find her a place to live separate from his first wife, equally provide for her living, and become fully prepared to provide for any offspring to come. Every time he decides to add a wife (until he reaches the maximum of four), he needs to find a way to multiply his fortune in order to sustain them all, along with all the children. In today's Islamic society, only a very wealthy man can support four wives and a gang of children.

Physical Capability

Scholars warn that a man who is infertile or sexually incompetent should not marry more than one woman (unless by some common agreement), as that would be a form of injustice to his wives. He should be satisfied with one woman who accepts his situation. Concealing the issue and marrying a second wife is the peak of injustice as she might have hopes of motherhood. Islam does not allow men to cheat women into marrying them and shattering their hopes, not to mention leaving them unsatisfied.

The husband must provide for each wife and her children in an equal amount. In this context, equal means fair division. In other words, if one wife has three children, and the other has two, the wife with three children must receive a little more. Similarly, if one wife is ill and the other is healthy, the husband should spend a little more for the sick wife's medical care until she gets better.

The other side of this is the husband's ability to sexually satisfy his wives on a constant basis. To achieve equality between wives, scholars define that he should dedicate a day for each wife during which he *has* to fulfill her needs. It is an offense in Islam to leave a wife physically unsatisfied, as this may steer her mind into seeking pleasure elsewhere. If he doesn't think he possesses the strength to satisfy more than one wife, then it is better for him to keep to only marrying one. Again, this requirement scares some men from indulging in multiple marriages.

Emotional Capability

True love has little to do with rationality, and no person can force himself to fall in love. It is not likely that a man with four wives will be in love with them all, and the Koran does not require it of him either. But for harmony's sake, he should at least be fond enough of them to enjoy their company. He should not display any coldness toward any of them. On the contrary, he should pamper each wife with plenty of affection even if he married out of humane concern. The husband should also treat all his children equally without giving preference to any of them, even if some are his stepchildren. Meeting these requirements is a tedious task to any man, and most men avoid putting themselves in this situation.

Equality and Fairness

Jealousy is an instinct deeply rooted in the human being. It would be nonsense to claim that two or three wives would happily accept sharing their husband without feelings of jealousy and resentment. That's why Allah warns in the Koran: "You will not be able to deal equally between (your) wives, however much you wish (to do so)." It is hard enough to please one woman—two or more would pose a serious challenge.

Allah knows that a man's heart will be more inclined toward one wife than the other, which may lead to a tendency to spend more time, attention, and money on the wife he loves most. The Koran does not ask a man to love his wives equally, but tells him to display his attention equally.

Scholars note that most important, his wives are better off housed separately from one another. Housing his wives in one place is asking for trouble. More likely than not, as has happened in many cases, the women will not display any tolerance toward each other. Clashes between the children of different mothers will arise, and the situation will become too stressful for all the people involved. Also, the husband should avoid getting affectionate with one wife in front of the other. That creates rivalry.

ALERT!

A woman has no right to prevent her husband from seeking a second wife, but a good husband should take her feelings into account. She does have the right to ask for divorce from her husband if he insists on marrying a second wife. However, if she exercises patience and does not break up her marriage, Allah will reward her.

Prophet Muhammad's Wives

Throughout the sixty-three years of his life, Prophet Muhammad married twelve women. His first wife was Khadijah, a wealthy widow. She died when he was forty-seven years old. After that, Muhammad married several women, and every marriage was a lesson and an example for Muslims. Muhammad married that often and practiced polygamy beyond the four-wife limit by Allah's guidance and consent. Muslims believe his case was an exception because he had twenty-three years to deliver a religion from Allah to all humankind, and had to provide as many examples as possible for Muslims to follow.

Khadija

Muhammad married Khadija, who was about fifteen years older than he was. At the time, Muhammad was a simple trader and Khadija was his rich employer. He was a bachelor, and she was a widow. Despite the differences, the couple had a blissful marriage that lasted more than twenty-six years. Muhammad did not marry anyone else during his commitment to Khadija. In their example, it is evident that differences in age, money, power, or social status are irrelevant when it comes to the marriage bond. Khadija was the wife closest to Muhammad's heart.

Aisha

Aisha was the daughter of Muhammad's close friend, Abu Bakr. When she was nine years old, she got engaged to Muhammad. As she matured, Aisha grew close to Muhammad, and the couple shared a real married life.

Aisha learned about the Koran firsthand from the Prophet. She was always present when he preached and she memorized the lessons well. Later when Muhammad fell ill due to advancing age, it was Aisha who took care of him and nursed him for the last few months before his death. When he died, Aisha repeated the lessons she learned from him, and recited many Hadith for others to learn and memorize. The wisdom in Muhammad's marriage to Aisha at such a tender age was to leave behind a legacy, a woman who grew up in the very heart of Islam as a wife of the Prophet himself.

Other Wives

Apart from Aisha and Khadija, Muhammad had another ten wives. Ramlah (also known as Umm Habiba) and Juwairiyah were daughters of Muhammad's worst enemies from Quraish. They were taken captives from battles and instead of being reduced to slaves, they became Muhammad's wives. This was to demonstrate Islam's desire for peace and reconciliation.

Maria was a Christian slave given to Muhammad as a gift from the ruler of Egypt, but she too became his wife. Safiya was a Jewish woman who also accepted the Prophet's marriage proposal. Muhammad's marriage to these women proved to Muslim men that they can marry women of other faiths.

Sawda was a kind and gentle widow who benefited from being taken as a wife to Muhammad, and in return looked after his children. Hafsa, Zainab Bint Khuzaimah, and Umm Salamah were three other widows that the Prophet married to sustain and protect. Another woman, Maymuna, had yearned to marry the Prophet, and when she was thirty-six, she proposed to him and he accepted. Finally, Zainab Bint Jahsh was a cousin that he married to show the people that Allah allows them to marry their cousins. The Koran mentions and supports all these types of marriages.

FACT

Many of Muhammad's wives were not Muslims when he married them, but later converted to Islam. They became known as the "Mothers of Believers" because they preached and taught to Muslims what they had learned about Islam during their lives with the Prophet.

Not for Imitation

Although Muslims are required by the Koran to emulate the Prophet, one of the things that was reserved for him alone was his marriage to more than four wives. Muhammad strove to demonstrate through example what Muslims can and can't do. The Koran tells men that they can marry free or enslaved women, women of other faiths, and cousins. So Muhammad married many times, mostly out of humane concern or to provide an example to Muslims. If he had not done so, a rich family might be reluctant to give their daughter's hand to a less fortunate husband, an older woman might not marry a younger man, or a Muslim man might refrain from marrying women of other faiths—even if it was all permitted by the Koran.

On the subject of the Prophet's multiple marriages, Allah says to him in the Koran that it is "a privilege for you only, not for the rest of the believers . . ." (33:50). What is generally meant by this verse and the few that follow in the same Surah is that only the Prophet was allowed to marry more than the limit of four wives, and that such a practice is strictly prohibited to other people.

The Koran adds that Muhammad was not to marry more than the women he had already wedded, and was not to divorce them to marry others. Even though he had more than four wives at the same time, Muslims know Prophet Muhammad was the only man in history to have ever treated all of his wives fairly and equally, that not one had ever complained. Such fairness was of course due to Muhammad's piety and exalted character, as described in the Koran.

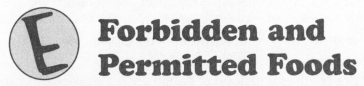

Chapter 8

Forbidden and Permitted Foods

The Koran states quite specifically what Muslims can and cannot eat. According to the Koran, Allah created everything, but because of some foods' adverse effects on health as well as some other reasons, Allah commanded people to avoid foods that are harmful, and eat only what He had made for human consumption. The Koran also sets rules on the method of slaughter of animals intended for consumption, defining the difference between *haram* and *halal* meats.

Why Forbid Certain Foods?

There are many reasons why Allah prohibits the consumption of certain foods—the most prominent of them is health. Back in the days of Prophet Muhammad, people knew little about healthful eating. They received their guidance from the Koran and Muhammad and did as they were told without question. As science advanced over the centuries, people discovered the adverse effects of the forbidden foods. Muslim scholars now believe that the Koran's main purpose for disallowing people from eating certain things is to protect their health.

The Koran defines a method of slaughtering animals for consumption, and an animal slaughtered any other way is considered *haram* to eat. Scientific experiments proved that the Islamic method is more humane and causes less pain to the animal than contemporary methods of stunning or strangling an animal. This shows that the Koran not only protects people's health, but also animal welfare.

FACT

Islam did not forget the importance of teaching people good table manners. These teachings are found in the Sunnah, where the Prophet Muhammad set an example for others to follow. There are numerous Hadith that tell people the do's and don'ts of table manners; the most famous of them is "Mention Allah's Name (i.e., In the name of Allah) before starting to eat, eat with your right hand, and eat from what is near you."

Alcohol and Other Addictions

The news reports alcohol as a major factor in social, criminal, and health problems. Alcohol damages the brain, slows down perception, weakens the liver, and leaves the body susceptible to many illnesses. Many Muslims feel that setting limits on the sales or distribution of alcohol is not likely to help much: if a little is allowed, people may push for more. The Koran does not tell people to drink a maximum of one glass a day; it bans it completely, as abuse is likely to result from any leeway.

Use of Alcohol

The Koran forbids consumption of wine, spirits, liquor, and any drink that contains alcohol. Violation of this law is a grave sin. The rules around alcohol are so strict that the Prophet said that Allah condemns all who participate in its manufacturing, buying, selling, and serving. You'd be sinning if you even lingered around a place where alcohol is served and people are drinking. The prohibition of alcohol is mentioned more than once in the Koran. Allah associates indulgence in it with the evil works of Satan:

> *O you who believe, intoxicants and games of chance and idols and divining arrows are only an infamy of Satan's handiwork. Leave it aside in order that you may succeed. Satan seeks only to cast among you enmity and hatred by means of strong drink and games of chance, and to turn you from remembrance of Allah and from (His) worship. Will you then have done? (5:90–91)*

In the previous verse, the Koran uses the Arabic word for "wine," but the translation uses "intoxicants." This is because the Koran does not refer to wine alone, but to every substance that damages the health and the mind. Prophet Muhammad confirmed this by forbidding any drink, cocktail, food, plant, or substance that causes a reaction in the brain similar to that of alcohol.

Use of Drugs

Drugs are not mentioned by name in the Koran, but are forbidden by reference. Drugs reduce perception and cause intoxication, and anything that falls under such classification is downright forbidden. Some of the less-knowledgeable Muslims use drugs like hashish and marijuana, claiming that the Koran does not mention them. However, Prophet Muhammad said, "Every consumable that causes intoxication is forbidden."

Consumables don't have to be consumed only through the mouth to be unlawful. According to Muslim sources, the rule covers all intoxicants, including any that are swallowed, inhaled, or injected. The Koran and the Sunnah exhibited no leniency toward intoxicants—partly because of their damaging effects on health, but more importantly because of their reduction of awareness and perception. The absence of the mind is the absence of reason, leading to an increased crime rate and a frail sense of security in society. Of course, the absence of the mind is also the absence of faith and belief in Allah.

Smoking

Smoking is an issue that has caused a lot of controversy among Islamic scholars. Since there is no direct prohibition of it in the Koran or the Sunnah, scholars had to rely on the effects of smoking on the health to understand how to better classify it. Their studies showed that nicotine is an addictive substance, and that smoking is the leading cause of lung cancer. It also increases the risk of heart disease and other illnesses that contribute to shortening a smoker's life.

With hundreds of thousands of people dying each year from smoke-induced diseases, the classification of tobacco as a toxic substance is unquestionable. Although there is no direct reference to it in the Koran or Sunnah, some scholars declare that smoking is forbidden, basing their decision on the Koran and Sunnah's warnings against self-destruction. Other scholars are content by declaring it a disliked, not recommended practice.

Islam has a scale of five classifications for all matters of life: *haram* (forbidden), *makrooh* (disliked), *mubaah* (permitted), *mustahab* (desirable), and *fard* (compulsory). For example, drinking alcohol is forbidden, smoking is disliked, polygamy is permitted, voluntary donations are preferred, and fasting Ramadan is compulsory. A Muslim loses or gains a certain measure of negative or positive points for engaging in each of those acts.

What's on the Menu

Allah's creation is vast. According to the Koran, He created thousands of species of animals and plants, and forbade humans only from consuming the few that are harmful to them: "O you who believe, eat of the good things wherewith We have provided you, and render thanks to Allah if it is (indeed) He whom ye worship" (2:172). Muslims who follow Allah's guidelines are well satisfied and have plenty of choices.

The Islamic Food Pyramid

The forbidden foods can be counted on your fingers. The permitted foods are almost limitless. Some religions forbid the eating of meat of any kind. In the Koran, the common belief is that both Earth and humans were created to serve each other. The circle of life would not be complete without each side giving to and taking from the other.

Everything that falls into the standard food pyramid designed by modern nutritionists is allowed by the Koran. Specifically, the Koran allows Muslims to eat red meat and poultry (with a few exceptions), vegetables, fruits, fish and sea creatures, grains, and carbohydrates. They can also eat eggs, dairy products, and honey.

This system allows Muslims to benefit from a balanced diet that includes all the elements of the food pyramid. The few things that the Koran tells people to avoid are not fundamental parts of the pyramid.

FACT

One of Prophet Muhammad's companions reported that on an expedition where food was scarce, Muhammad did not object to them eating locusts. Islam does not forbid this because locusts do not present any health risk. However, you are not likely to find locusts served in any Muslim house or restaurant these days!

Vegetarianism in Islam

There is a difference of opinion as to whether or not Muslims have the choice to be vegetarian. The Koran says that people should not forbid what Allah has permitted, or permit what Allah has forbidden. Some people use this as an argument against vegetarianism. Their opinion is that if Allah permitted meat and poultry, it is not anyone's place to refute it, and because Prophet Muhammad ate meat, all Muslims should emulate him.

Others use the word *permit* as the basis of their entire argument. They say that Allah presented a wide range of foods for the pleasure and benefit of humankind, but did not make it compulsory for people to eat from *all* that's permitted. This means, they say, that people can pick and choose what they like from the range presented, and that they can avoid meat if that's their preference. They do not believe they are forbidding what is permitted—they are simply making a personal choice among foods.

What's Not on the Menu

In forbidding certain foods, Muslims believe that Allah is not only saving them from health risks, but also testing them. Wine, for example, is a sweet indulgence for many people. Some may say a few sips are harmless. The real test for Muslims is in *resisting* the temptation of those few sips, and remaining faithful to Allah. Therein lies a test of human patience exercised as a form of worship. Every time a person resists a temptation for the sake of religion, Allah adds to the rewards of that person.

Apart from alcohol and intoxicants, what is *not* on the Islamic menu is as follows:

- Pork and its derivatives
- Carcasses of animals who died out of illness, injury, etc., or were left over by preying beasts (with the exception of fish and sea creatures)
- Blood
- All carnivores such as lions, tigers, wolves, etc.
- Birds of prey such as vultures, falcons, owls, etc.
- Animals slaughtered by means other than the Islamic *(halal)* method

There are a few other things that are questionable, and therefore are not included on the list; they will be described later. All the items in the previous list, with the exception of pork, are not commonly found in any non-Muslim American menu, so Muslims aren't missing out on much by avoiding these foods. In fact, they would gain the advantage of preserving their health from harmful side effects.

ALERT!

The Koran lists all the foods that Muslims are not allowed to eat, but also states that if one has a reasonable excuse, such as the absence of other foods, he or she can eat from what is forbidden without being a sinner.

Forbidden Pork

Muslims are known for never eating pork, based on the words of Allah in the Koran: "Forbidden unto you (for food) are carrion and blood and swine flesh and that which has been dedicated unto any other than Allah . . ." (5:3). Muslims believe that Allah did not forbid pork out of a mere test of people's self-restraint, but because He had sufficient reason to do so. Medical studies have shown that pork causes many different ailments to those who regularly eat it. Pig's flesh contains numerous parasites, bacteria, and germs. Although some of these parasites are found in other meats as well, most of them are unique to pigs and found in greater frequency in pig meat. Because of its high cholesterol and saturated fat content, pork is said to cause gallstones and obesity. With such a high health risk to humans, Muslims say it's no coincidence that the Koran forbade pig meat.

Animal Carcasses

An animal that died of natural causes such as illness or old age, or was killed in a fight or by a predator, is considered a forbidden carcass. If the animal was beaten to death, strangled, or even stabbed, it is considered unlawful to eat. Science can easily explain why it's unhealthy to eat an animal found dead or killed in the manner described here. When an animal is killed or slaughtered by means other than severing the throat, blood is retained in the body. The blood retention in the carcass is harmful and unhealthy for consumption by humans.

A dead body also rots very fast. The decomposition process forms armies of germs and bacteria that eat away at the flesh until it's reduced to bones. Rotten meat is poisonous and can be fatal to humans if eaten. The prohibition against eating carcasses is only stating the obvious. Muslims agree that humans were never meant to be scavengers, as do most people.

Beasts of Prey

Prophet Muhammad prohibited the eating of every fanged beast of prey. That not only includes lions, tigers, and similar predators, but also pets like dogs and cats. Carnivorous birds that hunt or scavenge on raw meat, like eagles, owls, crows, and vultures are included on the list of forbidden foods. Animals that feed on raw meat are generally unhealthy for people to eat because their bodies harbor parasites and bacteria that are particularly harmful to humans. These organisms as well as other viruses and microbes are also harbored in blood, which can transmit lethal diseases to humans.

FACT

Although Muslims are forbidden from eating blood, according to the teaching of the Koran, blood can be transmitted medically for health purposes.

Unconfirmed Foods

There are doubts surrounding a few other things that the Koran does not confirm as being forbidden for consumption. They include omnivores (such as chimpanzees), horses and donkeys, reptiles, and creatures that feed and live in filth, such as sewage rats. Allah says in the Koran: "O mankind! Eat of that which is lawful and wholesome in the earth . . ." (2:168). The Sunnah confirms this through Muhammad's Hadith: "If you see it appetizing, eat it, and if you don't, do not eat it."

This leaves a wide range of creatures to personal judgment. What the Hadith means is that if you are offered a worm sandwich, for example, and it doesn't appeal to your taste buds, the wise choice is not to eat it. There is a chronicle of the Prophet when some Bedouins invited him to a meal and served him a lizard, which he refused to eat. He said, "I am neither its eater nor do I prohibit it." Since Muslims emulate the Prophet, they ought to understand that they may be allowed to eat lizards and other exotic creatures, but that it is not recommended.

Slaughtering an Animal for Consumption

Meat only becomes permissible *(halal)* for a Muslim to eat when the animal is slaughtered according to the laws of Islam. With a very sharp knife, a swift deep incision is made in the animal's throat so that the veins and arteries are cut without severing the head. As the butcher brings down the sharpened knife, he must audibly say, "Bismillahi Arahman Araheem, Allahu Akbar," which translates as, "In the name of Allah, the Beneficent, the Merciful, the Greatest." Only then can the meat be declared *halal* for Muslims to eat.

Islamic belief is that every animal has a soul. Invoking the name of Allah at the moment of slaughter indicates that the animal's life is sacred for lawful purpose. The consumption of the animal's meat by humans is a lawful purpose sanctioned by Allah. Inevitably, the soul flies to the Heavens and returns to its Creator.

The Islamic slaughter method may seem brutal at first glance, but research suggests that it is a reasonably humane method. Professor Schultz of Hanover University, Germany, performed a comparative experiment between methods of slaughter. He compared the modern "captive bolt gun" (CBG) stunning method to the Islamic method, using electrodes to record the electrical brain activity of the animals.

With the Islamic method, the graph showed that the animal felt no pain at the point of the incision or for the following moments. A reflex of the spinal cord caused the body to convulse vigorously, which completely drained it of all blood. The graph showed zero level of pain during the entire process, and the end result was clean and hygienic meat for the consumer.

On the other hand, the stunning method rendered the animal unconscious for a second, which was immediately followed by severe pain. The stunning caused the animal's heart to stop sooner than that of the *halal* method. The result was that a lot of blood was retained inside the body—unhygienic meat for the consumer and a lot of pain for the animal.

Chapter 9

Legal Matters: Punishment, Politics, and Money

The criminal justice system described in the Koran is decisive and strict, and more than 1,400 years old. It may appear harsh to some, but Muslims see it as fair, reasonable, and applicable to any time and place. The Koran addresses both major and minor crimes with a penalty system devised to combat the very existence of crime. Islamic law also covers banking and financing, setting rules and limits for all types of transactions.

The Islamic Criminal Justice System

The Koran spells out specific punishments for many different crimes, both major and minor. Felonies in Islam are murder, fornication (premarital sex), adultery (extramarital sex), theft, apostasy, and slander. Other less serious crimes include drunkenness, assault, and fraud. Each one of these crimes is assigned a code of trial and punishment.

You may be surprised that fornication is a felony and that drunkenness is a punishable crime at all, but Muslims believe that Allah recognizes a danger imposed by these acts on the order and security of society, as each step taken in this direction opens the road to more crime. Islam aims to build and preserve an environment where society will prosper. To that end, the justice system described in the Koran has the following goals:

- To preserve life
- To preserve lineage
- To preserve property
- To preserve religion
- To preserve reason

Murder and assault are offenses against life; fornication and adultery are offenses against lineage; theft and robbery are offenses against property; apostasy is an offense against religion; and drunkenness is an offense against reason. This is why Allah devised a solid system to counter these crimes against society. The ideal environment would offer security and stability free from all these disturbances.

FACT

Islamic punishment is divided into three levels: fixed punishment, retribution, and discretionary punishment. Felonies and a few other crimes receive fixed punishment as defined by the Koran, while minor crimes receive either retribution or a discretionary punishment as judged by the state.

The Islamic system applies the philosophy that prevention is better than cure. Having a strict and effective penal system is only part of achieving peace and stability. The other half, Muslims trust, is in the lessons of the Koran, which arm the believer with a conviction against immorality. Allah makes it very clear in the Koran that He knows all and nothing escapes Him, and that punishment for the wrongdoers will be severe. Simultaneously, He describes the abundant rewards awaiting the righteous, filling believers with a desire to follow the straight path to Heaven. Ideally, people will be motivated by the desire to please Allah rather than the fear of punishment, but for those who are not, the punishment is harsh enough to make them think twice before committing a crime.

The other strategy of crime prevention taught by the Koran is the application of a healthy and balanced economic and social system that reduces the cause for crime in the first place. Islamic punishment is severe, but enforcement would rarely be necessary in a place where the governing body provides at least the minimum requirements of food, clothing, and shelter for every individual. Islam makes it the duty of the government to eliminate poverty and create an economic system in which everyone gets a chance to grow. Scholars say that the crime rate would drop significantly on its own in a society where these ideal conditions exist, along with a high sense of morality within the people.

Punishment for Felonies

Most of the crimes regarded as felonies in Islam are regarded as minor crimes in modern American or European law. If appropriately proven guilty, committers of these felonies receive a fixed penalty exactly as stated in the Koran.

The Penalty for Slander

Celebrity magazines and tabloids exploit the rich and famous on a daily basis. They write that this actress has a new boyfriend, or that singer cheated on his wife with her best friend. Such slander is damaging to people's reputations, but unless it inflicts damage against the victim's money or property, it can hardly be brought to court. On the other hand, the Koran views slander as a breach of respect and honesty and a serious offense against a person's honor.

Slander becomes a felony in Islam when it attacks the chastity of a woman. For example, if a man runs off to the press and claims to have seen this woman and that man in bed together and cannot provide sufficient evidence, he is committing felony slander. Also, if two, three, or four people testify against such a case, and their testimonies are not unanimous, this indicates slander, and they will be accused and charged with the fixed punishment specified by the Koran.

According to the Koran, the punishment for this type of slander is eighty lashes: "And those who accuse honorable women but bring no four witnesses, scourge them (with) eighty stripes and never (afterward) accept their testimony. They indeed are evil-doers" (24:4). It is no lenient punishment, but Muslims feel the damage that could have been caused by the false accusations against the people involved makes the punishment fair and just. What if the man in question had a wife and children? What if the woman was a young single virgin? Such slander could break up the man's family and ruin the woman's reputation and her chances of a good marriage proposal. The punishment prescribed is meant to deter people from rushing to authorities (or worse, to the press) with such news unless they have witnessed it firsthand and can present sufficient proof.

Punishment for Fornication

The Koran warns people against even toying with the idea of fornication (sex outside of marriage), much less engaging in it. That's why, according to the Koran, women are not allowed to display their beauty publicly, why men are commanded to lower their gaze, and why marriage is obligatory on all who can afford to get married.

In cases where fornication has been proven, the punishment of 100 lashes carried out in public must be given. Scholars explain that the punishment is applicable only to unmarried persons, as Islamic law defines a different punishment for adultery. For the fornicator, the punishment of 100 lashes cannot be waived or reduced in severity. But before the crime is confirmed, a strict set of conditions must be met.

ALERT!

Sex outside marriage is illegal in the Koran. Scholars argue that the damages incurred on society resulting from promiscuity are endless. They believe that diseases, broken families, illegitimate children, and crime are rampant in societies where promiscuity is the norm.

According to the Koran and Sunnah, the testimony of *four* reliable and honest eyewitnesses who have seen the act is taken. If a witness has a reputation of being unreliable or dishonest, his testimony would be invalid. Scholars say that witnesses must have been present at the moment of penetration and be able to describe the events as they happened. Any discrepancies in the testimonies will arouse doubts and may risk the witnesses being accused of slander. Finally, the accused must be a sane adult who committed the act under no pressure and out of his own free will.

Meeting each and every one of these conditions is an arduous task. Producing four reliable witnesses who actually saw the entire act of fornication is nearly impossible, unless the fornicators intentionally favored an audience. It is extremely rare for a case to be proven and for punishment to be carried out. Therefore, the 100-lash punishment serves more as deterrent than as a penalty. Muslims believe that Allah made it difficult to prove this crime in order to give a chance for the wrongdoers to repent under the safeguard of secrecy.

ESSENTIAL

Adultery and fornication are rare in truly Islamic communities. Even though almost all cases would never be revealed or convicted, people do not commit these acts due to the strength of their faith and their fear of Allah.

Punishment for Adultery

In Islam, adultery is worse than fornication and receives the severest, most intense of all punishments. Scholars argue that unlike the unmarried, a married person is not deprived of satisfaction and should not seek pleasure with someone other than a spouse. If he or she is not finding satisfaction with a spouse, they should seek a divorce instead of falling into the grievous sin of adultery. The punishment for adultery in Islam is stoning to death. This punishment is not mentioned in the Koran but is taught by Muhummad in the Sunnah.

The trial process of adultery is the same as that for fornication. Four trustworthy testimonies are needed to convict the adulterer. Again, the likelihood that four people bear witness to an act of infidelity that is usually carried out in total discretion is near zero, so it is as rare to prove a case of adultery as it is to prove a case of fornication. The only situation where the testimony of witnesses would not be required is when an adulterer confesses to his crime.

If the crime is not exposed and goes unnoticed, the adulterer may repent to Allah in discretion. If the repentance is sincere, Allah will forgive any sin, provided the person does not go back to it again and again. In the Koran, Allah encourages sinners not to expose themselves but to cower away from sin and ask forgiveness. In other words, he asks people not to publicize their sins, but keep them secret, as this gives them a chance to repent and lead a normal life. If a sinner does not repent in his lifetime, his punishment in the afterlife will be more severe than any he would have received on Earth.

FACT

Because it is extremely difficult to prove a case of fornication or adultery, records state that only fourteen adulterers were stoned to death from the time of Muhammad to the 1980s. The number illustrates that though the system is harsh in principle, it is very rare in practice.

Penalties for Theft

The Koran recognizes the effort people put into establishing a proper lifestyle for themselves. Their earnings are their property, which must be guarded. Theft is a transgression against property. Stealing people's possessions subjects a thief to a very severe punishment, which is the amputation of his hand: "As to the thief, both male and female, cut off their hands: a punishment by way of example from Allah for their crime, and Allah is Mighty, Wise" (5:38).

Like other crimes, the punishment for theft is applied only after fulfillment of a certain set of conditions as defined by the Sunnah. First, the money or property stolen must be taken from a safe place—taking an abandoned billfold of cash off a bench in a park is not theft, but breaking into a bank vault and filling bags with money is. Second, the value of the item stolen should equal at least a quarter of a dinar (a little short of a U.S. dollar) or more; the item must hold a financial value to the owner and not be something that could easily be thrown out. Third, the thief must be sane, mature, and fully aware of the crime he was committing. Fourth, the crime must have been committed out of greed rather than hunger or poverty. And finally, two reliable witnesses must have seen the crime taking place.

As is evident, fulfilling such criteria is not easy. However, if the case is proven against the thief, his hand must be amputated at the wrist. Again, it is so rare that such convictions ever occur that in a 400-year period in early Islamic times, only six cases of hand amputation were recorded. This supports the words of Allah, "a punishment by way of example," which serves more as deterrent than as regularly applicable punishment. Allah follows that verse with "But whoso repents after his wrongdoing and amends, Lo! Allah is Forgiving, Merciful" (5:39).

Highway and armed robbery are major felonies. Such crimes catch unsuspecting victims defenseless, and involve theft, injury, and possible loss of lives. The punishment prescribed by the Koran for such crimes is amputation and exile.

Punishment for Other Crimes

The Koran's criminal justice system contains punishment for many more crimes than the four felonies listed previously. The other punishments are less severe but do not lack effectiveness. The Koran applies the "eye for an eye" principle when dealing with violent crimes such as assault. Retribution is also applied when the victim demands a monetary compensation for the loss or damage inflicted. There are also prescribed punishments for apostasy and drunkenness. As for other various crimes, verdicts are left to knowledgeable and wise judges who base their judgments on the basic principles of the Islamic judicial system.

Islam does not assume that any person accused of a crime is guilty until sufficient proof is presented. This is similar to the familiar concept of "innocent until proven guilty" in the United States.

An Eye for an Eye

The Koran describes the concept of retribution as an effective means of combating different types of crime when Allah says:

> *And We prescribed for them therein: The life for life, the eye for the eye, the nose for the nose, the ear for the ear, the tooth for the tooth, and for wounds; retaliation. But whoso forgoes it (in the way of charity) it shall be expiation for him. Whoso judges not by that which Allah has revealed: such are wrongdoers. (5:45)*

This verse is to be taken in both a literal and metaphoric sense. In a literal sense, it would mean, for example, if somebody punches you in the face and breaks your nose, you have the right by Islamic law to break his nose, too, under the supervision of authority. Or if someone throws a rock at your glass window and breaks it, Islam allows you to do the same to his window. The "eye for an eye" reference is also a metaphor describing the idea that a victim of some types of crime has the right to demand some sort of retribution from the criminal.

Retribution is applicable when the damage inflicted is deliberate. Also, instead of returning the blow exactly the same way, you have the liberty to choose a ransom as compensation. Of course, if you find it in your heart to forgive, that would be even better, according to the Koran.

Deliberate, cold-blooded murder cannot be settled by ransom or simply forgiven. The life of the murderer must be taken. Like the legislation of many countries, the Koran requires capital punishment for murderers. As for accidents and manslaughter, Allah says about the person holding the blame: "He who has a killed a believer by mistake must set free a believing slave, and pay the blood money to the family of the slain, unless they remit it as a charity . . ." (4:92). The Koran goes on to say that if the deceased was not a believer, then freeing a slave would be enough, and if the blamed person cannot afford compensation or freeing a slave, then he must fast for two consecutive months as repentance to Allah.

ALERT!

The Koran does not define a method of capital punishment. In the United States, different methods of capital punishment are the electric chair, gas chamber, and lethal injection. Murderers in Islam used to be beheaded, as it is considered painless and quick. However, today most Islamic countries hang murderers.

Apostasy and Drunkenness

Apostasy is an abandonment of one's religion. According to Prophet Muhammad, "It is not permissible to take the life of a Muslim who bears testimony that there is no god but Allah, and that I am the Messenger of Allah, but in one of the three cases: the married adulterer, a life for life, and the deserter of his religion (Islam), who abandons the community."

This means that besides adultery and murder, the one last crime punishable by death is apostasy. Islam regards people who abandon it not as traitors, but as enemies of the religion who set out to distort its image before others. Also, Muslims feel that a believer who has learned of the thoroughness of the faith should know better than to turn away from it.

Drinking until the mind is wasted calls for due punishment in Islam. Alcohol is forbidden and any consumption of it is a sin, but Islam does not leave it entirely to the individual's conscience to drink or not to drink. It enforces the law with forty lashes—a punishment found in the Sunnah.

This does not apply to people drinking in the privacy of their own home, but to those who get drunk in public. Two witnesses are required to convict the drunkard.

QUESTION?

How does Islam deal with unproven criminal cases?
Prophet Muhammad used to release people from accused charges due to lack of evidence or witnesses. He said this was better than punishing a person who is possibly innocent. Since "Allah knows and sees all," crimes will be punished by Him in His time.

Islamic Law and Society

There is no doubt that criminal punishment in Islam is more severe than many systems around the world. To view the Islamic system in proper perspective, note that Islam does not fight crime on the surface and ignore the roots of society. Instead, the Koran calls for nurturing these roots through effective social, economic, and political systems. Children are to be raised in a loving home with their parents, all people are to be educated, virtues and morals are to be valued, and the government must work toward an economy where wealth is distributed as evenly as possible and opportunities are available for everyone. Scholars are convinced that when all these factors come together, the crime rate will naturally drop, and the few people who are insistent on harming society will be duly punished.

Many scholars agree that standing trial alone with the risk of getting a hand amputated is sometimes enough of a psychological torment to prevent a thief from ever crossing the line again. When Islamic punishment used to be applied, people usually avoided doing anything illegal due to the chance—however small—of being convicted. Muslims believe if one person every fifty years is lashed for fornication, the memory will stick in people's minds and deter them from committing the same crime. The system works "by way of example" according to Allah, and is very effective.

Harsh or Humane?

Lashing, stoning to death, amputation, and exile all sound extremely severe and degrading of human rights. Yet, from the Koran's perspective, the particular act of adultery, theft, or slander is the real violation of human rights. Muslims believe that Allah's purpose in setting these laws is only to preserve peace in society.

Also, even though the punishments are severe, they are rarely carried out, due to the complex trial system. Upon close inspection, you will also see that the penalties are harsher by name than in reality. Take lashing for example: a person is accused of fornicating, is proven guilty, and is sentenced to 100 lashes. According to the rules set by the Sunnah, the accused will not be thrown into the merciless hands of a vicious executioner who will tear his skin to shreds.

Instead, the punishment will be carried out in front of a crowd, the whip will be of medium size, the lashes should be of average intensity (the executioner should not raise the whip above his shoulder level to strike), the accused will be fully clothed, and the weather conditions should be tolerable. The executioner should avoid striking the head, face, or private parts, and should not strike hard enough to break the skin. Additionally, the 100 lashes could be given over a period of ten days and not necessarily on one day.

ALERT!

Although Allah prescribed severe punishment for certain crimes, He says in the Koran that whoever sincerely repents after wrongdoing, Allah will forgive him and he may be left alone without being punished for his crime.

Laws for All Times

The laws of the Koran are not constrained by time or place and are applicable anywhere until the end of time. They were meant to protect society from crimes that will cause instability and lack of order. Some crimes mentioned in the Koran used to be regarded as crimes 200 years ago in America and Europe, but due to changing views and opinions, they became publicly acceptable in those places. Such examples are fornication and adultery. The Koran will always regard them as felonies worthy of fixed punishment, whether committed 500 years ago, or 500 years from now.

Islamic Political System

When Allah created Adam, He told the angels He was sending a vicegerent to Earth. Humans are Allah's vicegerents responsible for running this world to the order of the Koran. The Arabic word for vicegerent is *khalifa*, or caliph. Islam has only one governing system: the caliphate. The caliphate ruled the Muslim world for a few hundred years following the reign of the Prophet Muhammad.

While all people are Allah's caliphs on Earth, they still need a superior caliph to organize them. A caliph by political definition is a Muslim ruler. In ancient times, the caliph was appointed by the people to govern the state. The people would propose some candidates who shared almost similar expertise in religion, politics, and social order, and vote for the one they thought was most suitable for the post. The election process was more primitive than today's elections, but followed the same basic principle.

FACT

The caliphate system is close to modern democracy in the United States but holds one major difference: the caliphate rules by Islamic law that is not amendable, while democracy continuously changes the law through votes by Congress. In other words, democracy rules by popular sovereignty while the caliphate rules by Allah's sovereignty.

The appointed caliph would rule based on the Koran and the teachings of the Prophet, which both strive for an ideal society. Because Islamic law is complete, thorough, and indisputable, the caliph would never need to make amendments to the governing, social, economic, or criminal justice system. In matters that would require judgment and decision, the caliph would consult his group of advisors (who were also men of great knowledge and wisdom), and take their vote in the matter. If the people felt the caliph was deviating in his ruling from the law of the Koran and the Sunnah, they would deny him his position and reappoint a new caliph.

Banking, Finance, and Trade

Islamic banking is radically different from universal banking in one major aspect: it neither charges nor awards interest to its clients. The Koran completely prohibits interest in all financial transactions. According to Muslim scholars, the reasons are that gaining interest involves oppression and exploitation of people's rights to their property, and that it causes uneven distribution of wealth, particularly from the needy to the wealthy.

Money earned through interest is considered unlawful money. The Koran also forbids fraud, cheating, and monopoly, promising Hell to all those involved in them. Such gains are deemed unlawful money, as they come from dishonest and oppressive means. Allah says in the Koran: "And of their taking usury when they were forbidden it, and of their devouring people's wealth by false pretenses. We have prepared for those of them who disbelieve a painful doom" (4:161).

Chapter 10

Abandoning Evil and Adopting Goodness

Every page of the Koran distinctly separates goodness from evil and the righteous from the wrongdoer. The Koran outlines all appropriate behavior, from general public conduct to personal hygiene. The most important thing is the purification of the soul and sincerity of the heart toward the faith. The Koran defines conduct toward friends, neighbors, strangers, and animals. It also warns about the luring path of Satan, describing its features and the scorching end to those who walk it.

The Good Muslim

Strong, sincere faith drives good Muslims toward perfecting their character and heightening their morality. The good Muslim is influenced by his faith in his everyday life, letting it be his guide and mentor in all matters. His faith strengthens his desire to become a better person and emulate the ideal character of Prophet Muhammad as closely as possible. With faith, purity, and a desire to please Allah, the general moral conduct of the Muslim is guaranteed to improve by vast measures.

Purity and Ablution

A rule in the Koran states that before praying or touching the Koran, the body must be washed and cleansed with water. Muslims believe this cleansing, called ablution, achieves several goals: first, cleanliness of the face, hands, arms, and feet is achieved through repeated ablutions throughout the day; second, small and minor sins are washed away with every ablution; and third, prayer or worship is approached in a state of mental, physical, and spiritual purity. Only in this state can a person commune with Allah through prayer, giving gratitude and asking His divine assistance, or by reading His words in the Koran.

FACT

According to the Koran, every person has an angel to his left jotting down his bad deeds, and an angel on the right jotting down his good deeds. Since the angel on the left cannot always be sure of the person's intentions, he writes down all the deeds except those that are definitely good, and leaves the final judgment to Allah.

Ablution is therefore not only an act of washing away everyday grime, but washing away sins as well. This is not to be taken in a literal sense—the sins are not washed off your skin, but rather are wiped off your record. Allah made it possible for anyone anywhere to wash, even if water is not available. In that case, a Muslim is allowed to rub with sand or clean earth as a form of ablution.

Muslims pray five times a day, so they perform ablution quite a few times, signifying Islam's high regard for purity and cleanliness. Why not cleanse just once every morning? Because ablution becomes invalid after responding to nature's call, passing air, having sexual intercourse, and even falling asleep.

Prophet Muhammad often said that he would recognize the devoted followers of the Sunnah on Judgment Day by the radiance and whiteness of their faces, hands, and feet, due to their frequent ablutions. He also said that a careful ablution could wash the sins from under your nails, which, in a metaphorical sense, means that even really bad sins can be wiped away. In Islam, ablution is a form of worship to Allah.

General Moral Conduct

The Koran guides every step a person takes, from the cradle to the grave. It describes the ideal character and behavior, urging people to strive toward purity of the mind and soul. High morality is the understanding of right from wrong, performing what's good, and avoiding what's evil. These days, most Muslims with high morality are still far from the Koran's description of a moral person. To come close to this description, one must also have the prerequisite of strong faith.

According to scholars, strong faith is both love and fear of Allah; you do good because you love Allah, and you shun evil because you fear Allah. The Koran preaches that morality should be practiced in all places and toward all people and animals. The Koran provides a stable, constant, and thorough moral system that is applicable to every person in the world and can be referred to in all aspects of life.

Practicing the Faith

Along with strong faith, a purified body and soul, and a sense of morality, worship is also essential. True Muslims spend their lives worshipping Allah. That does not mean they pray fifty times a day or fast all year. Worship is not limited to the Five Pillars of Islam (prayer, fasting, Hajj, charity, and belief in Allah and Muhammad). Muslims understand from the Koran that everything a person does in his or her life that is *good* is a form of worship. Patience and tolerance during a stubborn illness, feeding a hungry stray cat, greeting coworkers in the morning, maintaining calm in an aggravating situation, and keeping in close touch with your family are all acts of worship.

Prophet Muhammad once said, "Worship Allah as though you see him." He was indicating that worship should be pure, sincere, and overflowing with devotion. Muslims believe that those who pray out of love for Allah are closer to Him than those who pray as a fulfillment of obligation.

Piety

Piety is devotion to religion. Allah says in the Koran: "And vie one with another for forgiveness from your Lord, and for a Paradise as wide as are the heavens and the earth, prepared for those who ward off (evil), those who spend (of that which Allah has given them) in ease and in adversity, those who control their wrath and are forgiving toward mankind; Allah loves the good" (3:133–134). The "righteous" and "those who do good" are the pious people who remember Allah throughout every hour of the day, never forgetting what He considers good and what He considers sin.

Piety is also a fear of Allah. A Muslim knows that Allah can see every action and hear every thought. He or she can hide from the world, but not from Allah. Muslims believe that every little thing they do, from mere passing thoughts to performing good or evil deeds, is being recorded. All humankind will be questioned on Judgment Day and will probably find no excuse for whatever evil they did in life; they will not be able to hide or escape.

This belief creates awareness in true Muslims that affects how they live their life. Consider this scenario: A Muslim finds himself in a supermarket aisle tempted by a bar of chocolate, with long lines at the checkout counter and an appointment to fulfill. He faces one of three options: pick up the chocolate and wait in the line with risk of missing the appointment, turn away and leave with the intention of sating his appetite for chocolate later, or discreetly slip the bar in his pocket and walk out unnoticed. If he is pious, he will either wait in line or come back later, because even if no one spots him shoplifting, Allah will know and will be displeased.

ALERT!

In Islam, Muslims in prayer must not be disturbed, talked to, or walked around. During prayer, a Muslim concentrates her whole being of body, mind, and spirit in the ritual. She is not allowed to talk to anyone, look around, and shouldn't even let her thoughts trail away until the prayer is concluded.

Remembrance of Allah

All good deeds and worship are done through a remembrance of Allah. That's why five prayers are required from every Muslim. For further reward, a Muslim can add a voluntary prayer to every compulsory prayer as the Prophet used to do. He can also pray at night while everyone else sleeps, or at any other time during the day. From morning until night, a Muslim may pronounce little prayers such as, "Thanks to Allah who had fed, sheltered, and protected me" at the end of a meal. A Muslim can pray twenty times a day if she so chooses, as every prayer will earn her a better place in Heaven.

Prayer is emphasized dozens of times in the Koran for its merit and benefit for humankind. Allah says that prayer prevents a person from sinning or committing evil deeds. This is because praying is a spiritual experience in which the person praying speaks directly to Allah. When performed several times a day, prayer embeds the notion of Allah deep in the mind, driving the person to good deeds and helping him resist sinning. If Muslims were required to pray only once a week, there would be six days during which they would not feel particularly close to the Creator, which might weaken their resistance to sin.

Prayer is one way to remember Allah, but not the only one. Fasting is also another way to protect oneself from sinning. It may seem like a lot of worship, but Muslims believe it is the only way to live with an awareness of Allah, which in turn repels the devil and keeps people on the right track.

People who establish regular prayer as an integral part of their lives not only earn rewards in Heaven, but also on Earth. Prayer is a way of showing gratitude to Allah for His blessings, and He rewards those who pray with more blessings and good fortune.

Attitudes and Virtues

Ablution, piety, and remembrance are ways of Muslims, but anyone can benefit from the Koran's lessons in morality and righteousness. Muslims believe the Koran makes a perfect reference for molding an excellent personality. If it seems that an ideal character is beyond human capability, observe the conduct and personality of Prophet Muhammad. He was human, yet embodied the ideal character endorsed by the Koran. Allah says, "And lo! You (Muhammad) are on sublime morals" (68:4).

The virtues of good character mentioned in the Koran are too numerous to discuss within the limited context of one chapter. Some of the most important qualities of the ideal character described in the Koran are patience, kindness, truthfulness, and selflessness. Some other virtues and qualities are humility, justice, generosity, sympathy, tolerance, forgiveness, politeness, courage, decency, cooperation, modesty, and contentment. It's not easy for anyone to possess all these qualities and the many more in the Koran, but people can strive to become the best they can. If a person exerts a conscious effort in improving him or herself, Allah will be pleased.

Patience and Tranquility

Allah favors those who exercise patience throughout their lives. Allah talks about patience in the Koran with great emphasis: "And surely We shall try you with something of fear and hunger, and loss of wealth and lives and crops; but give glad tidings to the steadfast" (2:155). How a person tackles a certain loss or obstacle makes all the difference. For instance, take a man who worked very hard and suddenly lost his job. Does he curse his bad luck, or exercise patience and wait for his fortune to improve?

According to the Koran, patience is always rewarded: "Verily the steadfast will be paid their wages without stint" (39:10). If the man who lost his job prays for better fortune and remains calm, he is more likely to receive Allah's blessing than if he had cursed his luck in anger. Allah tells us in the Koran that we may hate something that is in fact good for us, and we may like something that is in fact bad for us. Consequently, people are better off exercising patience over their misfortunes as they do not know how events will unfold. In the Koran, patience is closely linked to faith in Allah, as those who believe that Allah can see them will find it easier to wait for His divine assistance.

Tranquility and dignity are two of the Koran's most endorsed characteristics, and Muhammad displayed both prominently. Allah says in the Koran: "The (faithful) slaves of the Beneficent are they who walk upon the earth modestly, and when the foolish ones address them answer: Peace" (25:63). Quick loss of temper is not favored in Islam as it results in temporary irrationality. The Koran preaches that a quiet, cool-tempered person is more likely to navigate intelligently through aggravating circumstances.

In His infinite wisdom, Allah distributed wealth variably among the people. Whether a person is among the less or more fortunate, his contentment with what he already has will be rewarded either in this life or the afterlife. Contentment is gratitude and will be rewarded, while greed is detested.

Truthfulness

The Koran and Sunnah address truthfulness repeatedly, emphasizing its importance as a virtue that every person should strive for. Truthfulness is not just a matter of speaking the truth—it applies to a wide array of situations, including keeping promises and guarding secrets. Because people often make promises they don't fulfill, Allah addresses them in the Koran: "O you who believe, why say you that which you do not do? It is most hateful in the sight of Allah that you say that which you do not" (61:2–3).

People should observe honesty in business and trade matters. A salesperson should never lure a customer into buying a product or service with an exaggerated and unfitting description. Even little things like cheating on school quizzes are a form of dishonesty that people should avoid. A truthful person is someone who is trustworthy and reliable, someone whose word is respected and believed.

Selflessness and Generosity

Selflessness is the love of others more than the love of oneself. It leads people to care enough to share their wealth with those who are needy. The Koran urges the more fortunate not to hold on to their money and possessions, but to share with others: "Those who spend their wealth in the cause of Allah, and afterward make not reproach and injury to follow that which they have spent, their reward is with their Lord; and there shall no fear come upon them, neither shall they grieve" (2:262). Note that the Koran promises reward to those who give without proudly publicizing or making an issue of the gift they gave.

Scholars describe selflessness as not only a sharing of wealth, but also a sharing of things like knowledge, shelter, food, and space. It is also about extending a hand of assistance where it is needed. Volunteer social work is an ideal example of selflessness as Islam would have it. Generosity falls under the same category. If your coworker has forgotten to bring along a sandwich for lunch, and you have two sandwiches, you would be doing a great deed to offer one of your sandwiches to him or her. This is an example of selflessness and generosity, where a person would not hesitate to help another.

FACT

People need to be modest and down-to-earth, but they should not neglect their outward appearance as a way of being humble. Prophet Muhammad proclaims, "Allah is beautiful and loves beauty," meaning that people should give importance to wearing neat and tidy attire and presenting themselves fresh and well-groomed.

Behavior Toward Others

In Islam, every man and woman is in debt to others. They owe one another politeness, kindness, truthfulness, tolerance, and respect. The Koran holds every person responsible for the welfare of the people close to him and those who are less fortunate. Treatment of friends, relatives, and neighbors must be honorable and respectful. Such good conduct is as essential as performing prayer, fasting, and giving to charity.

Protection of Orphans

The Koran commands people to give their "wealth, for love of Him, to kinsfolk and to orphans and the needy . . ." (2:177). Prophet Muhammad encourages the adoption of orphans, as long as lineage is not altered (see Chapter 5). Children without parents need a home even if they were left with a substantial inheritance. People who offer them a home, food, clothing, and education are guaranteeing themselves admission into Heaven according to the Koran and Sunnah.

If the orphan inherited a good sum, the adopter may spend this money on the upbringing of the orphan, as stated in the Koran: "And approach not the wealth of the orphan except with that which is better; till he reach maturity" (6:152). The age of maturity referred to in this verse would either be eighteen or twenty-one years, according to the law of the state. The Koran also warns against taking any of the orphan's money: "Lo! Those who devour the wealth of orphans wrongfully, they do but swallow fire into their bellies, and they will be exposed to burning flame" (4:10).

Duties Toward Neighbors

Prophet Muhammad preached that good treatment of neighbors is vital. In the Koran, Allah instructs people to "show kindness unto parents, and unto near kindred, and orphans, and the needy, and into the neighbor who is of kin (unto you) and the neighbor who is not of kin . . ." (4:36). Neighbors should treat each other with respect and politeness. Scholars advise that peace and privacy should be taken into consideration; neighbors should not spy on one another or turn up the TV so high that it would disturb the peace. Food sharing is an excellent deed between neighbors—those who eat their fill while their neighbors go to bed hungry are condemned.

ALERT!

A greeting is like an act of charity. Islam urges people to greet each other even if they are not on good terms. Surah 4 verse 86 says, "When you are greeted with a greeting, greet with better than it or return it. Lo! Allah takes count of all things." A common Muslim greeting is Assalam Alaykum, which translates to "peace and blessing be upon you."

Friends, Relatives, and Others

The Koran expects people to practice all the previously discussed qualities and virtues with all others, whether they are friends, relatives, colleagues, or strangers. Relatives should watch over each other and be prepared to help—financially or otherwise—if help is needed. In fact, the Koran says that relatives should be given priority (if a need exists) when someone is deciding where to give charity. Strengthening family bonds with things such as frequent visits, phone calls, or letters is a charitable and favorable act, while ignoring or cutting ties with relatives is a sin. Duties to family are not options, but obligations according to the Koran.

Friends and others should be treated similarly, with kindness, compassion, truthfulness, and respect. Hospitality and politeness are compulsory with guests even if they are secretly unwelcome. A Hadith of the Prophet says, "Do not disdain a good deed, even if it is your meeting with your Muslim brother with a cheerful face."

Treatment of Animals

Prophet Muhammad tells us that "[w]hoever is kind to the creatures of Allah is kind to himself." Islam recognizes animals as creatures of Allah deserving an equal share of space, food, and security. Humans might be Allah's vicegerents on Earth, but that does not give them the power to destroy it and kill its creatures. Just like humans, these animals possess a degree of consciousness. Allah says in the Koran: "The seven heavens and the earth and all that is therein praise Him; and there is not a thing but hymns his praise; but you understand not their praise. Lo! He is ever Clement, Forgiving" (17:44). This verse indicates that animals have some awareness of the Creator and they, too, praise Him.

The Koran and Sunnah instruct humans not to exploit animals for their own pleasure. Although Allah permits the consumption of some animals slaughtered under strict conditions, killing or hunting for pleasure is forbidden and anyone involved in it would be sinning. A Hadith by Muhammad says: "There is no man who kills even a sparrow or anything smaller, without its deserving it, but Allah will question him about it." Unjustified killing includes killing for fur, tusks, oil, skin, and other commodities.

The Koran and teachings of Muhammad do not directly address experimentation on animals, but the general guideline is that animals not used for consumption should be spared. Torturing or harming animals is a terrible sin. Mutilating animals is described in the Koran as the work of Satan.

The Major and Minor Sins

Just as the Koran and the Sunnah emphasize virtues and good deeds, they also emphasize a long list of bad and evil deeds. There is no fine line between good and evil; the border is thick and defined by Islam. However, sins vary from major to minor, and Allah judges each accordingly. According to Islamic belief, no one except the prophets is sinless; humans are weak by nature and easily seduced, as Allah created them.

Islam strictly forbids activities that cause harm or pain to the body or distort appearance. Surah 4 verse 119 quotes Satan as saying he will lead people to "change Allah's creation," which scholars have interpreted as mutilation of the body, whether animal or human. This includes tattooing and body piercing, and any intentional cutting, burning, or bruising of body parts.

Major Sins

In the Koran, the biggest sin is disbelieving in Allah or His oneness. It is the only sin that cannot be forgiven if taken to the grave. Other sins, no matter how big or small, can be forgiven. Some sins are forgiven through everyday worship rituals like ablution and prayers, and some others are forgiven only through sincere penitence. The Koran addresses the forgiving of sins repeatedly, as in the following verse: "If you avoid the great (things) which you are forbidden, We will remit from you your evil deeds and make you enter at a noble gate" (4:31).

There are several obvious sins, as described in Chapter 9: murder, theft, fornication, adultery, slander, drunkenness, and assault. Other obvious sins are in the negligence of one or all of the Five Pillars of Islam, as in not praying, not fasting, etc. Apart from the obvious sins and crimes, there are some fifty bad deeds to abstain from listed in Islamic books. Some of the other big evils are:

- Charging interest on loans and financial transactions
- Bribing or accepting bribes
- Disrespecting parents or abandoning relatives
- Practicing black magic
- Believing or consulting fortunetellers and astrologers
- Gambling in any form
- Running away from the battlefield
- Committing suicide
- Habitual lying, deceit, or betrayal of trust
- Consuming an orphan's property for personal purpose

There are many more evils mentioned in the Koran and Sunnah that people should avoid. The Koran explains that for Allah to forgive these sins, one must repent and refrain from falling into the same error again. Allah's mercy is vast, and all sins, regardless of how evil, can be forgiven.

Minor Sins

Little "harmless" lies, negative thoughts, and gossip are examples of sins that are more readily forgiven by Allah. These are the sins that can be washed away with ablution, regular prayer, or lots of general good deeds. The Koran says that even the best Muslim collects a number of small sins because they are mistakes everyone falls into.

According to the Koran, lying is undeniably a sin regardless of how big or small the lie is. The Koran also forbids gossip, particularly if it involves backstabbing or hypocrisy. Getting intimate with someone who's not a spouse—even if it does not result in fornication—is a sin, too.

Possessing a character that is opposite in many ways to the ideal Islamic character is a sin. Impatience, irritability, impoliteness, ignorance, and cruelty are traits that add quite a substantial amount of sins to a person's record when practiced. Indecent public behavior that disturbs or offends the public is sinful as well. Muslims believe that because Islam is based on logic, whatever logic dictates as being harmful or offensive to the self or to others is most likely a bad deed punishable by Allah if not offset by better deeds.

Chapter 11

Marriage and Sexuality

With each new marriage, a new family is formed. If the couple is incompatible, the family fails. Because Islam wants to limit family failure, it grants people the right to choose their partners in marriage. The proposal, engagement, and marriage procedure has been partially defined by the Koran and Sunnah, and partially by traditions based on the moral system of Islam.

Choosing a Partner

Both men and women have the freedom to choose a partner in marriage. As discussed in Chapter 6, forced marriages are prohibited by the Koran and Sunnah. The man and the woman must both consent to the marriage. This does not mean the marriage cannot be arranged, as is often done in the Middle East. An arranged marriage is not as awful as the phrase implies—more often it refers to a man and woman being introduced to each other. Family, relatives, or friends normally do the matchmaking in an arranged marriage. If sparks fly, the man formally proposes to the woman or her family, asking for her hand in marriage.

Who Will Choose the Partner?

Sometimes parents pressure children into a marriage they do not want. In such a case, if the son or daughter accepts despite his or her inner disapproval, the marriage is legal. However, Islamic tradition discourages pressuring a couple into marriage, as it sometimes results in the joining of two people who are incompatible, which may lead to a broken family.

Finding a partner through dating is possible. Dating is a sensitive issue to Muslims because it combines the togetherness of a man and woman who are strangers to each other (in this context, strangers are all nonrelatives, with the exception of cousins). Most scholars denounce dating, but dating may be permissible as long as it observes the rules of modesty found in the Koran. The couple should agree that the date is a chance to get to know each other with the honorable intention of possibly getting married, rather than a chance to make out. They must not touch each other. Modesty is not only limited to their gestures, but should rule their speech as well.

It is perfectly normal and acceptable if a couple wishes to marry for love. Although some conservative families frown upon a son or daughter who's in love prior to marriage, the Koran and Sunnah show no objection to love being the reason behind a marriage. On the contrary, many scholars say it is preferable if the couple shares warm emotions, as this guarantees some measure of harmony in their married life. The Koran describes the creation of man and woman so that they marry and live together in harmony: "And of His signs is this: He created for you mates from yourselves that you might find rest in them, and He ordained between you love and mercy" (30:21).

The Koran allows a Muslim man to marry a Christian or Jewish woman, but Muslim women are allowed to marry only Muslim men. This is possibly because the dominant religious environment in the household, which will influence the children, is attributed to the father.

The Engagement Period

The Sunnah approves and recommends an engagement period prior to the wedding. Since some couples don't know each other well enough before the proposal, the engagement period allows them to develop a close relationship. Often, the man may visit his fiancée under the supervision of her parents or guardians, or they may go out together in public places only, preferably with someone who's a relative of the bride.

Technically, an engaged couple is not yet married, and therefore the rules of modest conduct listed in the Koran apply. If they go out, they must remain within busy public areas, and not go near deserted or dark places. For example, it's okay to visit malls, restaurants, and parks, but places like movie theaters, the beach at night, or the car in a deserted parking lot are not allowed. Prophet Muhammad said that Satan is always in the company of a man and woman who are together in privacy, meaning that Satan will play with their minds until the two are drawn together inappropriately.

According to the Koran, the engaged couple certainly cannot engage in sex with each other. If they did sleep together, it would be considered fornication. They'd be sinning if they even kissed. *How do I know if we're a good match?* has no application in Islam—Muslims trust that if you find emotional harmony together, chances are you will find physical harmony as well. The Koran is very strict about limiting sexual intercourse to marital relationships.

Why is sex a sin for an engaged couple?
They may have every intention of getting married, but it's a common occurrence that engagements break up prior to marriage. The woman will have lost her virginity and might even end up pregnant by a man who's not her husband.

Adapting to the New Home

Islamic tradition dictates that mothers should give their marrying daughters a brief overview of married life and how they should treat their husbands and watch over their homes. Muslim boys are brought up knowing that a day will come when they will marry and become responsible for a home and family. The Koran holds the newlyweds responsible for their home and privacy from day one. Their lives are a private matter where no details are to be given to anyone, except in times when serious disputes arise between the couple.

Guarding Secrets

Both husband and wife are required to guard the home and its secrets. Allah addresses women in particular in the Koran: "[G]ood women are the obedient, guarding in secret that which Allah has guarded" (4:34). The things Allah wills the wife to guard are her chastity and virtue, her home, her husband's reputation, and her private life with him. For example, a woman guards her chastity by dressing and behaving appropriately in the presence of other men, and she guards her home by not letting in strangers or people her husband does not like.

According to the Koran and Sunnah, both husband and wife are required to keep their private life a private matter. For example, the wife should not consult a whole group of friends every time she has a little argument with her husband. And certainly, she should not advertise explicit details of a great night she shared with him. The same rules apply to the husband, as Prophet Muhammad instructed both husband and wife to keep their lives a private matter and as far as possible from the scrutinizing eyes of other people.

In a Hadith, Prophet Muhammad summarizes the mutual responsibility of husband and wife in this regard: "Amongst the lowest grades of people before Allah on Judgment Day is the man going to his wife (to have sex) and she going to him, then either of them divulging their common secret."

Dealing with Problems

There are sometimes small or major disputes in any marriage. Chapter 6 introduces the stages of approaching and solving marital problems caused by the wife. But if the husband misbehaves, the wife may request the help of her father or a close relative who is mature, diplomatic, and able to negotiate. This is the method described in the Koran: "And if you fear a breach between them twain (the man and wife), appoint an arbiter from his folk and an arbiter from her folk. If they desire amendment Allah will make them of one mind. Lo! Allah is ever Knower, Aware" (4:35).

Muslim families typically use this method to solve their children's marriage problems. Some couples prefer to settle their problems discreetly. However, when disputes are too complex to resolve on their own, a mediator from each side becomes involved to help out. This is not very different from marriage counseling, except in the Islamic case, the counselors are relatives rather than professional psychologists. The positive side to family counseling is that the family members have the couple's best interest in mind, and they don't charge a dime!

ALERT!

To avoid the sin of fornication, some Muslim men and women who are attracted to each other sexually but have no interest in long-term commitment agree to a short-term marriage of a few months to satisfy their urges. This is called "Pleasure Marriage" and is strictly forbidden in Islam as it fails the real objective of marriage.

In the Bedroom

Allah created sexual desire in humans just as He created desire for food and need for sleep. One of the main reasons for marriage in Islam is the fulfillment of this innate sexual need. Because fornication is a sin and a crime, people would not be able to sate their yearning except through marriage. As it is a main reason for Muslims to marry, Islam thoroughly describes the roles of the husband and wife in satisfying each other. It is mandatory that both pay great attention to each other's needs at every chance possible.

Rights of the Husband

The teachings of Islam make it abundantly clear to every wife that she should respond to her husband when he wants to make love unless she has an excuse (such as being ill or menstruating). Most of the teachings regarding this matter are derived from the Prophet's Hadith. In one Hadith, the Prophet says: "The right of the husband is that when he calls his wife to sex she should not deny him herself." In another Hadith, the Prophet instructs that if a woman does not respond to her husband's request for sex and that upsets him, Allah remains displeased with her until her husband forgives her. Because sex is not allowed during fasting (unless after sunset when a fast is broken) by the law of the Sunnah, a wife is not allowed to voluntarily fast beyond Ramadan without the consent of her husband.

Prophet Muhammad preaches that she should also make herself presentable and attractive to her husband. She may dress up, do her hair, apply makeup, and wear perfume. Cleanliness and personal hygiene must be taken into account; for example, it is unacceptable by Islam and offensive to her husband if she presents herself after a workout without first bathing.

The Koran and Sunnah set these rules to ensure that marriage truly serves a purpose of sexual fulfillment. If sexual urges were not satisfied in marriage, people would be tempted to commit adultery—a sin to be avoided at all costs. A wife should make herself available and attractive for her husband, not particularly to prevent him from infidelity, but to bless her marriage and keep the passion alive. If she does not love or want him, Muslims think it's better to divorce than to deprive him of sexual satisfaction.

FACT

If a married couple has sexual intercourse once and would like a repeat, the husband must wash his body before they do it again. Also, after having sex both husband and wife must shower from head to toe before praying or touching the Koran.

Rights of the Wife

The wife has similar rights to those of the husband. He, too, must respond to her call of desire. In the Koran, Allah instructs that husbands should "live with them on a footing of kindness and equity" (4:19). Just as a woman makes herself available and desirable to her husband, he should do the same out of kindness and for a harmonious relationship (although for men, it is not a sin if he does not answer the wife's request). The Koran describes the closeness and intimacy between a married couple through a metaphor: "They are raiment for you and you are raiment for them . . ." (2:187).

Permitted and Forbidden Pleasures

The Koran permits many pleasures and prohibits only a few. A husband and wife have the right to enjoy each other and express their sexuality in many different ways. Some acts are forbidden due to the health risk they impose on the couple. Islam fully acknowledges sex as physically and mentally healthy, and as an essential part of life, as long as it doesn't cross a few limits.

Permitted Pleasures

If husband and wife married to satisfy each other, then that satisfaction ought to be complete. According to the Koran, sex can take a variety of shapes: "Your women are as a tilth for you (to cultivate); go to your tilth as you will . . ." (2:223). This verse uses the imagery of a farmer taking care of his fields—the seeds are planted with care and nurtured until they grow. Scholars say that likewise, women are to be approached with love and care.

Forbidden Pleasures

A man is not allowed by the law of the Koran to have sex with his wife during her period. Allah says: "They question you (O Muhammad) concerning menstruation. Say: It is an illness, so let women alone at such time and go not in unto them till they are cleansed. And when they have purified themselves, then go in unto them as Allah has enjoined upon you. Truly Allah loves those who turn unto Him, and loves those who have a care for cleanness" (2:222).

Although polygamy is permitted in Islam, a man is forbidden from being married to two sisters at the same time. This ruling prevents the inevitable jealousy and resentment that would arise between the siblings (who should in fact be in harmony) if they shared the same husband.

During the few days of menstruation, a husband and wife may engage in foreplay or activities not related to intercourse as they please but must avoid intercourse. According to the previous verse, when the wife's period has ended, she must shower and thoroughly cleanse herself. Only then can the couple have sex again. Muslims believe the reasons for prohibiting sex during menstruation are that it is painful for the woman, messy, and unhygienic for both parties. This end of the previous verse, "loves those who have a care for cleanness," indicates the importance of physical purity in Islam.

The one other forbidden pleasure is anal sex. Scholars say this ruling is based on the logic that the rectum is unhygienic, and engaging in this act may cause health complications for the husband and the wife.

Islamic View of Homosexuality

When Allah created the human race, he created Adam and Eve, male and female. They were created from one soul for each other's psychological, biological, and sociological benefit. It was never Allah's intention to unite males or females together. The Koran approves only of heterosexuality. The ruling regarding homosexuality is very straightforward: it is prohibited and a major sin.

In one of the stories in the Koran, Prophet Lot was appalled at his people's rampant homosexuality: "What! Of all the creatures do you come unto the males, and leave the wives your Lord created for you? Nay but you are forward folk" (26:165–166). Lot's people laughed and mocked, and challenged Lot to send down a punishment from Allah if they were indeed sinning. Prophet Lot prayed to Allah, and soon Allah responded by eradicating them through natural disasters of unnatural magnitude.

Through Lot's story, the Koran demonstrates the severity of homosexuality as a sin. Islam regards attraction to the same sex a deviation of natural order that leads to corruption. Scholars advise that even if such homosexual thoughts run through some people's minds, they should not act upon them, just as they resist fornication and other temptations. This of course applies to both men and women.

Chapter 12

The Beginning of Creation

Allah makes it crystal clear in the Koran that He is the sole Creator of the universe and all forms of life present in it. The Koran covers such topics as how the world began, where the planets came from, and what the stars are made of. Additionally, the Koran narrates the story of Adam—how and why he was created, his time in Heaven, and his experience with Satan. Since it teaches that Adam was the first man, the Koran dismisses the theory of evolution, stating that all people are Adam's children.

The Creation of the Universe

A commonly accepted theory concerning the origin of the universe is the theory of the big bang. While scientists still work on this theory, the big bang concept was outlined in the Koran more than 1,400 years ago. Starting out as a single mass, the universe exploded into millions of fragments—a phenomenon that occurred billions of years ago. Since then, the universe has been expanding, getting bigger and bigger, until—as scientists speculate—it will stop expanding and begin to contract. As far as such matters of the universe are concerned, science and the Koran seem to be in mutual agreement.

The Big Bang

The modern discovery that the universe began as a single mass is noted in the Koran in the following verse: "Have not those who disbelieve known that the heavens and the earth were of one piece, then We parted them, and We made every living thing of water? Will they not then believe?" (21:30).

At the time the universe was forming, science dictates that space was full of hot gases, which the Koran also mentions: "Then turned He to the heaven when it was smoke . . ." (41:11). According to science, the word *smoke* is a very accurate description of these gaseous formations. Then Allah divided up the Heavens into seven Heavens, as He says in the Koran: "Then He ordained them seven heavens in two days and inspired in each heaven its mandate; and We decked the nether heaven with lamps, and rendered it inviolable" (41:12). These lamps that decorate the lowest Heaven are the stars that glitter across the galaxies.

Scientists speculate that the universe is about 18 billion years old. The Koran states that the universe was created in six days, or six periods. Based on the information in the Koran, some Islamic scholars have also calculated the universe to be 18.25 billion years old.

The two days Allah talks about here are not our standard twenty-four-hour days, but rather they are to be measured by a completely different scale. The Koran states that Allah's day is equivalent to a thousand years on our scale of time, and in some circumstances, equivalent to 50,000 years.

The single mass exploded and scattered its fragments across space, which formed stars, planets, solar systems, and galaxies. Astronomers calculate that this all happened spontaneously due to heat, gravitational forces, and other factors. However, the Koran says that the distribution of stars, planets, and other elements across the universe is the work of Allah, and that nothing happens without His will. In other words, it is understood from the Koran that there was nothing spontaneous about the organization of the universe.

The exquisite order of planets and their orbit around the sun is also described as the work of the Creator. The Koran says that Allah "compelled the sun and the moon to be of service, [and] each runs unto an appointed term; He orders the course . . ." (13:2). Scholars state that the appointed term here refers to a point in time when the sun will die (as science already predicts), and similarly the moon will perish. In the Koran, the end of the sun's and moon's appointed terms coincides with the end of the world.

The Koran also describes Allah's creation of the sky: "Allah it is who raised up the heavens without visible supports" (13:2). Allah also says that He placed in those Heavens a "great lamp" and a "moon giving light." Of course, life as we know it would not have been possible without the alternation of night and day—another piece of Allah's creation.

ALERT!

Science has successfully discovered that the universe was a single mass, but it fails to determine how the single mass came to be, and how space (i.e., void, emptiness) found itself. This is where some scientists come to accept the possibility of creation.

Expansion of the Universe

Modern scientific discoveries state that the universe has been expanding ever since the big bang, and will continue to do so until one day it stops and reverses the process by contracting. This is a fairly recent discovery in the scheme of time, dating back a few decades. However, Allah had already revealed this fact in the Koran: "We have built the heaven with might, and We it is who make it extend" (51:47). Science tells us that galaxies are driving further apart, and some stars die, while others are being born—another fact confirmed by the Koran: "So when the stars are put out . . ." (77:8). The process of the universe's birth at the big bang and its continued expansion indicate that a day will come when the universe will die. Death is a process integral to every living thing.

The Creation of Man

Unlike the formation of the universe, there isn't much agreement between science and the Koran on how man came to be. While science dwells on man's evolution from apes, the Koran explains that Adam was the first man, and that he was created from clay. Allah shaped man into human form, then breathed life into him. Allah's intention was to send to Earth a vicegerent—a plan the angels initially weren't happy with. The one creature that scorned Adam and refused to obey Allah's command was the Devil (Iblis, a *jinn*), who to this day and until the end of time will remain man's worst enemy.

The Angels' Dispute

According to the information presented in the Koran, angels were created prior to man. They are pure and sinless creatures, made to faithfully serve Allah. Unlike humans, angels are not capable of disobeying Allah's instruction or taking another god to worship. This gave them every reason to wonder when Allah informed them that He had chosen man over them to be His vicegerent on Earth.

The angels knew man's temper would destroy Earth as described in the Koran: "And when your Lord said unto the angels: Lo! I am about to place a viceroy in the earth, they said: will You place there in one who will do harm therein and will shed blood, while we hymn Your praise and sanctify You?" (2:30). This verse does not mean that the angels disapproved of Allah's will, but merely inquired of His reasons in His choice.

However, Allah only said to them: "Surely I know that which you know not" (2:30). Allah was just about to show them what He meant.

A devoted Muslim generally has utter faith in the Koran and doesn't wait for it to prove itself, but when Koranic verses relating to the origin of the universe are scientifically proven true, it helps support the case of the Koran as being the word of the Supreme Being.

Allah Creates Man

The Koran states that man was created from clay: "Who made all things good which He created, and He began the creation of man from clay" (32:7). There are various stories among scholars regarding the details of man's creation. Some say that Allah sent an angel to Earth to bring him a handful of dust, which He softened with a little moisture and left for some time until it became like clay. Then He shaped the clay into human form and breathed life into it.

Others say that dust was collected from various places around the earth to create diversity in physical traits among humans. The mud was left aside for a while before it was shaped into human form. These stories are based on various accounts and Hadith of Prophet Muhammad that were transmitted through his companions. None of this is for certain, but we do know from the Koran the following: "Then He fashioned him and breathed into him of His spirit; and appointed for you hearing and sight and hearts. Small thanks you give!" (32:9).

Upon breathing into man of His spirit, man came to life. He was named Adam—considered by Muslims to be the first prophet. Islamic sources say that Adam was lonely for a while, until Allah created Eve, the female counterpart. The Koran doesn't explain much about the creation of Eve except in a few verses, such as: "O mankind! Be careful of your duty to your Lord Who created you from a single soul and from it created its mate and from them twain has spread abroad a multitude of men and women" (4:1).

From this verse, it is understood that Adam's mate was created from him. She was named Ha-wa (Eve), an Arabic name derived from a root word that means "life," because she was created from a live being. Prophet Muhammad further elaborated by explaining that Eve was created out of Adam's rib.

FACT

Some Muslims believe that Allah chose dust to create man because people will be buried in the earth after their death, and will rise out of the earth on Resurrection Day. They also believe that dust, or clay, has good properties such as tangibility and calmness as opposed to fire, from which the jinn were created.

Angels Bow to Adam

The angels were still wondering why Adam was more deserving of adopting the earth than they were. Meanwhile, Allah instilled in Adam the knowledge of many things as well as the desire to learn. Then Allah called upon the angels and asked them a question: "Inform me of the names of these, if you are truthful" (2:31). Before them, Allah placed the objects, animals, or whatever else Adam had learned of.

But the angels were clueless: "They said: Be glorified! We have no knowledge except that which You have taught us. You, only You, are the Knower, the Wise" (2:32). Allah turned to Adam and asked him for the names of the objects. Accurately and efficiently, Adam addressed everything placed before him. The angels were surprised, and Allah said, "Did I not tell you that I know the secret of the heavens and the earth? And I know that which you disclose and which you hide?" (2:33).

Adam's ability to learn and his innate thirst for knowledge gave him superiority over the angels, which the angels faithfully admitted. With thousands of angels assembled to witness this miracle, Allah commanded them to bow before Adam. The Koran narrates: "And when We said unto the angels: Prostrate yourselves before Adam, they fell prostrate, all except Iblis; he demurred through pride, and so became a disbeliever" (2:34).

Iblis is the given name for Satan, one of the jinn. Before that day, Iblis was as faithful to Allah as the angels. However, when Allah commanded him to bow before Adam, he scorned and refused because he considered himself superior to man. Being a creature of fire, Iblis rejected the thought of bowing before a creature of clay: "Iblis said: I am better than him. You created me of fire while him You did create of mud" (7:12). Nevertheless, upon this refusal to Allah's command, he became a disbeliever in Allah's knowledge and wisdom.

ALERT!

Muslims believe that the angels' prostration before Adam does not signify worship, but merely respect. Adam had exhibited his superiority over the angels, which was why they bowed in admiration. According to Koranic teaching, prostration in worship is only to be done to Allah.

The Creation of Other Creatures

Although it is easy to determine from the Koran that the universe was created before Adam, it is not clear exactly when animals were created. Paleontologists say that animals have walked the earth for millions of years. Is Adam millions of years old, too? Islam can't tell, but it is possible that at least some animals existed before him for two reasons: first, archaeologists guess that Homo sapiens (humans) have been around some 25,000 years; and second, Allah taught Adam "names," which interpreters say were names of animals and plants, among other things.

If humans have been around for only 25,000 years, it is clear that animals have been walking the earth a bit longer. Also, if Allah had taught Adam names of animals, then they must have already existed when he was created. Apart from animals, it is almost certain that plants and trees existed before Adam, because, according to the Koran, the earth was brought to life when it came into its designated course around the sun.

Creation of Animals

The Koran indicates that Allah created the animals out of water: "Allah has created every animal of water. Of them is (a kind) that goes upon its belly, and (a kind) that goes upon two legs, and (a kind) that goes upon four. Allah creates what He will. Lo! Allah is able to do all things" (24:45). Science completely agrees that water is not only the key element in the survival of life, but in the actual physical makeup of living beings as well.

There's no specific information in the Koran about how each animal or bird was created, but Allah explains that many of these animals were created for the service and pleasure of humankind, such as in the following verse: "And the cattle has He created, whence you have warm clothing and uses, and whereof you eat" (16:5). Other animals such as horses are described as treasured assets to people.

In many parts of the Koran, Allah tells people to look at his creation to understand his might and power. Muslims often marvel at little creatures, such as ants or bees, seeing them as wonders of divine engineering. The bee, for example, being such a useful creature, is spoken of in the Koran: "And your Lord inspired the bee, saying: Choose your habitations in the hills and in the tree and in that which they hatch" (16:68).

QUESTION?

In the Koran, which came first: the chicken or the egg?
The chicken did. Just as Allah created man from raw material and gave him life, He created all other forms of life using the same concept. At one point, the chicken was nonexistent, and at the next, there it was!

Allah says in the Koran that everything He created glorifies Him, except for humans who choose other gods to glorify. Everything, including planets, stars, and the sun, glorifies the Lord. According to the Koran, even innocent and seemingly dumb animals know their Lord: "Have you not seen that Allah, He it is Whom all who are in the heavens and the earth praise; and the birds in their flight? Each one knows verily its worship and its praise; and Allah is aware of what they do" (24:41).

Other Beings

Other beings, such as Satan, the jinn, and creatures of the deep, are mentioned in the Koran—if not specifically, then by allusion. Every

Muslim believes in the existence of the jinn because they are made real in the Koran (for more about the jinn, see Chapter 17). They have their own world and do not ordinarily appear to humans, and they were created from fire before the creation of Adam: "And the jinn did We create aforetime of essential fire" (15:27).

Science freely admits that not every species on Earth has been discovered and documented. The Koran confirms this: "And He creates that which you know not" (16:8). Here, Allah declares that there are creatures unknown to humans. Might these creatures live in the depth of the oceans in places undiscovered? Could a lake monster be an example of an unknown species? Perhaps the Koran refers to inhabitants of other planets. Whichever it may be, the fact is, according to the Koran, there are creatures in this world of which we are unaware.

The Forbidden Tree

When Allah created Adam and Eve, he invited them to make a home of Paradise. Adam had everything he ever wanted in Heaven. But Allah put Adam through a test: He forbade him from eating from a certain tree. Due to Satan's luring, Adam and Eve's life in Heaven didn't last, and they were dismissed from Heaven and sent down to Earth.

Allah compares the creation of Adam to the creation of Jesus. He says that Adam was dust and He said to him, "Be!" And he was. Likewise, Allah said to Jesus, "Be!" And he was. This comparison is found in Surah 3, verse 59.

Before Adam and Eve were permitted into Heaven, Allah addressed them with a warning. Without giving them any particular reason, Allah forbade them from eating from a certain tree in Heaven: "[B]ut come not near this tree lest you become wrong-doers" (7:19). At the same time, Allah also warned them of the power of Satan: "Therefore We said: O Adam! This is an enemy unto you and unto your wife, so let him not drive you both out of the Garden so that thou come to toil" (20:117).

The forbidden tree may have been harmful or useful for all Adam knew, but he intended to obey Allah's instruction without questioning it. In Islam, it is believed that Allah forbade Adam and Eve from eating from that tree as a test of their faith in Him and their will against evil. Adam and Eve already had all they wanted in Heaven and there was no reason for them to turn to the forbidden tree—except out of curiosity or greed.

Satan's Lure and Adam's Descent

When Iblis (Satan) refused to prostrate himself before Adam, Allah banished him from the Heavens: "Go forth from hence, degraded, banished. As for such of them as follow you, surely I will fill hell with all of you" (7:18). Not only was Iblis banished from the Heavens, but he was also promised Hell for him and for all who follow his path. Angered, Iblis sought revenge on the first of mankind, Adam.

Iblis's conversation with Allah is depicted in the Koran more than once, where Iblis demonstrates arrogance and openly announces that he will drive humankind off the straight path: "He said: Now, because You have sent me astray, verily I shall lurk in ambush for them on Your Right Path. Then I shall come upon them from before and from behind them and from their right hands and from their left hands, and You will not find most of them beholden (unto You)" (7:17).

FACT

According to some Islamic scholars, Adam and Eve managed to get by many years without touching the forbidden tree. Every now and then, Iblis would crawl to them and whisper to them to eat from the tree. Adam and Eve managed to resist Iblis most of the time, but their resistance inevitably weakened as time progressed.

Satan Tempts Adam and Eve

Scholars aren't sure how long Adam and Eve resisted the temptation of the forbidden tree, but eventually, curiosity got the best of them. The

Koran narrates: "But the Devil whispered to him, saying: O Adam! Shall I show you the tree of immortality and power that wastes not away?" (20:120). To further induce them, Iblis swore to them that he was their sincere advisor. Despite Allah's warning about Iblis and the tree, Adam and Eve approached the forbidden tree and picked its fruit.

Adam and Eve had no chance to savor the fruit, for as soon as they tasted the fruit of the tree, "their shame became manifest to them" (they became aware of their nakedness). Shameful of their situation and remorseful for disobeying Allah, they hastily heaped leaves on themselves for cover. The Koran comments: "And their Lord called them, (saying): Did I not forbid you from that tree and tell you: Lo! Satan is an open enemy to you?" (7:22). It was too late, as Adam and Eve had failed the test by disobeying Allah and following Satan's path.

Adam and Eve Are Forgiven

Immediately after eating from the forbidden tree, Adam and Eve asked Allah for forgiveness: "They said: Our Lord! We have wronged ourselves. If You forgive us not and have not mercy on us, surely we are of the lost!" (7:23). Because Allah accepts sincere repentance, he forgave them for the sin and guided them once again onto the right path.

ALERT!

Adam and Eve's sin was forgiven, so they won't be charged for it on Judgment Day, but they were sent to Earth as punishment for disobeying Allah. According to the Koran and Sunnah, Adam and Eve's sin has already been wiped off the record.

Although they were forgiven for the sin, Adam and Eve were dismissed from Heaven and sent down to Earth. Since then, men and women have dwelled on Earth. Allah speaks to them in the Koran: "Go down (from whence), some of you a foe unto others. There will be for you on earth a habitation and provision for a while" (7:24). Here, Allah is addressing all of humankind, indicating to them that life on Earth won't be as blissful as it would have been in Heaven.

The Koran's Perspective of Evolution

The word *evolution* is not mentioned anywhere in the Koran. Almost every verse that speaks about a creature also hints of it being a complex and intelligent design by Allah. By studying the Koran, one can come to see that it firmly states that everything that exists in the world, from bacteria to animals to stars and planets, is a result of Allah's ingenuity and creation.

Based on this, Muslims refute the theory of evolution. This theory suggests that the first form of life made of single-celled organisms came about as a result of the right conditions and elements. These microorganisms evolved into more complex forms, such as insects, and eventually into animals. Over the course of millions of years, different species evolved out of one another, until the most efficient designs survived.

The Koran does not discuss evolution or even hint of it. It states that Allah is the Creator and that every living thing is his creation, including things that don't appear alive, such as planets, galaxies, and so on. According to the Koran, no creature evolved from another; every living thing received its engineered design from Allah.

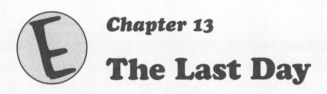

Chapter 13

The Last Day

Allah speaks about the Last Day extensively in the Koran and uses it as a reminder that all actions will be judged in the next world. Allah also revealed certain signs of the Last Day in the Koran and to Prophet Muhammad. Muslims recognize many of these signs today, and conclude that the Last Day is not all that far away. On that day, people will be terrified, and every person will think of no one but himself or herself, as humans march toward their final destination.

The End of the World Is Coming

The Koran makes it very clear that the world as we know it will eventually come to an end. In numerous places in the Koran, Allah enforces the fact that the Last Day will hit unexpectedly at a time only He knows of. One such verse warns of the final judgment of each human that will come with the Last Day:

> *They indeed are losers who deny their meeting with Allah until, when the hour comes on them suddenly, they cry: Alas for us, that we neglected it! They bear upon their backs their burdens. Ah! Evil is that which they bear! Naught is the life of the world but a pastime and a sport. Better far is the abode of the Hereafter for those who keep their duty (to Allah). Have you then no sense? (6:31–32)*

Although no one knows exactly when the world will end, Allah spoke of a few signs in the Koran and informed Prophet Muhammad of many more that aim to increase people's awareness of how far or close the Last Day may be. There are some ninety or more signs of the drawing near of the Last Day extracted from the Koran and the Hadith. They are divided into two categories: major and minor. Currently, the world is in a period in which nearly all the minor signs have occurred, and we await the first of the major signs. It is presumed that all the major signs will take place within a shorter period than the minor took place.

FACT

Prophet Muhammad's Hadith are the main source for learning about the signs of the Last Day. Muslims believe Angel Gabriel carried the messages down from the Heavens to the Prophet, telling him about those many signs. In turn, Muhammad narrated to the people what he had learned through Gabriel.

Signs That Have Occurred

The minor signs of the end of the world started to happen early in the days of Prophet Muhammad, such as the splitting of the moon (see

Chapter 2). The Prophet himself was a sign, as he tells of in a Hadith. Closely following the time of Muhammad came a series of signs that he mentioned in his Hadith. He said that thirty people along the time-line would claim to be messengers of Allah—one with the name of Musaylama had already done so before the death of the Prophet. He said that people would kill an Imam (an elite Islamic scholar and leader), which did happen to Caliph Othman. He said that a blazing fire would erupt in Hijaz (Medina), and in the year A.D. 1233 a huge fire erupted in the city and burned for two days before it was finally extinguished. There were more signs that took place over the course of the past centuries, all of which the Prophet had talked about in his days.

Signs That Are Happening

Muhammad spoke of many signs that are happening in our modern day. He didn't know their chronological order, so he listed them randomly in various Hadith. There are almost 100 minor signs, but you will find only a few of them discussed here. Most of these signs have occurred within the last fifty years, implying to some Muslims that the end of the world is approaching . . . fast!

The Koran gives the Last Day many names. The Hour, Resurrection Day, Day of Assembling, and Judgment Day all refer to the end of the world, but describe its different phases.

The Hadith of Prophet Muhammad summarize that a general lack of morality will prevail in the days before the Last Day. The Prophet said that illiteracy, promiscuity, alcoholism, fragility of blood ties, foul language, nudity, and abandonment of religion are indications of the nearing Last Day. Other signs prophesied are that children will cause agony to their families, and people will try to avoid pregnancies. Music will enter every household and most people will be involved in it in one way or another. Many will fall victim to depression that stirs thoughts of suicide, as Muhammad said: "People will pass by graves and wish to exchange places with the dead." Dishonesty in all aspects of life will be a common thing; people will find lying easier than telling the truth.

Honest and trustworthy people will be tossed aside and replaced by dishonest traitors. People will pay less and less attention to practicing the Islamic faith and become more consumed in the pleasures of life. Also, less knowledgeable people will become teachers, writing about subjects they are hardly familiar with. These signs are merely a sample of the many social signs known to Islam.

A very interesting sign that Muhammad mentioned is the construction revolution in Arabia. He said that a time would come when we will find "shoeless, unclothed, poverty-stricken shepherds" suddenly constructing high-rise buildings. Most of the countries in the Arabian Peninsula only came to exist in the second half of the twentieth century. The discovery of oil brought them instant wealth that elevated them from penniless shepherds to world-class businessmen. Money pooled into banks, and buildings grew taller. By the beginning of the twenty-first century, the Arab businessmen were competing at building the tallest skyscrapers.

FACT

When Muhammad relayed the information about the signs of the Last Day to his companions, they were astounded that humanity would experience an age of immorality. Muhammad also told them that one day, wealth will be so abundant that no one will accept charity anymore.

One of the terrifying signs that has already begun to appear is the increasing frequency of earthquakes. The Prophet said that as the Last Day draws nearer, earthquakes would hit more and more often. Quakes are neither new nor rare; they have been happening since the beginning of time. But just as quakes shook the earth vigorously millions of years ago before the beginning of human life, it is possible that a similar phenomenon will happen as the world runs closer to the end.

Armageddon

Christian and Jewish Scripture have both prophesied the war of Armageddon. When the minor signs have all appeared, the major signs begin. The link between the minor and major signs is the war of Armageddon, which will presumably take place in Israel and 200 miles of surrounding land.

The War of Armageddon

The word *Armageddon* comes from Hebrew. It refers to the land that will host the war, which other faiths predict will be near Mageddo Valley in Palestine. The Bible and the Torah mention Armageddon (also known as the Dragon War) and describe its war zone, but Islamic sources provide no information about its location. Muhammad's Hadith describe the conditions that will cause the war as well as the devastation of its aftermath.

One such Hadith addresses who will fight in the war: "You (Muslims) will form a safe alliance with the Romans then you will both battle a common enemy . . ." Scholars clarify that the "Romans" addressed here are the Christians resident in Europe at the time of the Prophet. Since most Caucasians in the United States come from European roots, scholars conclude that America and Europe will be the allies.

With the Americas, Europe, and the Middle East becoming allies against a common enemy, the devastation of the war could be global. The common enemy is not defined in the Koran or Sunnah, but some Muslims guess the opponents may be Russia and Asia. It is believed by many that the war of Armageddon will be the most destructive war the world will ever see.

ALERT!

Islamic scholars theorize through studies of some Hadith that the era of Muslims on Earth is a little over 1,400 years from the day of the first revelation to Muhammad. They say the end of the Muslim era is followed immediately by the end of the world. (As of 2004, it's been 1,438 years already.)

The Aftermath of the War

When the war comes to an end, victory will be declared to the Muslim-Western allies, according to a Hadith of Muhammad. In the second part of the Hadith, Muhammad says that a quarrel between a Christian and a Muslim will plant resentment in the hearts of the Americans and Europeans against Islam. Secretly, Europe and America will plot revenge against the Middle East. Nine months after the war of Armageddon (as indicated in another Hadith), armies composed of eighty sections will attack the Middle East with a total number of 960,000 soldiers.

Prophet Muhammad also foretold the coming of a man known as Al Mahdi, "the guided one," who will save the Muslim people from these soldiers. He will become a trusted leader and will reign for several years, during which other extraordinary signs will appear.

The Major Signs

There are ten major signs, which scholars believe will occur in the following chronological order: the appearance of an imposter called Al Dajjal; the descent of Jesus from the Heavens; the escape of Yagog and Magog; the sun rising from the west; the coming of the Beast; the Death Wind; three massive earthquakes; and last, a fire that will start in Yemen and crawl all the way to Syria. Some of the signs are mentioned in the Koran, some in the Sunnah, and some in both, but all are believed by Muslims to be the last major events to hit Earth immediately before the Last Day.

Prophet Muhammad narrated in great depth the expected appearance of a creature in the shape of a man, called Al Dajjal, the Imposter. Muslims believe he will appear during the wars lead by Al Mahdi. Al Dajjal is so named because he will trick people into believing he is God. During Al Dajjal's time on Earth, Jesus will descend from the Heavens to kill the imposter.

Armageddon is regarded in Islam as the "beginning of the end." As nearly all the minor signs of the Last Day have appeared, we watch the stage being set for the major battle, which will link the minor signs to a series of final and terrifying signs as we approach the end.

Sometime after the imposter Al Dajjal is killed, two communities of people named Yagog and Magog (sometimes named Gog and Magog) will emerge from their prison. Scholars say Yagog and Magog are human descendants from Yafith, a son of Noah, and the father of the Asian ethnic group. Prophet Muhammad described them as short people with round faces, small eyes, dark hair, and flat noses. Many millenniums ago, they were trapped behind an enormous wall built specifically to withhold them from their barbaric destruction of the earth. They are mentioned in the Koran, and some Muslims believe their prison is hidden somewhere in Asia. When they finally escape, they will eat and drink from the sources of the earth until they run out. (Some scholars believe the wall or prison mentioned in the Hadith is a metaphor for something else, perhaps economic sanctions.)

Al Mahdi and Jesus will pass away a little after Yagog and Magog emerge. Then will come three days and three nights when the sun will not rise at all, and on the fourth day it will rise from the west. That day marks the time when repentance is no longer accepted, and when deeds will cease to be recorded. Immediately, the Beast, known as the Dabba (animal), will rise up from somewhere near Mecca according to the Koran: "And when the word is fulfilled concerning them, We shall bring forth a beast of the earth to speak unto them because mankind had not faith in Our revelations" (27:82). The exact description of the animal is not available in Islamic texts, but Muslims believe it will be like no other creature on Earth, and it will have the ability to speak to people and mark the believer from the nonbeliever.

After the Dabba, Allah will send a cold, smooth wind that will take the lives of all Muslims and believers. With all the righteous gone, three massive earthquakes will follow: one in the East, one in the West, and one in Arabia. The last of all signs is the fire that will ignite in Yemen and spread until it reaches Syria. Immediately thereafter, this world will end.

QUESTION?

Why isn't repentance accepted after the sunrise from the west?
The Prophet said that the western sunrise is a sure sign that the world is ending soon. The earlier warnings are to alert the people, and the western sunrise serves as a deadline for them to repent.

Depiction of the Last Day

There are some twelve Surahs in the Koran describing the horrors of the Last Day, not taking into account other Surahs that include a few highlights here and there. Muslims have no illusions about how the Last Day will hit Earth, due to the Koran's vivid depiction. From the angel's announcement, to earthquakes, volcanoes, and a collapsing sky, the Koran thoroughly portrays the Last Day.

Why does Allah describe the Last Day in such detail? For the same reasons that He describes Heaven and Hell, Allah dedicates a substantial portion of the Koran to talk about the Last Day. Heaven is illustrated in a way that lures believers, and Hell is depicted in a way that frightens and repels. This way, Allah provides a path for those who wish to follow. In the same way, the horrific disasters of the Last Day are used to strike fear of Allah and of the day people will stand before Him for judgment.

The Angel and the Horn

The Koran states that the Last Day will not come until the horn is blown: "For when the trumpet shall sound, surely that day will be a day of anguish" (74:8–9). Although the English translation calls it a "trumpet," Prophet Muhammad describes it as a "horn." When the time comes for the Hour (the Last Day), the sounding of the horn will announce the beginning of it.

The angel in charge of blowing the horn, whose name is not given in the Koran but is known as Angel Israfil according to the Prophet's teachings, is among the highest-ranking angels, running close behind Angel Gabriel and the Angel of Death. His sole duty is to blow the horn when the Hour arrives.

When the time comes, Allah will command Angel Israfil to blow the horn. The Koran speaks about more than one blow—at least two, and possibly three. Because the Koran only mentions two blows specifically, many scholars believe there are only two blows. However, another group says there are three blows, basing their conclusion on slightly different interpretation of the text and on the Sunnah. Whether there are two or three blows is not a major issue in Islam because all Muslims agree that the blows will first kill every living thing, then resurrect all the dead from the time of Adam to the time of the Hour.

FACT

Muslims believe that although Angel Israfil's job seems relatively minor compared to the hectic jobs of Angel Gabriel in delivering revelations, and the Angel of Death in taking every soul, his witnessing of the Last Day is far more strenuous on his soul than the other angels' work combined.

The First Blow of the Horn

After the extraordinary signs of the Last Day have taken place, it will be only a matter of time before the first horn is sounded. Prophet Muhammad said that the horn will sound when the most evil people live and the world is deep in corruption. Allah sends a warning to humankind in the Koran: "O mankind! Fear your Lord. Lo! The earthquake of the Hour (of Doom) is a tremendous thing" (22:1). The Koran goes on to say that when the day arrives, people will be so stunned in fright that a nursing mother will forget her nursling, and a pregnant woman will drop her burden.

In Islam, the first blow of the horn is called the Blow of Fright, as concluded from the Koran: "And (remind them of) the Day when the Trumpet will be blown, and all who are in the heavens and the earth will start in fear, except him whom Allah wills. And all come unto Him, humbled" (27:87). The Blow of Fright is what the name implies: it will trigger a chain of universal disasters that will stun creation in fear.

Global Disasters

The Koran describes massive earthquakes, volcanoes, typhoons, hurricanes, and every type of natural disaster as the start of the Hour. When the first horn is sounded, the universe will respond in a violent shudder, causing the planets to go out of orbit. The direct link between the blow of the horn and the earthquakes is presented in the following verses: "And when the trumpet shall sound one blast, and the earth with the mountains shall be lifted up and crushed with one crash, then, on that day will the Event befall" (69:13–15).

Volcanoes will erupt everywhere, casting lava upon the surface of the earth. Oceans will burst and flood the land, drowning anything left standing. All this, of course, will happen simultaneously, as clearly understood from the Koran. It may be possible that asteroids will lend a hand in destroying the world at the same time—a theory supported by some scientists.

FACT

Before the catastrophic events of the Last Day, Allah will send a smooth but deadly wind that will kill the last of the believers painlessly. Muslims believe that the purpose of killing all the righteous before the Last Day is to save them from experiencing or witnessing its horrors.

Collapse of the Sky

Because the entire universe will be shaken from the first blow of the horn, Earth's atmosphere will be affected. The Koran relays that the heavens (skies) will split apart: "And the heaven will split asunder, for that day it will be frail" (69:16). Science tells us that the atmosphere and space beyond are composed of gases. On the Last Day, Allah says in the Koran that the sky as we know it will no longer exist, and it will be replaced by something else: "The day when the sky will become as molten copper" (70:8). Some scholars theorize that the gases making up the atmosphere will be liquefied or simply dispensed.

Not only will the atmosphere and space change composition, but they will also be driven apart to open a gate to another realm. According to the Koran, when the Heavens draw apart, "the angels will be on the sides thereof, and eight will uphold the Throne of your Lord that day, above them" (69:17). Here Allah says that as the Heavens split open to the world beyond, angels will be at either side, waiting to descend upon Earth.

The Second Blow of the Horn

Prophet Muhammad said in a Hadith that there are *forty* between two blows of the horn. "Forty what?" his companions asked. The Prophet did not give them an answer, which left the door open for one of three guesses: forty days, forty months, or forty years. It's also not certain which two blows the Prophet intended; they may have been the first and second blows, or the second and third—unless, as some believe, there are only two blows instead of three.

According to Islamic scholars, if there are three blows of the horn, the first would collapse the universe, the second would kill any survivors, and the third would resurrect creation. If there are only two blows, the first would kill all and collapse the universe, and the second would resurrect creation.

When Life Perishes

Assuming there are three blows, the second one would eradicate whatever life remains on Earth after the catastrophes of the first blow. This second blow is called the Blow of Death. When Angel Israfil blows the horn a second time, every living being on Earth and in the Heavens will receive a fatal shock. That's why the second blow can also be called the Stunner. Allah describes this blow in the Holy Koran: "And the trumpet is blown, and all who are in the heavens and the earth swoon away, except him whom Allah wills" (39:68).

The Stunner is made to kill *everything*, including animals, humans, demons, jinn, and angels, except a selected few as stated in the previous verse. No one knows exactly who the selected few will be; some say they are the martyrs who are mentioned in the Koran as alive and well near their Lord. Others say they are the servants and maidens of Heaven who were created for the service of Heaven's people. It is also said that the verse refers to the four angels Gabriel, Israfil, Mikail, and Azrael, along with the carriers of the Lord's throne.

The Last to Die

Through a detailed Hadith linked to the Prophet (although some resources doubt its authenticity), Muslims learn about the death of the very last remaining lives after the Stunner. The Hadith narrates that the only survivors of the blow of the horn will be four angels, Gabriel, Israfil, Mikail, and Azrael, and the carriers of Allah's throne. Then the Angel of Death (Azrael) will speak to Allah and tell him that everyone is dead except the four angels and the throne carriers. Allah will issue a series of instructions for taking their lives, and then He will command the Angel of Death to die, and instantaneously the angel will die. The only one remaining will be Allah, the immortal. With no trace of His creation left, Allah will declare, "Whose is the sovereignty this day? It is Allah's, the One, the Almighty" (40:16).

The Third Blow of the Horn

Prophet Muhammad explained that there will be a moment when all will be dead except the immortal Creator. To resurrect life for judgment, Allah will first resurrect Angel Israfil, whose duty it is to blow the horn one last time. This blow is called the Blow of Resurrection. With it, every creature that ever existed within the span of Earth and the Heavens will come back to life.

FACT

The Last Day is not necessarily *one* day. For the entire universe to collapse would take a long time. That's why the Prophet defined the number forty, which could be days, months, or years, to indicate the period it will take for the world to end.

The Resurrection

Allah describes the Resurrection in the Holy Koran: "Then it is blown a second time, and behold them standing, waiting!" (39:68). It doesn't matter if the dead were swallowed by a shark or burned to ashes and blown away; when the horn is blown, their bodies will re-form and grow out of the earth like a crop. Allah says that He will send rain clouds that will drench the earth, which resurrect life: "And He it is Who sends the winds as tidings heralding His mercy, till, when they bear a cloud heavy (with rain), We lead it to a dead land, and then cause water to descend thereon, and thereby bring forth fruits of every kind. Thus bring We forth the dead. Haply you may remember" (7:57).

When every soul finds its body, and the rain quenches the dead land, people will begin to rise out of the earth. As they shake off the dirt clinging to their skin, they will immediately realize their situation: "And say: Ah, woe for us! This is the Day of Judgment" (37:20). They will stand in silence and fear of Allah, each one concerned with nothing but his own self. According to the Prophet, every person will be naked and barefoot, but no one will notice others due to the terror of the situation. The Koran says that people will hardly be aware of each other, even among relatives and close friends: "On the day when a man flees from his brother, and his mother and his father, and his wife and his children. Every man that day will have concern enough to make him heedless (of others)" (80:34–37).

White Land

The earth will be flattened when the first horn is sounded. The Koran says that the earth as we know it will be substituted with another. It is unknown whether that means that people will find themselves in another realm altogether, or that this Earth will have suffered so much that it will look vastly different. However, the general interpretation is that the Koran is describing the condition of this Earth, and not another realm.

In support of this thought, Prophet Muhammad said that the Resurrection will take place on a plain white land. After the flattening of the earth on Judgment Day, the land will have no marking or indication of places or direction, such as a building, tree, or even rock. The whiteness is a symbol of purity and innocence, which Muslims believe will be characteristics of the land after its rebirth on the Last Day; the earth will be cleansed and become a land where no crime or evil has ever been committed.

A Time for Judgment

When all forms of life are brought back to life, judgment will commence. Every creature that walked the earth, including animals, demons, and jinn, will be judged. All creatures will rise from the dead with a drooping head and a downcast gaze in fear and obedience of the Lord, each one marching toward his doom or bliss. The Koran highlights the different treatment the righteous and the guilty will receive, which will begin from the moment of the Resurrection: "On the Day when We shall gather the righteous unto the Beneficent, a goodly company. And drive the guilty unto Hell, a weary herd" (19:85–86).

According to Prophet Muhammad, the Last Day will occur on a Friday. He said that Friday was the day that Adam was created, the day he entered Heaven, and the day he was cast out and sent to Earth. For these and other reasons, Friday is the sacred day of the week in Islam.

Distribution of the Books

Every person has a book in which all his or her deeds, good and bad, are recorded. On Judgment Day, these books will be distributed among the people like grade reports are distributed among school kids. According to the Koran some people will take their books by the right hand, and some will take them by the left hand. People will have no choice but to take hold of their books with the designated hand.

Those who take their books by the right hand will know they have been forgiven and will be admitted to Heaven. Proud of the good job they did in their lives, they will invite others to read their books: "Then as for him who is given his record in his right hand, he will say: Take, read my book! Surely I knew I should have to meet my reckoning. Then he will be in blissful state, in a high Garden" (69:19–22).

The opposite is true for those who take their books by the left hand. They will realize their bad deeds have earned them a place in Hell, and will shamefully hide their books from others. The Koran comments:

"But as for him who is given his record in his left hand, he will say: Oh, wish that I had not been given my book, and knew not my reckoning!" (69:25–26). In this situation, neither earthly wealth nor power will save this group from Hell. Allah says in the Koran that they will wish they would turn to dust.

Three Groups

Allah says in the Koran that on Judgment Day, there will be people whose faces are radiant with joy, and others whose faces are darkened with grief. In Surah 56, the Koran describes three distinct groups deserving three different destinies: "(First) those on the right hand; what of those on the right hand? And (then) those on the left hand; what of those on the left hand? And the foremost in the race; the foremost in the race" (56:8–10).

The Koran promises "the foremost in the race" the best and highest Heaven, and says that they will be closest to Allah. The Koran says this elite group is "[a] multitude of those of old, and a few of those of later time" (56:13–14). They are the purest and dearest people to Allah.

The second group is that on the right hand. They, too, will be admitted to Heaven, although their bliss is supposedly of a lower level than the foremost in the race. The Koran describes them as "[a] multitude of those old, and a multitude of those of later time" (56:39–40). They are generally the rest of the righteous people. Last, the group on the left hand is the remainder of humankind, who will be sent to Hell.

Chapter 14

Life after Death: The Soul's Journey

Life in this world is fragile and inevitably comes to an end. When death arrives, a grave is dug and the physical body is buried. While the body rots, the soul that once inhabited the body is alive in an unseen world. That world of the unseen terrifies some souls, and welcomes others with open arms. According to the Koran, every living being has a soul. All souls have full perception, awareness, and sensation of things in both this world and the unseen one.

What Is a Soul?

According to Islam, there is no denying the existence of a soul in every living being, from humans to insects. However, no one knows whether the composition of a soul is physical or not. The soul is invisible and undetectable by humans. Even with the latest technology and detection devices, people are not able to scientifically prove the existence of a soul in or outside a body.

Muslims believe that they will never learn anything more about what a soul is than what is said in the Koran, and that Allah's wisdom kept the matter beyond human reach, possibly because the human mind can't comprehend such a matter. The Koran relates Allah's words to Muhammad on this matter: "They will ask you concerning the spirit. Say: The spirit is by command of my Lord, and of knowledge you have been vouchsafed but little" (17:85). Simply, this means that the world of spirits is a mystery to humans and will always remain beyond our knowledge.

A spirit and a soul are essentially the same thing. In English contexts, a "spirit" refers to a soul released from its body. The Arabic word used for both is *Rooh*.

So what do Muslims know about a soul? They believe a soul is like a breath of air inhabiting a body, causing it to function. It is threaded through the physical body to the very tips, and saturates the mind down to the subconscious. It is like an invisible clone of the self, living inside the physical self. When the physical self dies, the spiritual self departs and leaves the body behind, yet carries with it all experiences the self underwent.

When describing the creation of man, Allah says in the Koran that man was a mass of clay that He shaped into human form. This human-shaped mass was lifeless until Allah blew into it, as it is written in the Holy Koran: "Then He fashioned him and breathed into him of His spirit; and appointed for you hearing and sight and hearts . . ." (32:9). This verse explains that the soul brought life to the physical mass, and without it the physical body dies.

While that verse explains where the very first soul came from, it doesn't mention anything about where babies get their souls. Are souls genetically transmitted? Certainly not! According to a Hadith of Muhammad, an angel descends and delivers the divine breath into the fetus sometime during the first few weeks of pregnancy, bestowing life upon it. Before that, the fetus is nothing but a cluster of cells with the potential to become a human.

FACT

The soul is like an electric current supplying life to the physical body. Think of your body as a computer that keeps running as long as it receives a supply of electricity, but as soon as the power is cut, it shuts down and remains switched off until the power returns. This power is the soul, but unlike electricity, once it's removed from the body, it cannot be returned until the Resurrection.

Death: The Soul's Departure

Death is a mystery and will always remain so. People often wonder if death is the end, or if there is some world beyond it. The Koran explains that death is not the end, but rather the beginning of eternal life. Death is not only a heart that stops beating; it's the departure of the soul from the body. That soul then enters a realm undetected by humans, but known to Muslims as the realm of the next life.

The great mystery of death can partly be resolved by understanding from the Koran and Sunnah what happens to the soul after it leaves the body. The Angel of Death receives the command from Allah to seize a soul, and arrives where he's due with a few other angels. These angels may appear beautiful and charming for the righteous souls, but may appear in a different, less-pleasant form for a person whose soul is destined for Hell. Once the soul is seized, it is carried off to the Heavens in the company of the angels.

The Angel of Death

Allah created only one angel with the sole duty of seizing the souls of the dead, and that is the Angel of Death. Although he has no name mentioned in the Koran, Muslims know him as Azrael. The Angel of Death seizes the soul of every single person—and possibly creature—that lives on Earth. Even if there was a death every second, the Angel of Death would be right there to seize the soul. He never tires or complains of this never-ending job that he's been doing since the world was created. In his work around the clock, he has diligently collected billions of souls.

ALERT!

Allah says in the Koran that he breathed His spirit into man and gave him life. However, the human soul is a creation of Allah and is as mortal as the body. Either would perish if Allah willed it.

The Angel of Death can only seize a soul by command of Allah. There are no definite records of how Azrael looks, but Muslims say it is unlikely that he is the Reaper that's often depicted in movies. There are claims that the Angel of Death is hideous and enormous with 4,000 wings, some of them the size of the earth itself. In a Hadith of Prophet Muhammad, the Angel of Death is described to be so enormous that he holds Earth between his knees, and with a mere glance, he can locate the next soul to be taken. However, Islamic sources say the angel can appear in any form, as he appeared for Prophet Abraham as a very handsome, very elegantly dressed man.

This angel is an intelligent, thoughtful being. He, too, possesses a soul, created in him by Allah. One Hadith tells of Prophet Muhammad's conversation with Azrael at the deathbed of a close friend. Muhammad asked the angel to be gentle in taking the soul of the man, as he was a righteous believer. The angel replied, "Be calm and do not worry, Muhammad. I am gentle and compassionate to every believer . . ." Then he said, "By Allah if I wanted to seize the soul of a mosquito I would not be able to do so without Allah's command."

The Last Breath

It is not only the Angel of Death who is present at the moment of death, but a group of other angels as well. There are two groups of these angels—the Angels of Mercy, and the Angels of Torment. The Angels of Mercy appear for the righteous soul as pleasant, comforting apparitions, while the other group appears for the nonbeliever as terrifying, disturbing apparitions. This information is available to Muslims through Prophet Muhammad's Hadith.

The righteous believers have their souls extracted painlessly. The angels would first greet the person, according to the Koran: "Those whom the angels cause to die (when they are) good. They say: Peace be unto you! Enter the Garden because of what you used to do" (16:32). Having been informed of his destiny in Paradise, the person's soul is seized by the Angel of Death as gently as a hair is pulled out of dough— an analogy courtesy of the Prophet. The Angel of Death then grants the soul of the believer to the Angels of Mercy.

The situation becomes different for an unbelieving wrongdoer whose bad deeds are greater than his good deeds. The Angel of Death descends upon such a nonbeliever in an unpleasant form accompanied by the Angels of Torment, who instill terror in the heart of the wrongdoer with their disturbing appearances and angry glares. Allah says in the Koran: "Whom the angels cause to die while they are wrongdoing themselves. Then will they make full submission saying: We used not to do any wrong. Nay! Surely Allah is Knower of what you used to do" (16:28). The Angel of Death extracts the nonbeliever's soul painfully and grants it to the Angels of Torment.

FACT

A soul goes through four stages from the time it is created: first in the mother's womb; then in this world as we know it; then in the next world, which is a realm for souls; and last, in its eternal home in Heaven or Hell. Muslims believe Allah determines when it's time for a soul to move from one stage to the next.

The Departure

Allah says in the Holy Koran to the soul of the righteous: "You soul at peace! Return to your Lord, content in his good pleasure! Enter among My bondmen! Enter My Garden!" (89:27–28). One of the basic beliefs in Islam is that all souls return to the Creator, just as they were delivered through him.

According to a Hadith, when the Angel of Death hands the righteous soul to the Angels of Mercy, they carry it up and ascend to the Heavens. All the gates of the seven Heavens open up to let the good soul pass through, until the soul reaches the seventh Heaven. There, Allah declares that the soul has been good and forgives its sins. Then the angels fly back down to the body of the dead person and let the soul watch the preparations for burial of the body.

The soul of the wrongdoer is handed to the Angels of Torment, who carry it up to the Heavens. There, the gates of all Heavens are closed to it, and the soul is not permitted to pass through. While it is down by the lowest Heaven, Allah declares the soul evil and tells the angels to carry it down to Earth and leave it in the grave.

Treatment of the Body

Islam requires rituals to be performed on the deceased body before its burial. These traditions are taken from the Sunnah and carried out with devotion at every Muslim's death. The rituals start with washing the body, then wrapping it in cloth, praying over it, and finally taking it to the cemetery for burial. These rituals serve two main purposes: the body is cleansed to enter death in purity, and the body is covered to retain its dignity and respect in front of others.

ALERT!

People who are killed in battle while defending the name of Allah are not washed before their burial even if their bodies are smeared with blood. Prophet Muhammad said that the angels would take care of the cleansing, as these people hold a special place in Heaven.

There is no coffin for the body in Islam. The wrapped-up body is carried on a flat board to the burial ground, with a group of the deceased's male family members and friends marching alongside. According to the Sunnah, the burial can take place at any time except at dawn, midday prayer, and sunset.

During the funeral, the soul of the deceased watches, with the good soul urging the people to hurry up so that it may be in bliss, and the bad soul urging them to slow down so that the grave's punishment may be delayed.

The Interrogation

When the funeral is over, the soul enters the grave and waits until it hears the last of the footsteps receding. Immediately, two angels with the names of Nakir and Munkar appear to the soul in the grave for the questioning. These angels' job is to interrogate every soul just after its body is buried. They would find the soul and interrogate it no matter how or where the body perished. Their interrogation is an important preliminary step before the soul receives its due punishment or bliss. Their mission is described in detail in a Hadith.

Interrogation of the Believer

The righteous believer's soul sits in the grave contently awaiting the angels' arrival. Once they arrive, they make no introductions. Two windows appear on each side of the grave, one that opens to Hell, and one that opens to Heaven. Instantly, they ask him, "Who is your Lord, and what is your religion?" Confidently, the soul answers, "My Lord is Allah and my religion is Islam." The window to Hell closes a little.

Then they ask, "Who is that man who was sent among you?" He replies, "The Messenger of Allah." The window to Hell closes up a little more. Finally, they ask, "What did he bring?" He replies, "The book of Allah which I read and believed." The window to Hell closes completely and only the window to Heaven remains open.

QUESTION?

What kind of world does a soul dwell in?
After Allah declares the soul good or bad, it goes into a realm called Al Barzakh—the next life. In Al Barzakh, the soul is aware of our world but cannot reach across, while we are not aware of the soul at all.

Then a voice from the Heavens announces, "My servant has spoken the truth, so spread out carpets from the Garden for him and open a gate of the Garden for him." Upon this, the grave expands to the size of a meadow and a scent of Heaven reaches the soul. The interrogation is then over, and a very handsome, well-dressed, well-fragranced man appears to the soul. The soul is charmed with his presence, but when the man introduces himself as the soul's good deeds and assures the soul of the Paradise awaiting, the soul becomes ecstatic and remains in bliss until the Last Day.

Interrogation of the Nonbeliever

The nonbelieving soul receives different treatment from that of the righteous soul. After the funeral, the terrified soul returns to the grave and waits for Nakir and Munkar. When they arrive, the same windows to Hell and Heaven open on each side of the grave. They ask the same questions, but, of course, his replies are different. When they ask, "Who is your Lord?" he replies in confusion, "I don't know." But they say, "Wrong, you do know."

The window to Heaven closes completely and only the window to Hell remains open. Its heat sears the soul as the grave draws tighter and tighter until the soul's ribs are scrunched together. Also, a hideous, foul-smelling creature appears before the soul, and introduces itself as its bad deeds. The ugly apparition informs the soul of the Hell prepared for it, and then hits it with a blow strong enough to turn a mountain to powder—a blow that all creatures but humans and jinn can hear.

The Grave's Tortures and Bliss

The grave can be a resting place or a torture chamber, depending on how the person lived his or her life. In Islam, there is no denying that a soul gets a taste of Hell or Heaven while it lies in its grave—this is mentioned in the Koran and described explicitly in the Sunnah. It doesn't matter if the body was reduced to ashes, torn to pieces, or eaten by lions—the soul would still find the body and go through the same experiences as those who are buried in the earth.

FACT

When the soul returns to the grave for questioning, it returns to the body and becomes aware of the realm of Al Barzakh with all its five senses. The bliss or chastisement of the grave is felt by the soul just as though it were a live body.

Why a Grave's Torture?

Allah says in the Holy Koran: "[I]f thou could see, when the wrongdoers reach the pangs of death and the angels stretch their hands out, saying: Deliver up your souls. This day you are awarded doom of degradation for that you spoke concerning Allah other than the truth, and scorned His portents" (6:93). Clearly, Allah states in this verse that on the day a person dies and his soul is taken by the angels, he will experience chastisement for being a wrongdoer during his life.

Prophet Muhammad's Hadith describe different tortures for different deeds. Generally, punishment in the grave is a result of a life full of bad deeds. People who habitually spread lies, collect interest money, fornicate, and above all, know the Koran but neglect its teachings will suffer intensively in their graves. Of course, people who were generally immoral will receive one form or another of chastisement in their afterlife. They will also receive unimaginable punishment when Judgment Day arrives, but until then, they will be chastised with a mere sample of Hell.

ALERT!

It wouldn't be fair for some people to be punished for 5,000 years and others who die closer to the Last Day to be punished for only 100 years. That's why in the realm of Al Barzakh, time as we know it doesn't exist, and everybody experiences it an equal length of time.

The Grave's Bliss

The soul of the righteous believer goes through a completely different experience from that of the wrongdoer. However, all Muslims, no matter how good, fear the grave and constantly pray for Allah to have mercy on them when they die. This is partly caused by their apprehension of Nakir and Munkar, the two firm interrogators. Sometimes a Muslim fears that the shock of death and the sight of the unpleasant apparitions might strike him silent to their questions, but Allah reassures the righteous in the Koran: "Allah confirms those who believe by a firm saying in the life of this world and in the Hereafter . . ." (14:27).

The verse implies that Allah will strengthen the heart of the believer and support him or her in the grave's interrogation. After passing this critical test, the grave expands and spreads out for the comfort of the righteous soul. This, of course, happens only in the next life's realm, and the soul remains out of reach of this world. The soul may rest in peace and sleep through death until the Last Day, or it may sample paradise, travel through the Heavens, mingle with souls of other people, and watch this world through the veil of Al Barzakh.

Communication Between the Worlds

Muslims believe two types of death happen to every human being in the world. It says in the Koran, "Allah receives men's souls at the time of their death and that soul which dies not yet in its sleep. He keeps that soul for which he has ordained death and dismisses the rest till an appointed term" (39:42).

According to this verse, the soul of a sleeping person travels through the worlds to a place where Allah holds the souls of the dead. After a certain time, Allah sends away the souls of those asleep until their time comes to stay in Al Barzakh.

When the soul of a sleeping person ascends to Allah and returns to the body after some time, it is known in Islam as the Minor Death. This might be the stage-four sleep defined by science to be REM (rapid eye movement), when dreams occur.

Dreams play a key role in connecting the souls of the living with the souls of the dead. Based on the information in the Koran and Hadith, scholars explain that when the soul of a living person travels to the other world, it can meet the souls of the dead. Sometimes, the souls speak to each other. It's not a rare event for a living person to dream of a dead person, and for the dead to share a bit of wit or advice with the living person. Also, sometimes the soul of the dead may have some unfinished business in this world, so it visits the soul of the living and tells it what to do. Such a dream is actually regarded in Islam as a vision.

According to the Koran, the souls of the dead are in Allah's custody. The souls of the dead cannot visit us in our world because they are held back in Al Barzakh. Islam does not believe in souls stuck in this world for one reason or another, and neither does it believe in calling upon the spirits as some people claim to do. However, only Allah has full knowledge of how the worlds operate, and it may be possible that occasionally the veil between the worlds thins out so the two sides just may catch a glimpse of each other.

Chapter 15

Gates of Heaven: Rewards for the Righteous

The promise of Heaven is present throughout the entire Koran. Allah describes Heaven as the eternal home for those who believe in Him and do good in their lives. Heaven is unlike any place on Earth—its beauty and luxury are beyond imagination. The Koran provides insights on its landscapes, palaces, and food, and makes a clear distinction between those who will be granted entry and those who will be doomed to another fate.

The Concept of Heaven in Islam

The existence of Heaven is a fact according to the Koran. Like everything else in the universe, Heaven is a creation of Allah: "He it is Who produced gardens (Heaven) trellised and untrellised, and the date palm, and crops of diverse flavor, and the olive and the pomegranate, like and unlike . . ." (6:141). Its purpose is to motivate people to do good deeds in their lives, and reward them when they die.

Heaven is described in the Koran as a garden with trees, flowers, fruits, rivers, birds, and more, all designed for the pleasure of the righteous. The Koran heavily emphasizes the subject of Heaven to provide a strong motive for people to stay on the right path. In the Koran, Allah promises His believers again and again that they will be rewarded for following His teachings. For example, He says, "But as for those who believe and do good works We shall bring them into gardens underneath which rivers flow, wherein they will abide forever. It is a promise from Allah in truth; and who can be more truthful than Allah in utterance?" (4:122).

This assures believers that life after death will bring them more luxury than this world can offer. Heaven is Allah's promise to those people, assuring them that they will abide in it forever. Since there's no death after the Resurrection, anyone who enters Heaven will enjoy its luxury to no end. In Heaven, there is no aging, suffering, difficulties, or challenges that are typical of this world.

The Arabic word for Heaven is *Jannah (Jannaat* is the plural form). Heaven has some other names in the Koran that have correspondents in English, such as *Aden* for Eden, and *Firdouse* for Paradise. The Koran often speaks of Heaven using different names and in plural form, indicating the diversity among the levels.

The Road to Heaven

In Surah Al Fatiha, the opening Surah of the Koran, there is a prayer asking Allah for Heaven: "Show us the straight path, the path of those whom

You have favored; not (the path) of those who earn Your anger nor of those who go astray" (1:6–7). In another Surah, Allah says, "And (He commands you, saying): This is My straight path, so follow it. Follow not other ways, lest you be parted from His way. This has He ordained for you, that you may ward off (evil)" (6:153).

The straight path Allah talks about in the Koran is the road to Heaven. It is not a physical road that people will walk on Judgment Day; instead, it refers to the time spent and choices made in this world. The straight path is the Koran, as presented in the second Surah, which answers the first by saying, "This is the scripture whereof there is no doubt, a guidance unto those who ward off evil . . ." (2:2). Following the Koran and its teachings, which are the straight path, will lead to Heaven.

Whether or not someone will find the straight path is a matter ordained by Allah, according to the Koran: "And Allah summons to the abode of peace, and leads whom He will to a straight path" (10:25). The "abode of peace" in this verse refers to Heaven. The implication here is that Allah will make finding the straight path easy for the devoted believer. In other words, the more a believer strives to please Allah, the stronger her faith will become, and the closer she will get to Heaven, a chain of events made possible by the will of Allah.

Belief Is the Key

Belief in Allah as the sole Creator and in Muhammad as his messenger can be a ticket to Heaven even for someone who has not strived hard enough in this world. The first requirement in the Pillars of Faith and in the Pillars of Islam (see Chapter 4) is belief in Allah. Although it is the foundation of Islam, according to the Koran it can possibly save a non-Muslim from hellfire on Judgment Day: "Lo! Those who say: Our Lord is Allah, and afterward are upright, the angels descend upon them, saying: Fear not nor grieve, but bear good tidings of the paradise which you are promised" (41:30). The word *upright* here means being righteous.

Further on, Allah says, "Lo! Those who believe and do good works and humble themselves before their Lord: such are rightful owners of the Garden; they will abide therein" (11:23). This verse addresses "those who believe" in Allah and promises them the Garden (Heaven). Doing good works is essential, but belief is given top priority. Take the example of the grave's interrogation discussed in Chapter 14, where the angel's first question is "Who is your Lord?" Prophet Muhammad emphasized the importance of belief by saying, "The key to Heaven is the Declaration of Faith in Allah."

Who Goes to Heaven?

Prophet Muhammad was once asked, "Isn't belief the key to Heaven?" He said, "True, but every key must have teeth in order to open." In the Koran, the value of good deeds is not forgotten: "Enter the Garden because of what you used to do" (16:32). Belief in Allah may be the key, but a person's deeds determine the measure of reward deserved. Those deeds are the teeth to the key to Heaven. Most Islamic scholars conclude that belief grants a person admission to Heaven, but with more bad deeds than good, reward could be postponed until a certain sentence in Hell is completed.

QUESTION?

What happens to a nonbeliever with good deeds?
Allah states in the Koran that he who performs a particle's worth of a good deed will duly receive reward or punishment. Forgiveness is up to Allah, and no one can presume who will and who won't go to Heaven.

Throughout the Koran, good deeds are consistently linked to a promised reward in Heaven, such as in the following verse: "[T]hose who believe and do good works (will be) in flowering meadows of the Gardens, having what they wish from their Lord. This is the great preferment" (42:22). Other verses of the Koran specifically state what good deeds admit a person to Heaven. Surah 33, verse 35, describes in detail the character and deeds of a person who would enter Heaven. According to that verse, a person who surrenders to and obeys Allah, speaks the truth, practices patience, gives alms, fasts, guards his or her modesty, is humble, and remembers Allah in thought and speech will be rewarded in Heaven. The Koran mentions more conditions and the list is long, but it all boils down to following the teachings of Allah's book: "Who so obeys

Allah and His messenger, He will make him enter Gardens underneath which rivers flow, where such will dwell forever" (4:13).

According to the Koran and Sunnah, admission to Heaven is granted, not earned: "If Allah took mankind to task for that which they earn, He would not leave a living creature on the surface of the earth . . ." (35:45). This means that if Allah judged people by their record of deeds alone, their sins would be so much that He would not leave a living soul on Earth. Muslims believe that Allah's forgiveness and graciousness allow people to go to Heaven, while good deeds determine the level of comfort awarded.

The Gates of Heaven

The Hadith of Prophet Muhammad state that Heaven has eight gates. Each gate opens to a particular group of people according to their deeds. The Prophet said that for some people all eight gates will open, giving them a choice of which one to enter through. This happens to a select group that has excelled in worship and dedication to Allah. For example, if one believer prayed, fasted, spent of his money on charity, protected the name of Allah, and lived a life of good deeds, all the gates will open up for him. In another Hadith, the Prophet said that all the gates open in welcome of a believer whose ablutions were frequent and accurate, and who followed every ablution with the Declaration of Faith and the prayer: "Allah, make me a repentant and make me pure."

The guards of Heaven are mentioned in the Koran in the following verse: "And those who keep their duty to their Lord are driven unto the Garden in troops till, when they reach it, and the gates thereof are opened, and the warders thereof say unto them: Peace be unto you! You are good, so enter you (the Garden of Delight), to dwell therein" (39:73). This verse mentions the warders, or guards, in plural form.

All the Different Heavens

Muslims understand from the Koran and Sunnah that Heaven is not a single place for all, but is composed of many levels ranging from lowest to highest. The exact number of Heavens is not clear. Although there are several verses in the Koran that refer to "seven heavens," this is where the translations are misleading. In these verses, *heaven* means "sky," not Paradise.

ALERT!

In English translations of the Koran, the word *Heaven* is used to describe Paradise—the reward of the righteous—and the Heavens—the sky or worlds above our world. However, the Arabic Koran uses two distinct words to differentiate between the two meanings: *Samaa* for sky, and *Jannah* for Paradise.

The lowest Heaven provides the least comfort level among Heavens, and as you go higher, the comfort level increases. The highest Heaven is reserved for the elite who are chosen by Allah, such as Prophet Muhammad and his companions. However, Islam makes it clear that the highest Heaven is within reach of anyone who works hard enough to please Allah.

Although the number of Heavens is not known, the Koran attributes twelve different names to Heaven, indicating the differences and similarities among the levels. The most common of these names simply is *Jannah*—Heaven.

Other famous names of Heaven found in the Koran are the Abode of Peace, the Mansion of Eternity, the Garden Home, Gardens of Eden, Paradise, and Gardens of Delight. Islamic scholars are unable to determine whether these names are merely descriptive, or are actual names of different levels of Heaven. However, it is accepted that every person will receive due reward according to his or her deeds, which indicates that not all people will be in the same Heaven.

Heavenly Landscapes

Heaven contains scenes of nature that are beyond this world in beauty. The Koran describes in detail the landscapes, trees, lakes, and rivers of Heaven, while making it clear that the most breathtaking views on Earth

cannot compete with what has been prepared in Heaven for the righteous. Heaven's rivers and springs flow uninterrupted, providing nourish-
ment for its dwellers.

Heavenly Rivers

The rivers of Heaven are described in the Koran in the following
verse: "A similitude of the Garden which those who keep their duty (to
Allah) are promised: Therein are rivers of water unpolluted, and rivers of
milk whereof the flavor changes not, and rivers of wine delicious to the
drinkers, and rivers of clear run honey . . ." (47:15). Through this verse,
one can conclude that the rivers of Heaven are not limited to water, but
that there are also rivers of milk, honey, and wine.

FACT

In Heaven, neither water nor milk ever becomes spoiled or polluted. Also,
the wine of Heaven is different from the wines of this world in that they
taste better ("delicious to drinkers") and do not cause drunkenness. The
honey river, too, is unique in its clarity and contains no beeswax or any
other impure substance.

In a Hadith of Prophet Muhammad, the rivers of Heaven are said to
start in Paradise and flow down like a waterfall to the lower Heavens.
Some sources say that the rivers flow in the same bed but do not get
mixed together. The Koran states that the people of Heaven can freely
drink from these rivers.

Apart from the rivers, there are also springs of various heavenly cocktails as mentioned in the Koran: "They are watered with a cup whereof
the mixture is of Zanjabil (ginger), the water of a spring therein, named
Salsabil" (76:17–18). Islam believes that these rivers and springs that flow
uninterrupted without becoming spoiled or polluted are a miraculous
creation of Allah.

Heavenly Soil and Greenery

Like the rivers, the soil and greenery of Heaven are beyond this world
in their beauty, fragrance, and size. Allah says in the Holy Koran that

"[n]o soul knows what is kept hid for them of joy, as a reward for what they used to do" (32:17). Prophet Muhammad further explains that the sand of Heaven is made of saffron. Based on other Hadith, some scholars say that Heaven's ground is made of silver (or they could mean that it looks like silver), its soil smells of musk, and its trees have bark of gold and silver, with branches adorned with pearls and gemstones.

Some Islamic resources say that the rivers of Heaven have no banks or shores. This concept is a little beyond human comprehension, but may well be one of Allah's miracles.

The trees of Heaven are described in many places in the Koran, but the following is one good example: "And those on the right hand; what of those on the right hand? Among thornless lote-trees, and clustered plantains, and spreading shade, and water gushing, and fruit in plenty, neither cut off nor forbidden" (56:27–33). Detailed description of these trees is found in the Prophet's Hadith, where he says that the trees are dense and contain an abundance of fruits in seventy different colors.

Heavenly Fruits

The Koran describes the fruits of Heaven in detail, emphasizing that they are very different from the fruits of Earth. Renowned Islamic scholars agree that these fruits emit a glow, are sweeter than honey, softer than butter, and contain no pits. Like the rivers of Heaven, the fruits are within easy reach and do not run out or change color or flavor, because Allah maintains their condition.

The Koran says, "[A]s often as they are regaled with food of the fruit thereof, they say: This is what was given us aforetime (on Earth); and it is given to them in resemblance . . ." (2:25). According to experts, the interpretation of this verse is that the people of Heaven will be offered fruits that look like the fruits they ate on Earth, but the resemblance will be limited to shape or color, not taste, as the flavor of heavenly fruits is more delicious than those that grow on Earth.

The fruits of Heaven are easily reached by hand as mentioned in the Koran: "[A]nd the clustered fruits thereof are made to bow down" (76:14). This has been interpreted to mean that all a person has to do is wish for the fruit, and it drops down to his or her reach. Other verses state that some branches are very low, making the picking of fruits possible even while lying down. The types of heavenly fruits mentioned by name in the Koran are grapes, pomegranates, and dates. However, the Koran affirms that all types of fruits will be available.

In the Koran, Allah promises the righteous that He will grant them all their wishes, regardless of how grand the wishes are. This is because Allah wants to fulfill their desires and not withhold anything from them, as Heaven is a place of satisfaction.

Lifestyle and Pleasures

Palaces, landscapes, food, in addition to the fulfillment of every wish are a promise from the Koran to the people of Heaven. They will wear silk embroidered with gold, and will be adorned with jewels and silver. Servants shall carry drinks in silver cups to people reclining on couches under the shade of trees. Food with heavenly flavor will be brought to them at the mere thought of it. Of course, all of this is for eternity, as the Koran says: "[T]here they will abide" (23:11).

Life in Heaven will be drastically different from that on Earth. Allah specifically says in the Koran that feelings such as envy, jealousy, and hatred will be removed from people's hearts. Since there will be no working for a living, there will be no competition for money, power, or status. This is because every wish will be fulfilled instantly as promised in the Koran: "[W]hile those who believe and do good works (will be) in flowering meadows of the Gardens, having what they wish from their Lord . . ." (42:22).

People in Heaven will not age and their health will never deteriorate. Youth will be preserved forever and all people will remain in their prime (some guess the age of everyone will be between late teens to early twenties). The Koran states that spouses will be reunited. Those with no spouses from their life on Earth will be offered mates from Heaven to marry.

Hoor Ein (also known as Houris in English) is the name the Koran gives to women Allah created in Heaven especially for men with no wives. These creatures are perpetual virgins, fair with beautiful dark eyes, eternally youthful, and their goal is to pamper and delight their husbands. Prophet Muhammad said that a man could have two Hoor Ein to marry. However, couples who were married on Earth and reunited in Heaven will be re-created in the most beautiful picture for each other's pleasure according to the Koran: "There for them are pure companions; there forever they abide" (2:25).

FACT

Muslims consider the opportunity to see and speak to Allah while they are in Heaven the ultimate reward. The Koran says in Surah 83, verse 15, that the people of Hell will not get a sighting of Allah, and for them that is the ultimate punishment.

Meeting the Creator

Allah makes it evident in the Koran that the righteous people of Heaven will receive the additional reward of seeing their Creator: "That day will faces be resplendent, looking toward their Lord" (75:22–23). It is not permitted in Islam to wish to see Allah during life in this world; any Muslim who deviates by asking Allah to reveal himself is committing a serious offense. Allah does not reveal Himself to people in this world because their mental and physical being would not tolerate such a sighting, as mentioned in the Koran.

However, in Heaven, people will not be quite the same as they were on Earth. They will be able to fill their eyes with the sight of their Creator and will even speak to Him. Prophet Muhammad said that when the righteous people enter Heaven, Allah will ask them, "Can I grant you anything else?" They'll say, "You have saved us from Hell and granted us Heaven, for that our faces are radiant." Then Allah will reveal Himself, which to them is the greatest reward.

Chapter 16

Flames of Another World: Hell for Sinners

Hell is mentioned almost as many times in the Koran as Heaven is. Every time the Koran describes the bliss of Heaven, it also describes the terrors of Hell. The Koran clearly defines who will go to Hell and explicitly illustrates how they will be made to suffer. There are, of course, different levels and various punishments, and a number of people may even be released to Heaven after some time. Nevertheless, the Hell the Koran talks about is a place no one would want to step into.

Hell in the Koran

In any given set of pages in the Koran, there are a few verses talking about Hell. Some verses simply mention that the wrongdoers will go to Hell, but other verses dive into vivid description of certain tortures awaiting those people. It is not a pretty picture, but Allah uses it to repel people from sinning. In the Koran, Allah promises the righteous Heaven, then promises the wrongdoers Hell, and assures that He will keep His promises.

The warnings against Hell ring loud and clear in the Koran, as in this example: "Lo! Hell lurks in ambush, a home for the rebellious. They will abide therein for ages" (78:21–23). Just like Heaven, Hell is an eternal place. Hell is commonly known as a fire that will burn those who enter it, but it is more than that according to the Koran. Hell is about the absence of every luxury or pleasure that was available on Earth, from food to shelter to companionship. Psychological torture is taken as seriously as the physical, as you will discover in the next few pages.

Because Hell is eternal, there is no death in it. A Hadith of Prophet Muhammad says that when the people of Heaven go to Heaven, and the people of Hell go to Hell, Death is brought forth between Heaven and Hell in the form of an animal. Then it will be slaughtered, and a voice will declare, "Oh, people of Heaven! Immortality from hereon. Oh, people of Hell! Immortality from hereon."

ALERT!

Because there is only Heaven and Hell after the Last Day, every person that ever walked the earth will end up in one or the other. The Koran does not mention a third option. However, there are some people who will be admitted into Heaven after serving a certain amount of time in Hell.

Therefore, even though the people of Hell will be burned until their flesh melts off their bones, they will be resurrected to endure another scorching, and so on. This cycle is presented throughout the Koran, such as in this verse: "Lo! Those who disbelieve Our revelations, We shall expose them to the Fire. As often as their skins are consumed We shall exchange them for fresh skins that they may taste the torment. Lo! Allah is ever Mighty, Wise" (4:56). In this and many other verses, it is evident that there is no escape from the pain and suffering prepared for the wrongdoers in Hell.

Avoiding Hell

The Koran defines *halal* (that which Muslims are allowed to do and eat) and *haram* (that which is forbidden). The safe route is to avoid everything *haram,* as that will bring a more positive verdict on Judgment Day according to the Koran: "These are the limits (imposed by) Allah. Whoso obeys Allah and His messenger, He will make him enter Gardens underneath which rivers flow, where such will dwell forever. That will be the great success" (4:13).

The limits imposed by Allah refer to the line that separates good from evil. When Allah tells people not to commit fornication, He is setting a limit to certain behavior. Also, when Allah describes alcohol as the work of Satan and commands people to avoid it, He is setting another limit. The wrongdoers are those who cross these limits, and they are promised eternal Hell: "And whoso disobeys Allah and His messenger and transgresses His limits, He will make him enter Fire, where such will dwell forever; his will be a shameful doom" (4:14).

The Koran says that disbelieving in Allah is also a ticket to Hell, that He will "hurl to Hell each rebel ingrate" (50:24). In Chapter 15, the ticket to Heaven is described as following the straight path; that is, the Koran and its teachings. According to the Koran, failure to follow the straight path is a good reason for Allah to send someone to Hell. However, Allah says that no soul will be judged unjustly, and everyone will receive deserved punishment or reward.

QUESTION?

What if someone is only half-dedicated to the straight path?
Allah's wisdom and judgment would decide whether the person should go to Hell or to Heaven. Allah says in the Koran that His forgiveness is infinite, so such a person may be forgiven and granted Heaven.

The Bridge of Hell

There is a statement in the Koran confirming that everyone, including those going to Heaven, will get a sight of Hell after judgment is through. That will happen when everyone crosses a bridge, called *Sirat*, that extends over Hell. The Koran only mentions this bridge briefly, while the Prophet's Hadith dwell a little more on the subject. The objectives of crossing this bridge are to show the righteous what could have been their destiny, and to drop the wrongdoers into the pit of hellfire.

By studying the Hadith, scholars conclude that the first to cross this bridge is Prophet Muhammad, followed by the people who lived by the Sunnah. The Koran continues: "On the day when you will see the believers, men and women, their light shining forth before them and on their right hands, (and will hear it said unto them): Glad news for you this day: Gardens underneath which rivers flow, wherein you are immortal. That is the supreme triumph" (57:12).

Scholars conclude that the people whose good deeds were of moderate measure will be provided with a similarly moderate light that barely reveals one step ahead. Their mission to cross will be slower and prone to a few terrors, but eventually they will make it to the other side. Worse in luck are those with no good deeds at all, who will receive no light to guide them forth. They will collapse right into the pit the moment they set foot on the bridge.

The Magnitude of Hell

Hell is a living creation of Allah with a thinking, feeling mind of its own, as is implied in the Koran. The Prophet depicts its size and might in some Hadith; he saw it when he flew through the seven Heavens on Isra Wal Miraj (see Chapter 2). Imams (Islamic scholars) say that on Judgment Day, Hell will come before Heaven, blocking any path to it except the bridge. The mere sights and sounds of Hell will strike terror in the hearts of all creation.

Hell is not only about fire, but, based on the Prophet's Hadith, scholars conclude that Hell may contain nightmarish creatures or monsters designed to inflict pain and suffering among its people. One such example is a long-necked blaze with facial features set out to punish certain groups of people.

Frightening Power

In-depth studies of the Prophet's Hadith reveal that Hell is enormous and vicious. Based on the Prophet's sayings, on Judgment Day Hell will be hauled near the land where people are judged. The literal translation of the Arabic text is that Hell will come "walking" on four supports, constrained by 70,000 chain ropes. Each rope will be held by another 70,000 angels. Each angel will hold onto the rope by a ring that would take more than the world's iron to make.

When Hell comes into sight of creation, everyone will crouch in fear, including the prophets (with the exception of Muhammad): "And you will see each nation crouching, each nation summoned to its record. (And it will be said to them): This day you are requited what you used to do" (45:28). Hell will approach with a raging appetite to consume all humanity, but according to the Hadith, Prophet Muhammad will speak to it and force it to retreat from sight of the righteous. Then Muhammad will ask the Lord to have mercy on the people who followed the Koran and the Sunnah, and his wish will be granted. Therefore, Allah says, "We sent you (Muhammad) not but as a mercy for the peoples (in the worlds) (21:107).

When Muhammad tells the fire to retreat until judgment is over, it listens to him because it fears him. Muhammad is the one person who will be able to stand up to Hell and not be shaken by its terrors, as he is protected by Allah. This is according to Muhammad's Hadith.

Scorching Heat

The Prophet once said that a rock dropped into the pit of Hell would fall for seventy years before it hits the bottom. Hell is large enough to hold the masses and enfold them with its fire: "Lo! We have prepared for disbelievers Fire. Its tent encloses them. If they ask for showers, they will be showered with water like to molten lead which burns the faces . . ." (18:29). This is only one example, as the Koran frequently depicts the heat of Hell, and describes the life its people will lead.

The bottom of Hell contains the fuel that keeps it alight. That fuel is not gas or coal, but is as follows: "Lo! You idolators and that which you worship beside Allah are fuel of Hell" (21:98). Those people and some from a few other categories will share the duty of becoming fuel—the severest punishment imposed by Allah. Others will wear clothes of fire, sleep in beds of fire, eat and drink fire, and feel no shade or coolness forever, all by promise of Allah in the Koran.

When Hell Speaks

It has been mentioned before that Hell is a living, thinking creation of Allah. On Judgment Day, Hell will boil and churn in rage at the waywardness of humanity, and seek to swallow them all, but will be stopped by Prophet Muhammad. The Koran says, "When it sees them from afar, they hear the crackling and the roar thereof." Like a seething dragon, Hell's fury will cause it to roar and growl as it waits for its appetite to be sated. Later, the Koran says that Hell will almost burst with rage at the people being sent to it.

But Hell has a big appetite because it is mentioned in the Koran that Allah will ask Hell if it has reached its fill, but it will simply answer: "Can there be more to come?" (50:30). A Hadith adds that it will continue to grow and ask for more, until Allah finally forces it to recede and be satisfied with the masses it is consuming.

Gates and Guardians

There are seven gates to Hell. Each gate is for a particular group of people who have shared similar sins in life and will now endure similar punishment. There are different levels to Hell and not all people are punished with equal severity—some are in the bottom pit and some are up near the surface, suffering from relatively mild punishment.

F A C T

There are seven gates to Hell, and there are seven Heavens between this world and the next. Muslims believe that Allah prefers odd numbers to even numbers. This can be found in many acts of worship, such as in ablution where one has to wash three times, or in prayer, when words of devotion are uttered in sets of three.

Allah says in the Holy Koran: "We have appointed only angels to be wardens of the fire . . ." (74:31). According to the Koran, there are nineteen guardians of Hell. They may be angels, but they're very different from our typical view of angels. These are not sweet-looking, white-winged creatures from Heaven—they are quite the opposite. The guardians of Hell are ferocious, mighty, and stern. Some Islamic resources say that each guardian holds a massive spiked club for a weapon.

In the Koran, Allah explains that the people of Hell will try speaking to the guardians, asking them for help. The people will say, "Entreat your Lord that He relieve us of a day of the torment" (40:49). But the guardians will reply, "Came not your messenger unto you with clear proofs?" (40:50). The people will admit they had been sent messengers from Allah, but the Koran makes it clear that in Hell, no repentance is accepted.

Who Goes to Hell?

From a general Koranic perspective, the people who go to Hell are those who neglect the Koran and its teachings. Disbelieving in Allah, ignoring the Prophet's teachings, killing an innocent person, hypocrisy, running away from the battlefield, and cutting blood ties are acts and behaviors that Allah takes very seriously on Judgment Day, stating in the Koran that committers of such acts gain quick access to hellfire. Other sins that send people to Hell are lying, cheating, stealing, betrayal, and other *haram* acts, particularly when committed persistently without repentance.

Murderers

Murder is viewed as a severe offense against Allah's laws, so the punishment for it is intense: "Whoso slays a believer of set purpose, his reward is Hell forever. Allah is wroth against him and He has cursed him and prepared for him an awful doom" (4:93). This verse leaves no doubt that a murderer will be sent to Hell for an eternal punishment.

Although Allah speaks here about the murderer who slays a *believer*, that doesn't mean that a murderer who kills a nonbeliever will go unpunished, because the Koran states that murder is *haram*. Committing an act that is *haram* is a sin, and all sins are punishable. Muslims' opinions vary on whether repentance for murder is accepted, but the general belief is that Allah forgives anything as long as repentance is sincere and happens before death.

ALERT!

The Koran describes a conversation between the nonbelievers in Hell and Allah, where the nonbelievers admit they had been wrong and beg for release from Hell. Allah's only response is "[b]e gone therein, and speak not unto Me" (23:108). The Koran is very straightforward about the situation of Hell's people, stating that Allah will not comfort or forgive them, and will simply veil Himself from their sight.

Disbelievers

The one thing that Allah will not forgive on Judgment Day is disbelieving in Him and the Koran. The Koran repeatedly refers to people who ignore Allah's signs of His existence, saying that their destiny is Hell. Those who die as nonbelievers will never catch a glimpse of Heaven according to this verse: "Lo! They who deny Our revelations and scorn them, for them the gates of Heaven will not be opened nor will they enter the Garden until the camel goes through the needle's eye. Thus do We requite the guilty" (7:40).

The Koran uses an interesting analogy in the previous verse, promising those guilty of denying the revelation that they will not be admitted to Heaven until a "camel goes through the needle's eye." In other words, they will never be admitted to Heaven. Also note that Allah says "those who deny Our revelations," and does not use the word "Koran" instead of "revelations." The revelations meant here are the signs of Him being the Creator, such as the orbiting of planets, the order of nature, or human intelligence.

Hypocrites

The type of hypocrite the Koran talks about is not the ordinary two-faced gossip, but the pretender who makes Muslims believe he is one of them, while remaining a nonbeliever in his heart. For such a person, the Koran predicts an ugly fate: "Lo! The hypocrites (will be) in the lowest deep of the fire, and you will find no helper for them" (4:146).

Why such severe punishment for them? The Koran explains that such people have been exposed to the Koran and know a lot about it, yet when they are away from Muslims, they mock it and insist on following the path of the devil. Additionally, hypocrites are like a virus in a Muslim society, aiming to destroy it from within. In the Koran, Allah warns Muslims against befriending hypocrites, telling them that they will receive the same fate as the pretenders in Hell if they do.

Other Sinners

A miserable place in Hell is reserved for a soldier who runs away from the battlefield in cowardice. The Koran says that whoever does so has bestowed Allah's wrath upon himself and will dwell in Hell. Disobeying or deliberately ignoring the teachings of the Prophet Muhammad is another quick way to Hell, as Allah says in the Koran. Such a person would find himself in his own hellfire on Judgment Day, sentenced to abide in it forever. The punishment is severe because Allah defines obeying the Prophet as a rule, which if broken, is considered trespassing over Allah's limits.

In previous chapters, the importance of family in Islam is discussed. Islam makes the maintenance of family bonds an obligation. If this obligation is neglected and family ties are cut intentionally, Allah takes another measure of action: "Would you then, if you were given the command, work corruption in the land and sever your ties of kinship? Such are they whom Allah curses so that he deafens them and makes blind their eyes" (47:23–25). This is further confirmed in a Hadith, where Muhammad says, "He who cuts blood-ties does not enter Heaven."

The mildest form of punishment is reserved for Prophet Muhammad's uncle, Abu Talib. Although the man refused to believe in the Prophet's message, he protected his nephew dearly from the tribe's hostilities. For that, Muhammad said that Allah has given him the least punishment in Hell: standing on hot coal with bare feet.

Life in Hell

While the people of Heaven recline against luxurious cushions with heavenly cocktails in their hands, the people of Hell are chained and dragged, scorched to ashes then re-formed, and offered boiling water to drink and sharp thorns to eat. Their suffering will be nonstop, with no time off to sleep, have a meal, or even take a breather.

Food, Drink, and Clothing

The people of Hell will be wearing clothes described in the following verse: "But as for those who disbelieve, their garments of fire will be cut out for them" (22:19). This means that in addition to being immersed in Hell, they will be clothed in fire. They will never feel coolness, shade, or peace again. If they get thirsty, they will be given boiling water that will melt their insides, and if they yearn for a refreshing cold splash, they will be showered in acid water that will dissolve their skins.

For food, the people of Hell will eat out of a tree called *Zaqqum*. According to the Koran, this tree grows out of the core of Hell, and "[i]ts crop is as it were the heads of devils" (37:65). The people will eat against their will, and the food will shred them from the inside. They will also be eating filth and thorns. Every time that they nearly perish, they will be brought back to full form to endure another suffering.

Isolation and Torment

Through careful interpretation of the Koran, scholars discovered that the people of Heaven will live together in families with freedom to wander through the Heavens, but each person in Hell will be held to one place that's like an individual cell, where he or she will be separated from the comfort of companionship. This difference is more prominent in the Arabic Koran than the translations. For example, when Allah talks about life in Heaven, He says that the people will be in Heavens, but when He talks about Hell, He sometimes says that *he* (the wrongdoer) will be in *a* fire—singular form. This concept can also be found in verses where the Koran explains how a wrongdoer will be enveloped in fire from all sides, which scholars believe will prevent him from seeing others.

Is Hell's Punishment Eternal?

Prophet Muhammad said that no one who ever said *there is no God but Allah* with sincerity would remain in Hell forever. The Koran consistently talks about believers being the ones who will be rewarded with Heaven. Based on that, a believer who goes to Hell due to a long record of bad deeds will eventually be released and admitted into Heaven.

How long such a person would have to dwell in Hell before he is released depends on his deeds. Allah will judge and sentence him to a definitive period in Hell at a certain level of punishment. When the person has thoroughly paid for his bad deeds, Allah may then release him and grant him Heaven. An interesting Hadith narrates that the last person to leave Hell will literally crawl out of it, with Hell reaching for him persistently to drag him back inside. When he makes it out of Hell's reach, he will exhale and thank Allah for His graciousness.

Chapter 17

The Jinn

The jinn have long been misunderstood, wrapped in a variety of myths and beliefs in societies around the world. The movie business has made monsters and cartoon characters out of them, but according to the Koran, they are neither. The jinn are creations of Allah, like humans, and are the only other intelligent life form discussed in the Koran. Among them are decent Muslim jinn, as well as evil ones whose job it is to steer humankind off the path to Heaven. More important, their existence is no myth to Muslims.

The Existence of the Jinn

Although in many cases the Koran presents itself as a reliable source of scientific information through verses that correspond with scientific fact, as demonstrated in Chapters 19 and 20, the subject of this chapter is beyond science. Like creation, the soul, life after death, and Heaven and Hell, the jinn cannot be studied or proven scientifically—at least not yet.

The jinn are creatures that share the earth with us, but are not seen or detected by humans. The Koran leaves no doubt about their existence, referring to them numerous times throughout the text. It says they are intelligent and possess a free will like that of humans, and can either believe or not believe in Allah, although according to Allah they are expected to believe: "I created the jinn and humankind only that they might worship Me" (51:56).

Information about the jinn is derived from the Koran and Sunnah, and occasionally from less reliable sources, such as personal accounts. Based on the two main sources, Muslims believe the jinn live among us and can see us, but we don't see them. The creatures may or may not have the form of humans—their shape is changeable. Through the Koran, it is understood that there are good jinn and evil jinn. Evil jinn are evil personified. Although they work under the cover of invisibility, they're very effective in luring people toward sinful acts.

Under ordinary circumstances, people and jinn don't interact. According to scholars, the jinn are quite happy going about their business without introducing themselves. In some situations, though, a person may form an alliance with the jinn, such as for sorcery, and are able to interact with or see the jinn. Also, in areas where the jinn gather, an occasional sighting or experience between human and jinn may occur.

The word *jinn* is used for both singular and plural form. *Jinni* is used to describe a male jinn, and *jinniya* a female jinn. Evils ones are called *shayateen,* in the plural, and *shaitan,* in the singular, in Arabic. A particularly powerful jinn is called *efreet.* These terms can be found in the Koran.

The Creation of the Jinn

Man is created from clay, as the Koran clearly states. Muslims believe that angels are created from light. The jinn are from a more intense element, fire, as described in the Koran: "And the jinn did He create of smokeless fire" (55:15) Of course, the jinn are no more flaming creatures than we are muddy creatures; they have taken on another shape that only Allah knows of.

Scholars believe the jinn were created before Adam, based on the account of Iblis (Satan) in the Koran. When Allah created Adam, he asked all creatures to bow before him, but Iblis refused. This indicates that Iblis already existed when Adam was formed. Since Iblis is a jinn, we can conclude that these creatures existed before humans. The Koran explains that man was created as a vicegerent on Earth, but doesn't say much about why the jinn were created. The Koran does mention that man is superior to the jinn, because when Iblis was ordered to prostrate before Adam, he said, "[S]ee You this (creature) whom You have honored above me . . ." (17:62).

Satan is very effective even with the most devoted believer. At times of prayer, Muslims believe that Satan sneaks up and whispers things that cause the mind to wander off from the task at hand. Many Muslims conclude their prayer realizing that their mind was elsewhere during praying.

There's no description in the Koran of what a jinn looks like. In a Hadith of Prophet Muhammad, however, three types of jinn are described: one that has wings and can fly, one that impersonates certain animals, and one that is a slow traveler or mainly stationed in one place. From the Sunnah, Muslims understand that a jinn can appear in many different forms, from reptiles to humans. Some personal accounts claim that a jinn can stretch a limb to various lengths or even appear as half-human, and the other half something else.

Muslims don't know why they are unable to see the jinn on a normal basis, but the majority feel it's in their best interest that they don't mingle with the world of the jinn. The Koran warns people to stay away from the evil ways of the jinn—they usually aim to trap people under Satan's possession. As for the good jinn, Muslims believe they generally keep to their own world and avoid direct confrontation with us.

Satan and His Children

The first jinn recorded in the Koran is Iblis (Satan). Scholars guess that Iblis is the father of the jinn, just as Adam is the father of humankind. He was created with free will, and chose to disobey Allah, and therefore "became a disbeliever." (2:34)

A Whole World of Demons

Many verses in the Koran clearly indicate that the jinn have an ability to reproduce just like humans, although there is no mention of a female Iblis in the Koran. However, the Koran often refers to them in the plural form, meaning that they have multiplied since Iblis. Usually, they are called *shayateen*—satans. The term *shaitan* translates as "demon" or "devil" in English. From the line of Iblis came a whole tribe of jinn. Some of these creatures are demons, and some are believers. Since they can multiply, scholars believe their numbers are approximately equal to the number of humans on the planet, as the Koran suggests in its reference to "nations of the Jinn and mankind . . ." (46:18). Scholars also figure the jinn probably have a life cycle similar to that of humans, that they are born, grow old, and die (although they probably live much longer than humans). This conclusion is based on the Koran's explanation that the jinn will be resurrected on the Last Day and will either be thrown into Hell or sent to Heaven.

Satan's Promise to Mislead Humankind

Through his arrogance and refusal to obey Allah, Iblis was cursed until the Last Day: "And lo! The curse shall be upon you until the Day of Judgment" (15:35). Iblis was then cast out of the Heavens and descended to Earth. His plan for vengeance was to lead humankind to

Hell: "I verily shall adorn the path of error for them in the earth, and shall mislead them every one" (15:39). Iblis became Satan, the devil, who could lurk under cover and whisper evil thoughts to humankind. Muslims believe the worldwide view of the devil as the heart of evil to be true. Every reference to Satan in the Koran is associated with evil. That's why Allah instructs Muhammad of the following: "Lo! The devil sows discord among them. Lo! The devil is for man an open foe." (17:53). According to the Koran, Satan's sole objective is to lead as many people as possible to Hell, so he won't burn there alone on the Last Day.

Because demons are intelligent, free-willed creatures, they work to push every single human toward the way of evil at every moment of his or her life. How do they arrange that? Prophet Muhammad explains that a demon is appointed to follow every person like a shadow from the moment of his birth to his death. Islam calls such a creature *qareen*, an evil associate. The Koran says that even the prophets are not free from qareens: "Thus We have appointed unto every Prophet an adversary— devils of humankind and jinn . . ." (6:112).

FACT

When the Koran talks about devils, it sometimes states that they can also be human. A human devil referred to in the Koran is fully human, not a supernatural creature, but is being described as a devil because of its exceptionally evil and corrupt nature. On the other hand, a jinn devil is an evil supernatural creature.

Satan's Followers

Occasionally, the devil succeeds in completely trapping a person under his possession. The Koran teaches that Satanism—worshipping the devil—is a grievous sin leading straight to Hell. On Judgment Day, Allah will gather a group of sinners and ask the angels, "Did these worship you? They will say: Be You glorified. You are our Protector from them. No, but they worshipped the jinn; most of them were believers in them" (34:40–41). To this group, Allah will say, "Taste the doom of the Fire which you used to deny" (34:42).

However, the devil can overtake someone's mind without gaining his complete submission, such as by causing him to indulge in worldly pleasures and forget about Allah. According to the Koran, Allah will punish such people: "The devil has engrossed them and so has caused them to forget remembrance of Allah. They are the devil's party. Beware! Surely, it is the devil's party who will be the losers" (58:19).

Satan on Judgment Day

The Koran leaves no question that, along with certain people, some of the jinn will go to Hell: "Verily I shall fill Hell with the jinn and mankind together" (11:119). While this verse refers to jinn in general, the following verse addresses Iblis in particular: "He (Allah) said: Go forth from hence, degraded, banished. As for such of them as follow you, surely I will fill hell with all of you" (7:18).

The Koran promises Hell to Iblis, his demon children, and his followers. A follower in this context does not have to be a worshipper of Satan, but is anyone who listens to his evil whispers and strays off the right path. On Judgment Day, these followers of Satan will complain and try to put the blame on Satan to save themselves from hellfire. However, Satan will defend himself, arguing that they listened to him with their own free will. This story is narrated in the Koran: "And Satan says, when the matter has been decided: Lo! Allah promised you a promise of truth; and I promised you, then failed you. And I had no power over you except that I called unto you and you obeyed me. So blame me not, but blame yourselves. I cannot help you, nor can you help me" (14:22).

QUESTION?

Why does Allah allow Satan to mislead humankind?
In the Koran, it is evident that Allah has the upper hand in everything, and if He willed it, He could stop Satan. By letting Satan whisper evil to people, Allah is providing them with a choice of following His path to Heaven, or Satan's path to Hell.

The promise of Satan mentioned in this verse refers to his lies and deception in his attempts to lure people into sin. For example, Satan may talk someone into shoplifting, promising her that no one will catch her. But before the person walks out of the store, she is detected and arrested, and Satan's promise proves false. The Koran confirms Satan's deceit: "He promises them and stirs up desires in them, and Satan promises them only to beguile" (4:120).

The World of the Jinn

Most of the Muslim beliefs about the society of the jinn were acquired through encounters with them over the ages. The Koran confirms their existence, but doesn't describe them much. This is because Allah wants people to avoid crossing paths with the jinn. According to the Koran, getting involved with the jinn is possible through magic, but magic is almost a sure way to Hell.

The nations of the jinn are mentioned several times in the Koran. They do not have political nations like we do, but they are divided into groups that follow different paths, which they admit in the Koran: "And among us there are righteous folk and among us there are far from that. We are sects having different rules" (72:11). They have permission from Allah to share our homes, our food, and anything they can get their hands on. According to the Sunnah, the jinn are so close by that they could be watching while you change your clothes. Prophet Muhammad advised his companions to mention Allah's name before getting undressed or eating because it keeps the jinn away.

Power of the Jinn

The jinn can have power over humans, but the opposite is not possible. Prophet Solomon—also known as King Solomon—was the only man to ever have power over the jinn. The Koran narrates his story: "He (Solomon) said: My Lord! Forgive me and bestow on me sovereignty such shall not belong to any after me. Lo! You are the Bestower. So We made the wind subservient unto him, setting fair by his command whithersoever he intended. And the devils, every builder and diver (made We subservient)" (38:35–37).

The devils—or jinn—were made obedient by Allah's will as an exclusive miracle for Prophet Solomon. Solomon's story also illustrates that the jinn possess supernatural powers. Solomon had asked his soldiers to bring him the queen of Sheba, when a stalwart of the jinn offered to do it: "I will bring it to you before your gaze returns unto you [i.e., before you blink]" (27:40). Keeping his word, the jinn did fetch the queen of Sheba and brought her to Solomon's court before he blinked.

FACT

Common Islamic belief states that Muslim jinn generally prefer to mind their own business rather than mingle with our world. However, sources say that sometimes friction between the two worlds is inevitable, and an encounter might occur. But when a Muslim jinn is involved, the encounter is probably more likely to scare the wits out of the human and leave the jinn laughing, rather than cause any harm to either party.

Where They Live

Allah speaks to Satan in the Koran, saying, "And excite any of them whom you can with your voice, and urge your horse and foot against them, and be a partner in their wealth and children, and promise them. Satan promises only to deceive" (17:64). Here, Allah has given permission to Satan to interfere with people's lives and also live in their homes ("a partner in their wealth"). Having a qareen following you like a shadow is one thing, but according to scholars, there could be other jinn who live in your home as well. Some say any deserted place like a graveyard, the desert, a cottage in the woods, or an empty highway is a target for jinn occupation.

The Jinn and Free Will

Because the jinn have freedom of choice like humans, they can opt to believe in and submit to Allah, or remain in the line of Iblis, destined for Hell. And also like humans, the jinn were sent prophets to preach and invite them to believe in Allah. During the events of Judgment Day, Allah will speak to both people and jinn: "Oh you assembly of the jinn and humankind! Came there not unto you messengers of your own who recounted unto you My tokens and warned you of the meeting of this (Judgment) Day?" (6:130).

Islamic sources recount an incident where a group of jinn listened to the Koran's recitation at Prophet Muhammad's quarters without his knowledge. The Koran inspired them to believe in Allah, and—this is mentioned in the Koran—they hurried back to their community, preaching for Allah, and warning of Hell. In another Surah called "The Jinn," the creatures are again influenced by the recitation of the Koran:

> [S]ay (O Muhammad): It is revealed unto me that a company of the jinn gave ear, and they said: Lo! We have heard a marvelous Koran. Which guides unto righteousness, so we believe in it and we ascribe unto our Lord no partner. And (we believe) that He—exalted be the glory of our Lord—has taken neither wife nor son. (72:1–3)

Black Magic and Evil Jinn

Black magic, witchcraft, or sorcery—whichever you want to call it—is a real, effective practice according to the Koran. It is used to inflict harm upon people, bringing them physical, emotional, or social distress. Magic is made possible through the assistance of the jinn, specifically demons who thrive on evil. There's an outright prohibition of practicing magic in the Koran, warning that those who do so will receive punishment in the hereafter equivalent to that of a disbeliever.

Lying Soothsayers

Consulting a fortuneteller is unlawful and a sin because, according to the Koran, only Allah has knowledge of the future. Believing that a fortuneteller can obtain information about the future from a deck of cards is like disbelieving Allah's word that He is the sole All-Knower. Based on the Koran, Islam considers all forms of fortunetelling, including astrology, a lie.

If you argue that sometimes these fortunetellers hit the truth, you are not alone, as Prophet Muhammad's companions asked him the same thing. Muhammad explained that a fortuneteller may receive a hint from his jinn assistant, and build on it a story that makes it ring true. Of course, the jinn himself has no knowledge of the future either, but Muslims believe he is able to learn more about a situation by traveling quickly from one spot to another. For example, the jinn may have heard you talking to your friend before you met with the fortuneteller, and passed on the information discreetly. (This applies in the case of a serious sorcerer who utilizes the jinn, and not the type of psychic you would call on the phone, who, according to Muslims, relies on guesswork.)

FACT

Prophet Muhammad specifically said that a jinn can appear as a snake. If you find a snake in or near your home and you chase it away, but it keeps coming back for three consecutive days, it's possible it is a demon embodied in a snake. Perhaps this is because a demon likes to linger around human habitats to stir up trouble. Some Muslims also fear black dogs, particularly loose ones in the middle of the night, thinking that they might be demons in disguise.

Evil Spells

In the Koran, magic is the work of the devil: "[B]ut the devils disbelieved, teaching mankind magic . . ." (2:102). It was Satan who had taught humankind sorcery and witchcraft, indicating that all forms of real magic (not magic tricks) are evil. The type of magic referred to here is usually performed as a spell—a combination of various materials and odd-looking Scripture wrapped together in a piece of cloth. The spell would then be concealed in the home of the victim, and immediately the jinn would go to work, doing exactly what the spell tells them to do. This recipe is not found in the Koran. It's the secret of the sorcerers' trade, who use the devil to help them achieve what they want.

Remember, though, that the Koran says the devil does not service people, but merely manipulates and deceives. According to Islamic belief, the devil only helps a person who has submitted to his will. The Koran warns such people: "O you who believe! Follow not the footsteps of the devil. Unto whomsoever follows the footsteps of the devil, he commands filthiness and wrong" (24:21). Getting involved in magic, whether as a sorcerer or a customer, is a hideous sin according to the Koran and Sunnah.

The Evil Eye

The evil eye is not an easy concept to define, but is as real in the Koran as the jinn. Basically it's a kind of envy that inflicts harm. Imagine that your neighbor bought a new sleek sports car, while you're stuck with your old rusty shambles of a vehicle. You take a good long look at his new car, admiring its beauty, jealous of his fortune, and cursing your luck. A day later, another driver crashes into your neighbor's new car, and the cost of damage repair is a few thousand dollars.

This is an example of an evil eye. According to Islamic belief, admiring something, wishing it was your own, or feeling that person doesn't deserve it, can result in an evil eye. Anything can be a target: an intelligent child, your friend's beautiful hair, a piece of furniture, or even a pet. The evil eye is not always intentional; you may admire something in good will, but harm would come upon it anyway.

ALERT!

Prophet Muhammad once advised people to seek refuge in Allah when they hear a dog bark or a donkey bray because it's an indication that the animal had seen a demon. On the other hand, if they hear the call of a rooster, it's an indication that the bird has seen an angel.

How does the evil eye work? The Koran doesn't explain, but some scholars say it's the work of the devil. When a hint of a negative thought crosses your mind, such as, "I wish this was mine instead of his," the devil jumps at the chance of harming that thing so that the other person can't enjoy it. He interferes in all the ways that he can to cause trouble and satisfy himself.

Protection from the evil eye is easy. When Muslims feel that something is in danger of receiving an evil eye, they frequently repeat, "I seek refuge in Allah from the outcast Satan. In the name of Allah, the Most

Merciful." Although the Koran as a whole ought to scare Satan away, the last three Surahs directly address this issue (see Chapter 3). One of them is as follows: "[S]ay: I seek refuge in the Lord of Daybreak, from the evil of that which He created, from the evil of the darkness when it is intense, and from the evil of malignant witchcraft, and from the evil of the envier when he envies" (Surah 113).

The envier himself can protect the subject from the evil eye by saying "In the name of Allah" and a few other prayers. Reciting the last three Surahs of the Koran will protect anything from evil, whether it is the evil eye or the lingering of the devil nearby. In summary, the devil is Allah's creation, his power is limited, and his destiny is Hell. Allah advises in the Koran: "It is only the devil who would make (man) fear his partisans. Fear them not; fear Me, if you are true believers" (3:175).

Chapter 18

Unholy Wars: Affairs of Our Modern World

In recent times, Islam's image has been particularly disfigured due to terrorist attacks that were traced to Islamic influence. Islam has been labeled a religion that promotes hostilities and violence. However, Islam rejects the blame and confronts the accusations with evidence from the Koran and Sunnah that Islam is all about peaceful coexistence between Muslims and non-Muslims.

Islam Accused of Terrorism

In the world today, many acts of terrorism are blamed on Muslims, even before sufficient proof is present. No doubt, quite a number of attacks were the work of Muslims, but the fact that is often forgotten is that these people are either driven by nonreligious objectives, or are extremists who have misunderstood their faith. Scholars of Islam agree that Muslim terrorists have deviated from the basic teachings of the Koran.

The Current Image of Islam

Passenger airplane hijackings, suicide bombings, tourist massacres, and finally the World Trade Center attacks have all come together to paint a violent image of Islam for the average person. Many non-Muslims look at Islam as a bloodthirsty religion calling for violence, mass killings, and war against other communities. This image has been cultivated by the media, which covers incidents in what Muslims consider a biased, stereotypical manner.

The media is quick to accuse Muslims of violent attacks, with or without evidence. Such was the situation with the Oklahoma bombing in 1995, when it was immediately thought of as the work of a Muslim terrorist group, as newspaper headlines stated. Later, however, the real criminal was caught and turned out to be an American non-Muslim. Also, most attacks launched by Muslims have nothing to do with religious objectives, but the media hastens to label them "Muslims" instead of, for example, "Arabs from such and such region." Many times, the terrorists happen to be Muslims, but commit their crime for another cause entirely.

To build a strong case against Islam, sometimes the media pulls out verses from the Koran that talk about war and battle. It is undeniable that some Koranic verses do tell Muslims to fight the enemy, but such verses must be taken in the complete context of the Surah to be understood. Just as the Koran discusses war, it mentions causes, methods, rules, and most important, conditions that apply. When a single verse is looked at without the surrounding text, it gives the impression that Allah tells Muslims to fight mercilessly, which leads to more misconceptions about Islam.

The media cannot take all the blame, however. Muslims have been in conflict with others and with themselves for a long time, tarnishing the image of Islam with their own hands. But their restlessness is not in response to their faith. On the contrary, if they followed their faith devotedly, they would exist in peaceful harmony. Mostly, violent individuals are either aggravated by political circumstances or misled by another misguided extremist.

ALERT!

Islamic fundamentalism is the adherence to the teachings of the Koran and Sunnah. Every devoted Muslim is a fundamentalist. Since the Koran preaches against terrorism, fundamentalism cannot be blamed for terrorist attacks.

What Motivates the Terrorists?

When innocent civilians are killed in a plane hijacking or in their beds at night, they become a means to pressure governments to accept certain issues or legislations. Groups that massacre helpless villagers are not intending to eradicate villages and build cities in their place, but experts figure they are trying to pressure the government in a certain direction.

When unsuspecting tourists are suddenly bombed, authorities rush to resolve the issue before their entire tourism industry is affected. The authorities face a choice of either accepting the terrorists' terms, or fighting them. In these cases, experts believe the terrorists have utilized terror to attain a certain political goal that is not driven by Islam.

Some misguided terrorists think that they are committing an act that Allah will reward them for. The suicide bomber, for example, blows himself up thinking that he'll go straight to Heaven as a martyr for killing members of the enemy with him. Perhaps they take the verses like the following out of context: "Those who believe do battle for the cause of Allah; and those who disbelieve do battle for the cause of idols. So fight the minions of the devil" (4:76). There is no truth in the interpretation that this means killing leads to reward, as the rule regarding killing of the innocent is crystal clear in the Koran: "[W]hosoever kills a human being for other than manslaughter or corruption in the earth, it shall be as if he had killed all mankind" (5:32).

According to this verse, the killing of a person who's not a convicted criminal is regarded as if all humankind had been killed. This means that Allah would hold the terrorist guilty of killing all humankind, multiplied by the number of people killed; in other words, if a terrorist killed ten people, Allah would judge the terrorist as though he had killed all of humankind ten times over. There is no excuse in the Koran for killing the innocent, even if they belong to an enemy group.

Killing is allowed only in face-to-face combat in Islam. Bombing civilians, whether in war or terror, is against the teachings of Allah in the Koran. Prophet Muhammad's battles serve as proof of this, as he never attacked civilians or killed war captives.

The Concept of Jihad

The term *Jihad* has caused a stir in recent years due to its presumed relationship to terrorism. Jihad is part of Islam, no doubt, but it is not all about violence, as many believe. The term *holy war* is incorrectly applied to Jihad, because the scope of Jihad reaches beyond fighting. Jihad is taught to children in schools in the Middle East as part of their Islamic education. Are the children being trained for battle? On the contrary, they are learning that the true meaning of Jihad is in exerting an effort for the cause of Allah.

What Is Jihad?

The word *Jihad* literally means "striving" or "struggling." In Islam, the word refers to striving for the cause of Allah, spreading knowledge about His religion, and protecting His believers. Using the word *Jihad* as a synonym for "holy war," which is often done by the media, is inaccurate and misleading. The Arabic word for war is *harb*, and the word for fighting is *qital*, neither of which has anything to do with Jihad. The image of Jihad as an army of unruly fighters calling out "To Jihad!" set out to massacre the Jewish or Christians is completely misguided.

Although Jihad *can* take the form of physical struggle, in Islam, the word is more commonly used to describe different, nonviolent forms of Jihad. Jihad is within easy reach of any Muslim and is rewarded abundantly in Heaven. The nonconfrontational types of Jihad, such as when a Muslim tells his non-Muslim friends about the Koran, or when a scholar appears on TV to answer questions about Islam, are all excellent deeds according to the Koran.

Types of Jihad

Based on the Koran and Sunnah, Jihad can basically be divided into four categories:

- Jihad of the mind and heart
- Jihad of the tongue
- Jihad of the pen
- Jihad in battle

Jihad of the mind and heart is a secretive, personal endeavor. When a Muslim sees someone sinning, but knows that a verbal confrontation is not a wise approach, she can silently reject the injustice. Also, things like fasting regularly, memorizing the Koran, and spending the night in prayer qualify as forms of Jihad of the mind and heart. This is because these practices take an effort to produce, and whatever requires an effort to draw a believer closer to Allah is Jihad.

The Koran mentions Jihad of the tongue in the following verse: "Call unto the way of your Lord with wisdom and fair exhortation, and reason with them in the better way" (16:125). This is for the more daring—or perhaps more eloquent—to verbally confront non-Muslims with the Koran, asking them to take a glance at it, with the hope that they will believe it. It is also more of an effort than Jihad of the heart, which involves keeping thoughts to oneself, so it could receive better reward in Heaven.

Jihad of the pen is also called *Daawah*—preaching for Islam. If a Muslim living in a non-Muslim community writes up a flyer about Allah and distributes it among his neighbors, he is performing Jihad of the pen. It doesn't matter if the flyers are rejected or tossed away; what matters is that the Muslim exerted a real effort in calling non-Muslims to Islam. His striving for the cause of Allah is a valuable deed that Allah will reward. This applies to anyone who strives to spread knowledge about the Koran.

Jihad in battle is the type often mistaken as holy war. Since the Koran clearly forbids initiating hostility, the term *holy war* is better changed to "defensive war." It is this type of war that is acceptable to Allah as stated in the Koran. In general, Muslims are encouraged by the Koran to strive in the cause of Allah by the heart, mind, tongue, and pen, and then, only if needed, in battle. This conclusion is based on Prophet Muhammad's thirteen years of peaceful preaching in Mecca, where he avoided violent confrontation, and limited his Jihad to the mind, heart, and tongue (no pen, as he did not write).

FACT

In Islam, a person who performs any type of Jihad is called *Mujahid*, or *Mujahideen,* in the plural form. However, this term mostly applies to soldiers in a defensive battle to protect Islam. If a Mujahid dies in confrontation, he becomes a *shaheed*—martyr.

Martyrs in Heaven

Prophet Muhammad said, "He who is killed in defense of his belongings, or in self-defense, or for his religion, is a martyr." A martyr is called *shaheed* in Arabic. Nearly every day in Palestine, the news transmits the images of a funeral of a new shaheed. Most often, the shaheed died from gunshot while rebelling against Israeli forces. He died in defense of his land, home, and family; therefore, he is a martyr.

A martyr's soul flies straight to Heaven according to the Koran: "Think not of those who are slain in the way of Allah, as dead. Nay, they are living. With their Lord they have provision" (3:169). This promise by Allah that all shaheeds go to Heaven strengthens the will of soldiers in battle. They know that if they die, Allah will take their soul right up to Heaven.

The Laws of War

Being a religion of peace, the Koran's war policy is well defined with a list of rules and conditions that protect the interest of Muslims while avoiding unnecessary aggression. The Sunnah dictate that if the decision for violent confrontation is made, it must be agreed upon by the ruler of the nation (not decided by a minor group of radicals). Once war is declared, Muslims must adhere to certain rules from the Koran and Sunnah that protect both parties.

ALERT!

During wartime, many surviving Muslim soldiers report that they felt little fear while they were combating the enemy because they had no fear of death. The reason they have no fear of death is the Koran, which guarantees every martyr a place in Heaven.

Defensive Action Only

The Koran forbids Muslims from being aggressors in Surah 2, verse 190, but fully pushes them toward battle in verse 191: "And slay them wherever you find them, and drive them out of the places whence they drove you out, for persecution is worse than slaughter." Here, the Koran gives permission to battle the enemy, but in the context of the entire Holy Book, Muslims are allowed to fight only under one of the following three conditions:

- Muslims are being oppressed and prevented from practicing their faith.
- There are efforts to eject Muslims from their property.
- A clear violent attack against Muslims is under way.

While the Koran preaches peace and justice, it also confirms the need for battle on certain occasions. "Fight them back" is what the Koran orders Muslims to do. However, the rule applies that slaying the enemy occurs only on the battlefield. The Koran states that if members of the enemy seek Muslim protection, then they must be protected. Any prisoners taken must be treated humanely and with dignity—under no condition would they be killed or tortured. Consider the following verse: "And if anyone of the idolaters seeks your protection (O Muhammad), then protect him so he may hear the word of Allah; and afterward convey him to his place of safety. That is because they are a folk who know not" (9:6).

Muhammad and later scholars defined weapons to be used in battle. Although the rule hardly applies nowadays, soldiers were forbidden from dipping their spears, arrows, and swords in poison. During the battle itself, the Prophet instructed his troops to kill swiftly and avoid causing unnecessary pain or suffering against enemy soldiers.

FACT

At some critical times in history, Muslim Imams (elite scholars) declared that Jihad in battle is compulsory on every Muslim. One recent example is the 2003 war on Iraq, when scholars agreed that this was a case of hostility against Muslim land, and it is the duty of Muslims to protect the land.

Women, Children, and Others

Prophet Muhammad said, "Do not commit breach of trust nor treachery nor mutilate anybody nor kill any minor or child." He also prohibited the killing of women, the elderly, any noncombatant, or monks in their monasteries. Captives and those under Muslim protection must be given adequate clothing and provisions, and must never be treated with cruelty. The Koran says that captives in the hands of Muslims will become exposed to Islam and may choose to believe it, which is why kindness and fairness are foremost in their treatment.

The Koran strictly forbids excessive actions such as destroying crops, knocking down trees, and killing animals that belong to the enemy: "[A]nd work not confusion in the earth after the fair ordering thereof. That will be better for you, if you are believers" (7:85). Once order has been established, the Koran requires Muslims to work once again toward a peaceful coexistence with non-Muslims.

What does the Koran say about peace treaties?
The Koran fully endorses peace treaties between parties to prevent hostilities—a concept that the Prophet applied during his lifetime on several occasions. If peace is possible, Islam dictates that it should be established rather than neglected for violent confrontation.

Peace in the Koran

Islam comes from the root word *silm*, meaning "peace"; *Islam* means "peaceful surrender." With peace at the very core of the faith, hostility becomes an unacceptable notion to Allah. In the Koran, peace and harmony are described in the following verse: "Lo! Allah enjoins justice and kindness, and giving to kinsfolk, and forbids lewdness and abomination and wickedness. He exhorts you in order that you may take heed" (16:90).

With justice, kindness, and giving being an integral part of Muslim conduct, it is apparent that terrorism is not linked to Koranic teachings. Killing an innocent person is illegal according to the Koran, while saving a life is a great deed: "[A]nd whoso saves the life of one, it shall be as if he had saved the life of all mankind" (5:32). The Koran is not lenient toward murder, and promises Hell to anyone who commits this crime.

The Koran implies that peace pleases Allah: "Whereby Allah guides him who seeks His good pleasure unto paths of peace" (5:16). Another verse states: "Allah loves not mischief" (2:205). Even if a Muslim is angered, the Koran tells him to practice patience and tolerance, following the example of Prophet Muhammad. He was often verbally abused, threatened, and assaulted by idolaters who rejected his preaching, but never snapped or struck back at them; instead, he maintained his temper and looked the other way.

Tolerance and Harmony in the Koran

The Koran does two things to ensure a level of tolerance and harmony among diverse groups: first, it emphasizes the importance of exercising patience, and second, it forbids transgression. The Koran promotes patience for the sake of peace, because if every person is angered by minor and major incidents, people will spend more time at conflict than at peace.

The Koran also warns against initiating hostilities: "Fight in the way of Allah against those who fight against you, but begin not hostilities. Lo! Allah loves not aggressors" (2:190). Here, Allah clearly gives instruction not to begin hostilities. In other words, the Koran is telling people to avoid violence and restrain from initiating attacks. However, if confrontation is inevitable, the Koran gives instructions to fight back in self-defense.

An aspect of peace in the Koran is that it encourages reconciliation rather than vengeance. For example, retribution is allowed in the justice system, but the Koran says that if you forgive, it is better for you.

As for peaceful coexistence among diverse groups of various religions, the Koran says, "Allah forbids you not those who warred not against you on account of religion and drive you not out from your homes, that you should show them kindness and deal justly with them. Lo! Allah loves the just dealers" (60:8). This verse makes it compulsory for every Muslim to be kind and just to his or her neighboring non-Muslim.

In regard to tolerance, Allah also says, "Unto each nation have We given sacred rites which they are to perform; so let them not dispute with you of the matter, but summon yourself unto your Lord. Lo! You indeed follow right guidance. And if they wrangle with you, say: Allah is best aware of what you do. Allah will judge between you on the Day of Resurrection concerning that wherein you used to differ" (22:67–69). In these verses, the Koran makes it clear that Muslims should let other groups practice their religion in peace.

Even if the other group is stirring trouble, the Koran tells Muslims to avoid conflict and be forgiving: "Many of the People of the Scripture (Jewish and Christian people) long to make you disbelievers after your belief, through envy on their own account, after the truth has become manifest unto them. Forgive and be indulgent (toward them) until Allah give command. Lo! Allah is able to do all things" (2:109).

ALERT!

There is a belief among some people that the Koran tells Muslims to convert others to Islam by force. This is a misconception and completely against Allah's teaching. The Koran says, "There is no compulsion in religion" (2:256). This is a famous verse used to remind Muslims that they are not allowed to force or pressure anyone into Islam against their will.

Human Rights in the Koran

The Koran sets rules that protect peoples' rights. A concept like racism has no place in Islam, as Muslims believe all people are the children of Adam. The Koran further commands: "Oh you who believe! Be steadfast witnesses for Allah in equity, and let not hatred of any people seduce you that you deal not justly. Deal justly, that is nearer to your duty. Observe your duty to Allah. Lo! Allah is Aware of what you do" (5:8).

Honor and dignity are protected in the Koran in the following verse: "O you who believe! Let not a folk deride a folk who may be better than they (are), nor let women (deride) women who may be better than they are; neither defame one another, nor insult one another by nicknames" (49:11). The Koran also adds, "Shun much suspicion, for lo! Some suspicion is a crime. And spy not, neither backbite one another. Would one of you love to eat the flesh of his dead brother that you would abhor it?" (49:12). In these verses, Allah is telling people not to insult each other, not to harbor negative ideas about each other (i.e., suspicion), not to spy, and not to backbite.

Contrary to the practices of some Islamic nations, the Koran states that no one should be forced to adhere to a certain religion or follow its rules. In some areas, women wear the hijab by compulsion. If they took it off, they'd be charged and convicted of a public offense. That is against the teaching of the Koran.

The Koran designed a system that ought to distribute wealth evenly, thus providing the basic life requirements to the needy. However, Islamic governments leave this matter to the generosity of the wealthy. Prophet Muhammad reminds that Allah destroyed previous nations (such as Noah's people) because their rulers punished the weak, yet freely committed crimes themselves. This is an indication that in Islam, the ruler is not supposed to be above the law.

Muslims believe they are granted the right to live in a stable, secure environment as a result of the Koran's decisive justice system (see Chapter 9). It ensures to a high degree that their lives, honor, property, and families are protected. The most basic human right is the right to live, which the Koran protects by saying that one murder is to Allah like the murder of all of humanity.

Chapter 19

The Koran:
A Miracle in Itself

Muslims believe in miracles because they are revealed in the Koran. Allah's work of creation is considered to be a miracle. Possibly all known prophets were granted the ability to perform miracles to convince their people that they indeed carried a divine message. While these were big, astounding miracles, there are other smaller miracles. Muslims believe that the Koran is a miracle in itself, since it presents evidence that it is the word of Allah.

What Is a Miracle?

The commonly accepted meaning of the word *miracle* in Islam is—very briefly—an action or deed that is beyond normal human capabilities. Such miracles are believed to be limited to the prophets alone. For example, Prophet Moses turned a stick into a snake—a task that is impossible for an ordinary human to perform. This type of miracle was necessary to make the people of the time believe in the Prophet, and it worked quite efficiently.

Islamic scholars say that for a prophet's miracle to be considered a true miracle, it must fulfill all the following conditions:

- It is beyond human ability and breaks the laws of nature.
- It can only be made to happen by Allah's intervention.
- It supports the Prophet's claim and true message.
- It is performed by the Prophet himself.

This list of conditions is somewhat specific. The *Oxford English Dictionary* defines the word *miracle* as an "event so remarkable that it is attributed to a supernatural agency." So prophets' miracles aside, by general definition a miracle is still considered the work of a supernatural presence, such as a twist of fate at a critical time, the clocklike orbiting of planets, or the superior engineering of the human body.

Small Miracles in Our Time

Small miracles and fate sometimes work together to produce an event that would otherwise seem impossible. According to the Koran, Allah can make anything happen just by telling it to be so. Consider this scenario: A child runs off from her backyard to chase a frog down the road. The frog lies still in the middle of the road, and the child bends down to inspect it, unaware of the truck approaching her at high speed.

The parents shout in panic, but they are too far away to reach the child in time. Suddenly, a dog barks and the child looks up, finding it to be the neighbor's—her favorite dog. The child gets up and runs onto the pavement to play with the dog just as the truck screeches past her, barely missing a deadly collision. If analyzed from the Koran's perspective, this story is fate at work to produce a miracle. The child's fate is to live, and the miracle is that divine intervention caused her to run off and leave death behind.

FACT

Some Muslims search for a scientific explanation for miracles, but scholars argue that the laws of nature are Allah's creation, and He has the ability to break them as He pleases to create miracles. This means that the laws only appear fixed to us, but can be changed by Allah's command as He requires.

Miracles as Signs

Allah uses His miracles as examples to lead people to ponder the likelihood of a Creator. If you pick up a copy of the Koran and open it to any random page, there's a chance you will come across a verse that mentions one of Allah's creations or miracles. The verse will usually end with "that haply you may reflect," or something similar.

Such an example is found in the following verse:

> *Lo! In the creation of the heavens and the earth, and the difference of night and day, and ships which sail upon the sea with that which is of use to men, and the water which Allah sends down from the sky, thereby reviving the earth after its death, and dispersing all kinds of beasts therein, and (in) the ordinance of the winds, and the clouds obedient between heaven and earth: are signs (of Allah's sovereignty) for people who have sense. (2:164)*

The Koran as a Miracle

Muslims believe that the Koran itself is a miracle. Prophet Muhammad said, "Every prophet was given miracles because of which people believed, but what I have been given is divine inspiration which Allah has revealed to me, so I hope that my followers will outnumber the followers of the other prophets on Resurrection Day." Muhammad was implying that the Koran itself is the greatest miracle of all time, which Muslims see as evidence that *it* is the right path.

To Muslims, the Koran is a big miracle full of smaller miracles. The process of revelation, the literary excellence, and the content of the Koran contribute to its classification as a big miracle. The smaller miracles are within the text, such as the correctness of scientific information and historical recollections. These and other miracles will be described in more detail later in this chapter. Altogether, the big and small miracles constitute a number of signs demonstrating the existence of the Supreme Being.

Miracles of Prophets

The Koran states that every nation was sent a messenger. Every messenger also possessed some supernatural talent that Allah had given to him so he could gain people's trust. One of the most talented prophets of all time was Prophet Solomon, better known as King Solomon. His kingdom was the largest that had ever been on Earth. Allah bestowed upon him more power than that of any other king—a special kind of power unique to Solomon alone, as described in the Koran: "And unto Solomon (We gave) the wind, whereof the morning course was a month's journey and the evening course a month's journey, and We caused the fount of copper to gush forth for him, and (We gave him) certain of the jinn who worked before him by permission of his Lord" (34:12).

From this verse, Muslims understand that Solomon had the skill to utilize the wind to his demand. Also, the jinn were made loyal to him and fulfilled his requests (see more about the jinn in Chapter 17). Elsewhere in the Koran it also states that Allah gave King Solomon the ability to speak to and understand animals. These miraculous skills reinforced his position as king of the nation and messenger of Allah.

Prophet Noah is known for his ark in the Gospel and Koran. According to the Koran, he was sent to a nation where corruption prevailed. He preached consistently, but very few believed in what he said. So Allah inspired him to build the ark—an enormous ship—and load a pair of every species of animal to save them from the flood that would eradicate the nation. The Koran narrates: "We said: Load therein two of every kind, a pair (the male and female), and your household . . ." (11:40). When Noah's ark set sail, Allah drowned the earth in a flood, and only the ark and its passengers survived—a miracle made possible by Allah.

QUESTION?

Is the age of divine miracles over?
Some Muslims say that the age of miracles ended with Prophet Muhammad's death. Others believe that there are small miracles happening every day around the world. According to basic Islamic belief, Allah can allow miracles to happen whenever he wishes.

Miracles in Creation

From a gnat to the cosmos, the Koran describes examples of the superior engineering of everything in creation. The seemingly simplest creatures are mentioned in the Koran for their certain qualities. Insects, such as mosquitoes and bees, are considered little miracles of creation. The creation of the human being is a miracle that the Koran refers to as a work worthy of our constant gratitude. On a larger scale, the perfect orbiting of planets, the placement of the stars, and the balance of gravity are examples of creations that are even more miraculous.

The Human Body

In the Holy Koran it is written: "And Allah brought you forth from the wombs of your mothers knowing nothing, and gave you hearing and sight and hearts that haply you might give thanks" (16:78). Hearing and sight are mentioned in sixteen verses throughout the Koran, and always in the order of "hearing and sight," never as "sight and hearing." Medical studies have shown that the hearing mechanism begins to develop in an embryo in the third to fourth week of pregnancy, while sight develops in or after the fourth week. Given this information, Islamic scholars say the Koran specifically refers to them in that order because it is the order in which they develop.

The human brain is another example of divine engineering referred to many times in the Koran, such as: "Keep your duty toward Him who has aided you with (the good things) that you know" (26:132). A better translation of the verse would probably be "who has provided you with knowledge." This verse refers to humankind's ability to perceive and understand, a gift provided by Allah.

It is common practice in modern times to use fingerprints as a method of identification. The Koran noted the significance of the fingertip many centuries ago: "Does man think that We shall not assemble his bones? Yes, verily. Yes, We are able to restore his very finger tips" (75:3–4). This verse refers to resurrection on the Last Day, where Allah will put the scattered remains of a person back together in perfect order down to the fingertips. Scholars say the emphasis on the fingertips is an acknowledgment of the importance of a fingertip in identification. Like the rest of the human body, Islam considers the fingerprint a miracle.

Putting all the parts of the human body together, Allah simply declares: "[S]urely We created man of the best stature" (95:4). Then He challenges: "This is the Creation of Allah. Now show me that which those (you worship) beside Him have created" (31:11).

The Koran says that the human being itself is a sign of the Lord's existence, because of the complexity and efficiency of the human body. The human ear, for example, can detect 40,000 different sounds, while the eyeball contains about 158 million rods and cones—tiny components responsible for detecting light and color.

Miraculous Creatures

Throughout the Koran, Allah mentions His creation as proof of His superiority. For example: "Have they not seen the birds obedient in midair? None holds them but Allah" (16:79). This particular verse indicates that the ability of birds to fly is a miracle in creation. Allah says that this miracle is a sign of His divine achievement.

The honeybee is a creature mentioned by name in the Koran:

And your Lord inspired the bee, saying: Choose your habitations in the hills and in the trees and in that which they hatch. Then eat of all fruits, and follow the ways of your Lord, made smooth (for you). There comes forth from their bellies a drink diverse of hues, wherein is healing for mankind. Lo! Herein is indeed a portent for people who reflect." (16:68–69)

Scholars believe the mentioning of the bee in the Koran is not a random choice by Allah, but is specifically used as an example of a small but highly skilled creature that ought to be seen as a sign of Allah's sovereignty.

Then there is the camel. Allah says in the Koran, "Will they not regard the camels, how they are created?" (88:17). Why did Allah choose the camel as an example? The camel is a desert creature, often surviving in temperatures over 120°, and can go for weeks without water. When water is available, the camel drinks enough to fill an internal storage facility (like a water tank), and is able to survive on that supply for long periods. Also, camels are very hardy; these animals are able to tolerate harsh desert conditions, walk long distances on scorching sand, and keep sand out of its eyes in sandstorms.

The Order of the Universe

Allah refers to "the heaven full of paths" (51:7) in the Koran. According to astronomers, there are some 200 billion galaxies in the universe. Each galaxy contains its own stars, planets, and moons, all running in smooth perfect orbit. The galaxies themselves are gliding along computed paths and orbits. Muslims take this as a miracle in creation.

The Koran also describes the course of the sun: "And the sun runs on unto a resting place for it. That is the measuring of the Mighty, the Wise" (36:38). This verse literally translates as "the sun runs toward its destiny." In recent astronomical studies, scientists discovered that the sun travels at blinding speed in an orbit called the solar apex. As the sun glides around, our entire solar system travels along to maintain its orbit around the sun. The average Muslim probably has no knowledge of this fact, but scholars see it as another miracle in creation as well as reinforcement of the divine origin of the Koran.

The Literary Miracle

The Koran is widely believed among Muslims to be impossible to imitate, and therefore a miracle. In Arabic, the word for this miraculous inimitability is *ihjaz*. Muslims believe the Koran is impossible to imitate in language, style, form, content, and all other aspects. They also believe that its inimitability means that it cannot be the work of a human being (even Muhammad, as thought by some non-Muslims). These beliefs are not only based on the eloquence and accurate information in the Koran, but also on the Koran's literal assertion that it is the word of Allah.

The Koran says that its origin is self-explanatory. By presenting plenty of evidence, it insists that it is the word of Allah. This evidence sometimes takes the form of a revelation that is supported by science. Evidence can also be found in the accuracy of its historical recollection, the prophecies that have been fulfilled, its literary excellence, and many other aspects of the Holy Book. Muslims call these verses of evidence "miracles" that Allah has sent down to prove the divine origin of the Koran.

ALERT!

There are two views concerning the inimitability of the Koran. Some scholars say that the language and style are simply above and beyond human ability to match, while others say that the inimitability is a result of Allah's protection of the Koran from corruption, meaning that Allah prevents anyone's attempt to imitate it.

Eloquence and Style

Most Arabic speakers would agree to the literary excellence of the Koran. Its language is rich yet understandable, and it rhymes yet it is not poetry. This was made possible by its full use of Arabic vocabulary. Allah says in the Koran, "Lo! We have revealed it, a Lecture (Koran) in Arabic, that you may understand" (12:2), and He describes the text of the Koran as "clear Arabic speech" (16:103).

It is important to note that Prophet Muhammad was unlettered; that is, he could not read or write. This fact is supported in the Koran: "He it is Who has sent among the unlettered ones a messenger of their own, to recite unto them His revelations and to make them grow, and to teach them the Scripture and Wisdom (Koran) . . ." (62:2). This further indicates that Muhammad did not have the skill or knowledge to produce such a book himself.

Exempt from Errors

Although the Koran was revealed over a period of twenty-three years and averages 600 pages in Arabic print, studies have shown that it contains no errors or contradictions. Over the centuries, experts have inspected the Koran repeatedly for discrepancies and have found none. Mostly, they were looking for a verse here that contradicts a verse there, or a statement that scientific fact proves false, but they found the Koran to be clear and concise, even in its many revelations about nature, astronomy, and medicine.

That this research would take place did not escape Allah's notice, as He reveals in the Koran: "Will they not then ponder on the Koran? If it had been from other than Allah they would have found therein much incongruity" (4:82). Here, the Koran acknowledges itself as perfect and free of errors.

The Challenge

At the time of Prophet Muhammad, the nonbelievers and idolaters questioned the source of the revelations he received and accused Muhammad of inventing them, but Allah denies this possibility: "And this Koran is not such as could ever be invented in despite of Allah" (10:37). However, the people still disbelieved in Muhammad's message, claiming it was not of a divine source. Mostly, they doubted that Allah's messenger would be human like them, as the Koran explained he would be.

Nevertheless, Allah had full confidence in the text He revealed and knew it could never be matched. As such, in the Koran Allah offers a challenge to doubters: "And if you are in doubt concerning that which We reveal unto Our slave (Muhammad), then produce a Surah or like thereof, and call your witnesses beside Allah if you are truthful" (2:23). In this verse, Allah presents an open challenge to anyone at the time of Muhammad or after to try to produce a Surah similar to those in the Koran.

Muslims proudly consider themselves slaves of Allah, although in some translations the word is substituted with "servants." Being Allah's slaves gives them a type of devotion and bondage to Him. The Koran also describes people as vicegerents who are in charge of nurturing and looking after our planet.

Failure to Meet the Challenge

Time passed, and no one was able to meet Allah's challenge. Although they initially accepted the challenge, the people at the time of the Prophet could not produce a similar Surah to those in the Koran despite their eloquence and poetic skills. Allah knew that they would fail: "Verily, though mankind and the Jinn should assemble to produce the like of this Koran, they could not produce the like thereof though they were helpers one of another" (17:88).

The challenge is still open to whomever wishes to attempt it, but Allah warns: "And if you do it not—and you can never do it—then guard yourselves against the fire prepared for disbelievers, whose fuel is of men and stones" (2:24). Muslims interpret the failure to meet the challenge as evidence that the Koran is extremely difficult, if not impossible, to imitate.

The Numerical Miracle

The recent discovery of numerical patterns in the Koran astounded Islamic scholars with the genius of the Creator. The first discovery is about the number nineteen. A verse in the Koran says, "Above it are nineteen" (74:30). Taken in the context of the text surrounding this line, it is clear that the Koran is describing some aspect of Hell, and most scholars have interpreted it to be a reference to nineteen guardians over Hell. For some reason, some scholars were mystified by this number; they set out on a search for more appearances of it in the Koran. With the aid of computers, scholars searched the text for clues. They found that the number nineteen indeed has some significance, as it appeared that its multiples occurred in key places throughout the Koran. For example, the word *Bismillah* (In the name of Allah) in Arabic contains nineteen letters. That word occurs 114 times in the Koran: the number 114 is a multiple of nineteen.

ALERT!

Some people who attempt to count words and uncover the truth of the numerical miracle themselves fail because they attempt the research in an English translation of the Koran. Only an original Arabic version would be valid for a correct count, because a translation is not word for word.

Scholars also realized that certain antonyms occur an equal number of times. For example, both the words *angels* and *satan* appear eighty-eight times, and the words *life* and *death* appear fifty times each. They believe this pattern is a miracle that was waiting to be discovered to prove the Koran's divine origin. However, other scholars who are also devoted believers do not take these calculations seriously, and feel they are inaccurate and irrelevant to proving the message of the Koran.

Prophecies and History in the Koran

A number of prophecies in the Koran have come true; the most famous of them is the prophecy about the Roman-Persian struggle in A.D. 614 to 622 over Jerusalem. The prophecy in the Koran is as follows: "The Romans have been defeated, in the nearer land, and they, after their defeat, will be victorious" (30:2–3). In A.D. 614, the Romans were defeated in battle by the Persians. In A.D. 627, a decisive battle took place, and the Romans gained victory over the Persians.

Then there is the prophecy about the return of the Muslims to Mecca after being exiled by the idolators: "You shall indeed enter the Inviolable Place of Worship (Mecca), if Allah will, secure, (having your hair) shaven and cut, not fearing" (48:27). This prophecy came true when Prophet Muhammad reopened Mecca for Muslims shortly before his death. (The shaving or cutting of hair mentioned in this verse is a standard ritual of pilgrimage.) The Koran also prophesies the spread of Islam, and the fate of certain characters, such as Abu Lahab, who died an idolater as prophesied.

One accurate historical account in the Koran is that of Moses and the Pharaoh. The Koran also mentions that the Pharaoh had a close friend named Haman, but that information was not available in any other source until the nineteenth century, when hieroglyphics of ancient Egypt were decoded and understood.

Prophecies aside, the Koran narrates historical accounts with precision that surprises historians and archaeologists. For example, the Koran narrates the story of Prophet Moses and the Pharaoh of Egypt: "Therefore We seized him and his hosts, and abandoned them unto the sea" (28:40). In his attempt to get to Moses and kill him and his followers, the Pharaoh followed him into the sea, where the Pharaoh drowned. These events took place nearly 1,500 years before the revelation of the Koran. Today, in the Egyptian Museum in Cairo lies the mummy of a Pharaoh that archaeologists claim had died of drowning. Using the Koran for reference, they believe it's very likely that this is the same Pharaoh that had chased Moses into the sea.

Chapter 20

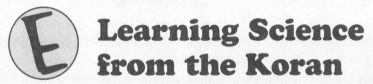 Learning Science from the Koran

In the years following the revelation of the Koran, Muslims were pioneers in the fields of astronomy, math, physics, and medicine. They led the way to new discoveries at the same fast pace that the Islamic nation was spreading. Being well versed with the Koran, they used the information it provided to learn about the world around them. The Koran proved to be a handy reference for a vast array of topics, such as embryology, geology, and astronomy. It is still being studied today for tips and insights.

The Koran and Science

When the Koran was revealed a millennium and a half ago, people didn't know much about science. The Koran described certain things in detail that people could hardly grasp, but they believed in it anyway. After some time, a few intellectuals decided to study the insights it provided. Eventually, it reached a point at which both scientists and Islamic scholars agreed on many scientific facts presented in the Koran.

Some centuries ago, when Islam was at its peak in political power, Muslims reached new frontiers in many fields, such as astronomy, physics, math, and particularly medicine. For example, they knew Earth was round—a discovery that took other scientists a few more centuries to note. In physiology and pathology, Ibn Sina was one Muslim doctor who excelled by using the Koran for reference.

Allah says in the Koran that He did not create the universe in vain or as a pastime, and that if He was looking for a pastime He would find it merely in His presence. This statement serves to signify the importance of this world (see 21:16–17).

The Koran on the Cosmos

The universe was once a single gigantic mass that exploded and threw its fragments across space (see Chapter 12 for more on the origin of the universe). Slowly, these fragments drew together to form galaxies. There are now almost 100 billion galaxies and thousands of billions of stars across the universe. Although the Koran did not provide these exact figures, it opened the gateway to their discovery through some surprisingly accurate insights.

Perfect Orbit

A few centuries ago, scientists began to study the size of the universe. They discovered planets other than Earth, thousands of stars, and hundreds of comets. Today, we know that the size of the universe is incomprehensible. There are billions of objects in space from stars to planets, each gliding along its own designated path in a miracle worthy of Allah's oath, "By the heaven full of paths" (51:7).

Muslims believe that it is indeed a miracle that the universe is in such impeccable order. The Koran points to the greatness of the universe: "Lo! Allah grasps the heavens and earth that they deviate not, and if they were to deviate there is not one that could grasp them after Him. Lo! He is ever Clement, Forgiving" (35:41). Not only does Allah swear by the places of stars, but He also declares that it is a great oath, indicating the precision of the orbiting system: "Nay, I swear by the places of the stars, and lo! That verily is a tremendous oath, if you only knew" (56:75–76).

FACT

Allah says in the Koran that humankind has only been granted a small measure of knowledge compared to the knowledge available in the universe. This means that no matter how far humans conquer the world with their knowledge, it will always be just a small portion of ultimate knowledge.

The Stars

Around the middle of the twentieth century, astronomers made a new discovery while observing the sky. They learned that a star goes through stages: birth, growth, maturity, and death. Prior to this discovery, people had been witnessing spectacularly bright stars that suddenly appeared in the night sky and continued to shine for months, if not years. They thought that these were new stars, while in fact they were dying stars. Science verified that the strong radiance of a star is a result of its explosion and death.

While the death of stars is a fairly recent discovery, the Koran had already described it in the following verses: "By the star when it sets" (53:1); "so when the stars are put out" (77:8). Although the translation here uses the word *sets*, a more accurate correspondent to the Arabic word used in the Koran is "collapse."

Another interesting story about stars is that in 1963, scientists detected a strong signal similar to radio waves coming from somewhere in the universe. The waves had the capacity to pass through the thickest, most dense walls and materials. The source of these waves remained unknown until ten years later, when advances in technology pointed out the source to be right at the edge of the universe—some 100 billion light years away. The waves were coming from a type of celestial object named a *quasar*—short for quasi-stellar.

Some of these quasars are 100,000 *billion* times brighter than the sun. They emanate an enormous amount of radiation that would be lethal to life on Earth if it weren't for the layers of the atmosphere. Some Islamic scholars have noticed a connection between these quasars and a few verses in the Koran: "By the heaven and the Morning Star—Ah, what will tell you what the Morning Star is! The Piercing Star!" (86:1–3). Because of the quasars' waves that pierce through any substance, and their radiation that is prevented from reaching Earth by the atmosphere, scholars figure that perhaps the quasar is the "Piercing Star." Some opinions are far simpler, describing the Piercing Star as shooting stars or other astronomical objects, but opposing views argue that for Allah to swear by the Piercing Star means it is more significant than something such as a shooting star or planet.

ALERT!

When Allah swears in the Koran by certain creations, such as dying stars, or the Piercing Star, it serves as an affirmation in the absolute truth of their existence. Muslims have long believed in those creations even before they fully understood them.

The Atmosphere, Clouds, and Rain

Our knowledge of the layers of the atmosphere, the formation of clouds, and rainfall has only been perfected in recent years with the invention of satellites, radar, and various sensors and detectors. Prior to that, scientists could only theorize, and their theories were sometimes off-track. However, the Koran depicts the process of cloud formation in a way that conforms to modern scientific discovery, and it also briefly describes the layers and functions of the atmosphere.

A Protected Roof

Allah says in the Holy Koran: "And We have made the sky a protected roof" (21:32). Twentieth-century research has proved this statement to be true. Earth's atmosphere is like a shell that preserves and protects life. The Koran also describes the creation of the Heavens: "He it is Who created for you all that is in the earth. Then turned He to the heaven, and fashioned it as seven heavens" (2:29).

There are scholars who, based on their interpretation of the Koran, believe there are two types of Heavens: the ones within our atmosphere, and the ones that lead to the world beyond (that is, where the angels, Heaven, Hell, and the Lord's throne are). These scholars believe that both types of Heavens are created in seven layers. Science cannot tell us about the world beyond, but it has already made discoveries about our atmosphere. The fact is that there are six layers to Earth's atmosphere, plus the ozone layer, which adds up to seven. They are: troposphere, stratosphere, ozonosphere, mesosphere, thermosphere, ionosphere, and exosphere. Together, these layers form a protective shell around Earth, sending away dangerous rays, and returning water (rain) to Earth. Their tasks support the Koran's revelation: "By Heaven with its cyclical systems" (86:11). Scholars believe that the atmosphere is like a roof over Earth, allowing life to flourish, and confirming the Koran's description of Heaven as a roof.

FACT

The discovery of new things in the world and across the universe is prophesied in the Koran as follows: "For every announcement there is a term, and you will come to know" (6:67). It is understood from this verse that people will learn more and more with the passage of time.

Clouds and Rain

The formation of rain clouds was only understood in the twentieth century through satellites and other equipment. Meteorologists state that there are stages to the process. First, tiny droplets of water vapor are carried high in the air by updrafts, which begin to form small clouds. Eventually wind causes these small clouds to stack up into dark, thick rain clouds. Updrafts in the center of the clouds cause them to grow thousands of feet high into the atmosphere. As the clouds grow vertically into cooler regions of the atmosphere, fat rain droplets formulate near the peaks and become too heavy to remain suspended, so they fall back to Earth. Long ago, the Koran revealed: "Allah is He who sends the winds so that they raise clouds, and spreads them along the sky as pleases Him, and causes them to break and you see the rain down pouring from within them" (30:48). This verse explains that wind is responsible for joining small clouds together until they are stacked up, causing rainfall.

The Koran adds: "Have you not seen how Allah wafts the clouds, then gathers them, then makes them layers, and you see the rain come forth from between them; He sends down from the heaven mountains wherein is hail . . ." (24:43). Notice that the Koran describes storm clouds as "heaven mountains," indicating the height of their gigantic masses. Studies have shown that some clouds can reach a height of 25,000 feet, making them as tall as some of the tallest mountains on Earth.

Muslims believe that clouds and rainfall are a blessing from Allah. In them is a genius plan to evenly distribute water across the land, and in turn allow life to flourish in as many places as possible.

Geological Revelations

Things like the shape of Earth, the role of mountains, and the nonmingling of seawater remained unknown for a long time. At the time when people in some parts of the world imagined Earth to be flat, Muslim scientists were studying the rotation of the globe. How did they come to know this? By closely observing the Koran, they discovered many insights about Earth, the mountains, and other geological matters.

Earth Is Round

For centuries, people thought that Earth was flat and feared falling off its edge if they sailed too far, but thanks to scientists like Galileo, the fact that Earth is round became known. Yet centuries before science admitted that fact, the Koran stated: "He has created the heavens and the earth with truth. He makes the night cover the day, and He makes the day cover the night" (39:5). In the original Arabic, this verse reveals that Earth is round. Unfortunately, the true meaning is lost in the translation due to the lack of exact correspondents in the English vocabulary.

Instead of the word *cover*, the Koran uses an Arabic term from the root word *kora*, meaning "ball," or "globe." By making a verb out of the noun, the meaning changes to "to make round" or "to wrap around a ball." Looking at the verse again, it would read: "He makes the night wrap around the day." This explains the meaning a little better, but doesn't take it completely out of the shadows. However, in its original Arabic, the Koran reveals not only that Earth is spherical in shape, but that night and day are a result of its rotation around its axis.

The Function of Mountains

The function of mountains is described quite clearly in the Koran: "And We have placed in the earth firm hills lest it quake with them . . ." (21:31). According to the Koran, the role of mountains is to prevent earthquakes and stabilize the surface of the earth. This is a fact confirmed by science. To understand why mountains prevent earthquakes, it's important to understand how they form.

A mountain is the result of two massive plates of the earth's crust colliding. When they collide, the weaker plate is stretched skyward, and the denser plate is embedded downward into the earth's mantle. Geologists explain that underneath every mountain is an equally massive rock—somewhat like the tip of an iceberg emerging above the water with the rest of it hidden underneath. When plates merge, their deeply embedded roots stabilize the earth's crust, preventing it from moving over magma found deeper near the core. In other words, mountains are like nails—or pegs—as stated in the Koran: "Have we not made the earth an expanse, and the high hills as pegs?" (78:6–7).

A verse in the Koran (27:88) states that people think that mountains are firmly stationed in their place, but in fact they are moving along like clouds. Scholars have interpreted this verse as an indication that Earth is constantly rotating around its axis, which means that everything on its surface, including mountains, is moving around with it.

Oceans Don't Mingle

Have you ever wondered why seawater doesn't mix with freshwater at intersections, or seawater doesn't mix with ocean water? Although it was impossible in past centuries to find out, we now have the facts due to advances in technology. The properties of water from different bodies, such as Mediterranean seawater and Atlantic Ocean water, differ. For one thing, they have different density. At the point where the two meet, each sea, due to its properties, remains as a separate entity, much like oil floats on water without getting mixed.

The Koran already knew this: "He has loosed the two seas, flowing together (side by side). There is a barrier between them. They encroach not (one upon the other). Which is it, of the favors of your Lord, that you deny?" (55:19–21). But this is not the only insight about oceans, because the Koran also describes other aspects of oceans: "Or as darkness on a vast, abysmal sea. There covers it a wave, above which is a wave, above which is a cloud. Layer upon layer of darkness" (24:40).

This verse discusses another notion that remained unconfirmed until recently. According to oceanographers, light barely penetrates at depths of about 200 meters below the surface of the ocean, and is completely lost at depths of 1,000 meters; this corresponds with the Koran's description of a "vast, abysmal sea." Also, it's been acknowledged that within those depths are internal waves occurring between layers of density, similar to the waves that occur upon the surface—also confirming the Koran's description in the previous verse.

Human Embryology in the Koran

Scholars say that more than forty verses in the Koran deal with conception and embryology of humans—a subject that was not researched until the seventeenth century. It wasn't until the mid-nineteenth century that some facts were established. Before then, there was a list of bizarre theories, some claiming that a female's egg already contains a microscopic human that is "activated" by sperm, and others claiming that the sperm contains the human and injects it into the egg. (These theories were formulated during the 1600s and 1700s.) But back in the 600s, the Koran had already explained the real process.

Conception

Allah presents a wise statement in the Koran: "We created you. Will you then admit the truth? Have you seen that (seed) which you emit? Do you create it or are We the Creator?" (56:57–59). Here, Allah is clearly stating that He created humankind as well as its ability to multiply. The Koran explains that semen causes pregnancy—a fact well known even to the people at the time of Muhammad. But the Koran goes on further to say that it is not the semen itself, but merely a drop (one sperm) of it that is needed: "Was he (man) not a drop of fluid which gushed forth?" (75:37).

ALERT!

Renowned Islamic scholars are not only experts on Islamic faith, but are also scientists. This conforms to the general Muslim belief that religion and science go hand in hand, and that whoever studies the Koran will learn a great deal of science.

Another characteristic of semen is that it determines the sex of the baby. For centuries, people around the world thought that women were responsible for the baby's sex, but science eventually proved them wrong. Surah 42:49 claims that Allah "bestows children male or female according to His Will." The Koran makes further note of the issue: "And that He creates the two spouses, the male and the female, from a drop (of seed) when it is poured forth" (53:45–46).

When sperm meets egg, fertilization occurs, forming a single cell called a zygote. Instantly, it begins to divide and multiply until it forms a tiny clot called an embryo. The Koran confirms: "We have created you from dust, then from a drop of seed, then from a clot . . ." (22:5). The Arabic word in the Koran for "clot" is *alaq*, which also means "clung to." Scholars believe the Koran is describing the next step after fertilization, when the clot clings to the uterus for its supply of blood and nutrients.

Development of the Embryo

After conception, the embryo, clinging to the uterus for life, begins to develop in stages. According to the interpretation of some scholars, a verse in the Koran describes three stages of early development: "He created you in the wombs of your mothers, creation after creation, in a three-fold gloom" (39:6).

There are three early stages of human development. First is the pre-embryonic stage, when the zygote divides into multiple cells and attaches itself to the wall of the uterus. Next is the embryonic stage, which lasts about five and a half weeks, during which the basic organs begin to develop. Finally, there is the fetal stage, which lasts throughout the rest of the pregnancy as the fetus continues to develop into a baby. The Koran describes the same process of development: "Then fashioned We the drop a clot, then fashioned We the clot a little lump, then fashioned We the little lump bones, then clothed the bones with flesh, and then produced it as another creation. So blessed be Allah, the Best of Creators!" (23:14).

More Scientific Facts in the Koran

Astronomy, geology, meteorology, and embryology are just a few of the topics discussed in the Koran. Upon closer inspection, one will come across an insight here or there about something that relates to our universe. The creation of pairs and the real source of iron are two interesting topics picked from an array of others.

Creation of Pairs

Allah says in the Koran: "Glory be to Him Who created all the pairs, of that which the earth grows, and of themselves, and of that which they know not" (36:36). At first glance, this verse appears to be talking about the creation of the male and female in all species, including humans. Upon further study, however, scholars conclude that there is a hidden meaning in "that which they know not."

In 1933, British scientist Paul Dirac was awarded the Nobel Prize for his discovery of antimatter. He proposed that matter is paired with its opposite: antimatter. For example, matter contains positively charged protons and negatively charged electrons, while antimatter contains negatively charged protons and positively charged electrons. The pair of matter and antimatter is believed by scholars to be the creation "that which they know not." Nevertheless, there could be more examples of hidden pairs of creation that are yet undiscovered.

Alien Element

Modern astronomical findings have documented that iron found on Earth has come from outer space. When stars explode, they throw their fragments in every direction. These fragments are often made up of about 90 percent iron. A fragment travels through space until it comes within a gravitational force, such as Earth's, pierces through the atmosphere like a fireball, and hits the ground at a tremendous force. This is called a meteorite.

Years ago—nearly 30,000 years and earlier—Earth was frequently pummeled by these meteorites. Scientists theorize these meteorites are responsible for the extinction of some species. With each meteorite, the earth's supply of iron increased. The Koran agrees: "We sent down iron, wherein is mighty power and (many) uses for mankind . . ." (57:25). According to this verse, iron found in the earth came from above, conforming to scientific fact.

Chapter 21

The Bible and the Torah: The Other Holy Books

The Koran confirms the existence of the Christian and Jewish Scriptures and demands belief in Jesus, Moses, and all other prophets. As the last Holy Book, the Koran carries a vision of Christianity and Judaism, stating that although these religions had once been similar to Islam, they were tampered with and altered to the form they are in today. There are many verses in the Koran that directly address Christian and Jewish people, refuting their beliefs, and inviting them to submit to Allah.

Muslims' Belief in the Holy Books

A Muslim is not a Muslim until he or she fully believes in all of Allah's Holy Books, which include the Christian Gospel and the Jewish Torah. Allah reveals this in the Koran:

> [S]ay (O Muslims): We believe in Allah and that which is revealed unto us, and that which was revealed unto Abraham and Ishmael, and Isaac, and Jacob, and the tribes, and that which Moses and Jesus received, and that which the prophets received from their Lord. We make no distinction between any of them, and unto Him we have surrendered. (2:136)

Believing is one thing, however, and following is another. Although Muslims believe in the Gospel and Torah (they know they exist), they do not believe them (that is, they do not subscribe to or follow the lessons and stories found in the books). Allah states in the Koran that these books were once His word, but some people have altered their text and twisted their meaning. So Muslims believe that these books were originally from Allah, but are no longer valid references. In other words, the Koran denies any truth to the Christian and Jewish Scriptures, except the parts that are in accordance with the Koran.

Interestingly, the Koran states that neither Jewish nor Christian people believe in the other's revelations: "And the Jews say the Christians follow nothing (true), and the Christians say the Jews follow nothing (true); yet both are readers of the Scriptures. Even thus speak those who know not. Allah will judge between them on the Day of Resurrection concerning that wherein they differ" (2:113).

Prophet Moses and the Torah

Moses was in Egypt when he received his first revelation. The Koran says that, like many other prophets, he hadn't known he was a messenger of Allah until adulthood. Moses is known as the prophet who brought Judaism, just like Muhammad is known as the prophet who brought

Islam. Moses was born sometime after Abraham and a few centuries before Jesus. He is famous among Muslims for his dealings with the savage Pharaoh of Egypt—a story related in detail in the Koran.

Along with their belief in Prophets Jesus and Moses, Muslims show them due respect by pronouncing "peace and blessing be upon him" with any mention of either name. Muslims apply this to every prophet and not only Jesus and Moses.

Prophet Moses and His Followers

When Moses saw a fire at a distance in the holy valley of Tuwa, he found himself drawn to it. The Koran narrates the incident, saying that at the site of the fire, Allah spoke directly to him: "And I have chosen you, so listen unto that which is inspired" (20:13). Moses recognized his duty as a prophet and fulfilled his Lord's request by visiting the Pharaoh's court to invite him to believe. The Pharaoh of Egypt at the time of Moses had been a brutal and arrogant man. He mocked Moses and rejected his message. However, with his God-given cane that changed into a snake, Moses was able to challenge the sorcerers of Pharaoh, and cause them to declare their belief in Allah.

Enraged, the Pharaoh showed no mercy to the sorcerers, then set out after Moses to hunt him down. The Koran continues: "And verily we inspired Moses, saying: Take away My slaves by night and strike for them a dry path in the sea, fearing not to be overtaken, neither being afraid (of the sea)" (20:77).

With Allah's will, the sea parted and let Moses and the believers through. The Pharaoh followed straight in with his soldiers, but his was a different fate: "[A]nd when We brought you through the sea and rescued you, and drowned the folk of the Pharaoh in your sight" (2:50). Allah had drowned the Pharaoh and saved the people of Moses.

The Children of Israel

Shortly after the people of Moses were saved, Prophet Moses left them under observance of his brother Aaron and was gone for several weeks to receive the revelation of the Torah. Upon his return, Moses discovered that his people were indulged in worshipping a calf of gold. A man named Samiri had taken the people's gold and possessions and melted them together, then produced a golden, hollow calf, which surprisingly made a sound like a real animal. Because of this account and a few others, the Koran speaks in a bitter tone about the children of Israel. In many verses, it relates that Allah's instructions were ignored, and his prophets were mistreated, such as in the following verse: "We made a covenant of old with the Children of Israel and We sent unto them messengers. As often as a messenger came unto them with that which their souls desired not (they became rebellious). Some (of them) they denied and some they slew" (5:70).

Jesus in the Koran

Muslims believe Jesus is a prophet like Moses and Muhammad. According to Islamic teachings, he is not God or the son of God, nor does he have any blood relation to God. However, there is no doubt in the Koran that Jesus is one of the most prominent prophets sent by Allah. The Koran confirms that Jesus was conceived miraculously and that his mother, Mary, carried him as a virgin. Jesus lived a life full of miracles to support his message, and according to the Koran, he never died on the cross, as Allah would not have allowed his prophet to suffer such a terrible death.

Mary's Pregnancy

Mary, known as Mariam in the Koran, has the honor of a Surah named after her. Surah Mariam contains ninety-eight verses, a decent portion of them narrating her story. The Virgin Mary is the mother of Jesus, a fact accepted by both Muslims and Christians. Mary was raised a devout Jewess. Prior to her pregnancy, Mary sought a quiet place far from her people: "And make mention of Mary in the Scripture, when she had withdrawn from her people to a chamber looking East, and had chosen seclusion from them" (19:16–17).

FACT

The birth and life of Mary, mother of Jesus, is recorded in the Koran. She was the daughter of the Imran family, which along with the families of Adam, Noah, and Abraham, is preferred by Allah above all families, as stated in the Koran. Mary's mother wanted a son to devote to Allah, but when a girl was born, she didn't hesitate to offer her to Allah.

Then the angels came to Mary, telling her: "O Mary! Allah has chosen you and made you pure, and has preferred you above (all) the women of creation" (3:42). Allah had chosen her to be the mother of the only unconceived child in the world. Naturally, Mary was dismayed and could not comprehend how she would be pregnant without having been with a man. Her words are quoted in the Koran: "[S]he said: How can I have a son when no human has touched me, neither have I been unchaste?" (19:20).

An angel answered her, saying, "Allah creates what He will. If He decrees a thing, He says unto it only: Be! And it is" (3:47). According to the Koran, all Allah did was say, "Be!" And that was enough to create a baby boy inside Mary. The angels also informed Mary of the child's name and his special role: "[T]he Messiah, Jesus, son of Mary, illustrious in the world and the Hereafter, and one of those brought near (unto Allah)" (3:45). They told her that Jesus would speak in his cradle, be a messenger for the children of Israel, and be inspired with knowledge of the Gospel and Torah.

The Birth of Jesus

Mary was pregnant, a virgin, and alone. When the time came, Mary sought the shade of a palm tree to deliver the baby. So intense was her pain that she wished she'd died before living that day: "[S]he said: Oh, would that I had died before this and had become a thing of naught, forgotten!" (19:23).

In several parts of the Koran, Allah says that he sent the holy spirit to Mary to deliver the news of her pregnancy. The Koran explains that this holy spirit is Angel Gabriel, who is the highest-ranking angel. Non-Muslims sometimes misinterpret the name, thinking it is the same spirit of God that the Bible talks about.

After the birth, Mary was weak and exhausted. Miraculously, her new-born baby tried to comfort her: "The (one) cried unto her from below her, saying: Grieve not! Your Lord has placed a rivulet beneath you; and shake the trunk of the palm tree toward you. That will cause ripe dates to fall upon you. So eat and drink and be consoled" (19:24–26). The angels' prophecy had come true, and the baby had spoken in his cradle.

When she regained her strength, Mary took the baby and returned to her people. They were not pleased to see her after so long, baby in her arms, and no husband. Apparently, the people thought Mary had an illegitimate relationship with a man—an act not readily tolerated by the Jewish people of the time. Mary didn't utter a word in her own defense, but pointed to her son instead. The Koran narrates: "He spoke: Lo! I am the slave of Allah. He has given me the Scripture and has appointed me a prophet, and has made me blessed wheresoever I may be, and has enjoined upon me prayer and alms giving so long as I remain alive, and (has made me) dutiful toward her who bore me, and has not made me arrogant, undisciplined. Peace on me the day I was born, and the day I die, and the day I shall be raised alive!" (19:29–33).

FACT

A Hadith states that Jesus was one of 124,000 prophets sent to human-kind before Muhammad. The Koran only mentions a few (35) and leaves the total number of prophets indefinite, but assures that every nation, tribe, or community of people had been sent a messenger who preached for the belief in Allah.

The Life of Jesus

The childhood and early manhood of Jesus are not mentioned in the Koran. However, his message is confirmed in the following verse: "And (I come) confirming that which was before me of the Torah, and to make lawful some of that which was forbidden unto you. I come unto you with a sign from your Lord, so keep your duty to Allah and obey me" (3:50). Jesus' message was clear as he continued: "Allah is my Lord and your Lord, so worship Him. That is the straight path" (3:51).

The people's reaction to the message of Jesus was like any other through history to any prophet: some accepted, but most rejected.

During his life, Jesus performed a number of miracles made possible by Allah's will. These miracles are described in the Koran in more than one Surah. Following every description is a confirmation that Allah permitted the performance of these miracles to convince the people of Jesus' divine message.

The Crucifixion

When rivalry began to sizzle against Jesus, a plot was devised to kill him. Those who disbelieved plotted to crucify him on the cross. The prelude to the crucifixion is not described in the Koran, and neither is the event itself. But Allah knew that the people were plotting to kill his prophet: "And they (the disbelievers) schemed, and Allah schemed (against them), and Allah is the best of schemers" (3:54). Just before they went to get Jesus, Allah raised him up to the Heavens and, as Muslims believe, replaced him with a look-alike. The look-alike was seized and crucified, while Jesus was safe in the Heavens with Allah.

The Koran narrates this story in the following verses: "And because of their saying: We slew the Messiah Jesus, son of Mary, Allah's messenger. They slew him not nor crucified, but it appeared so unto them" (4:157). Jesus was not crucified because he ascended, alive and healthy, to the Heavens: "(And remember) when Allah said: O Jesus! I am gathering you and causing you to ascend to Me, and am cleansing you of those who disbelieve and am setting those who follow you above those who disbelieve until the Day of Resurrection" (3:55).

Unoriginal Scriptures

Muslims believe that the Torah was sent to Moses and the Gospel to Jesus because it is mentioned in the Koran: "And verily We gave unto Moses the Scripture and We caused a train of messengers to follow after him, and We gave unto Jesus, son of Mary, clear proofs (of Allah's sovereignty)" (2:87). However, it is not possible for a Muslim to take up the Bible or Torah as a guide of faith because the Koran says these books are no longer in their original form. The alterations made were fundamental and are a far deviation from the teachings of the Koran.

FACT

The first five books of the Bible compose the Torah. These books are Genesis, Exodus, Leviticus, Numbers, and Deuteronomy. They are also part of what is known as the Old Testament. They were later incorporated into the Bible, and are used for reference by Christians.

Unoriginal Gospel

The Koran states quite clearly: "Therefore woe be unto those who write the scripture with their own hands and then say, 'This is from Allah,' that they may purchase a small gain therewith. Woe unto them for that their hands have written, and woe unto them for that they earn thereby" (2:79). The Koran does not say, "those who *will* write," or "those who *may* write." Instead, it speaks in the present tense, "those who write," indicating that writing the Scripture is an ongoing activity. The Koran further confirms that changes were already applied to the Scripture before the Koran was revealed when it says, "Woe unto them for that their hands *have* written."

According to the Koran, the Gospel contains information that goes against the teachings of the Koran. The Koran does not point out certain passages that do not agree, but it specifically rejects the Christian belief of the Trinity:

O People of the Scripture! Do not exaggerate in your religion nor utter aught concerning Allah but the truth. The Messiah, Jesus, son of Mary, was only a messenger of Allah, and His word, which He conveyed unto Mary, and a spirit (Angel Gabriel) from Him. So believe in Allah and His messengers, and say not "three." Cease! (It is) better for you! Allah is only One God. Far is it removed from His transcendent majesty that He should have a son. His is all that is in the heavens and all that is in the earth. And Allah is sufficient as Defender. (4:171)

Unoriginal Torah

According to the Koran, a Scripture was revealed to Moses, prophet of Judaism: "And when We gave unto Moses the Scripture and the Criterion (of right and wrong), that you might be led aright" (2:53). This "Scripture" is called the Torah by the Koran as well as Judaism. The Koran accuses the Torah of inconsistency and alteration. The Koran tells what Allah says about the Jews: "They change words from their context and forget a part of that whereof they were admonished. You will not cease to discover treachery from all, except a few of them. But bear with them and pardon them. Lo! Allah loves the kindly" (5:13).

There are many other differences between the Torah and the Koran, but the Koran only mentions a few. According to the teachings of the Koran, differences between the teachings of a previous Scripture and the Koran is clear evidence that the older text was subjected to alteration.

ALERT!

The Koran speaks of the "people of the Book (or Scripture)" numerous times throughout. This phrase refers to both Christians and Jews. When it is used in the Koran, Allah is usually addressing both groups.

Comparison of Beliefs

The Koran, Gospel, and Torah have many things in common, yet they also have many differences. Essentially, they all preach good conduct. They forbid things like murder, theft, adultery, lying, and preach of being kind to parents and neighbors. The differences among them lie on a more fundamental level, where each presents a different view of the Supreme Being. For example, the Bible suggests the Trinity (God the father, the son, and the Holy Ghost), and the Koran suggests one Supreme Being who has no family or partners.

Similarities Between Koran and Others

The command to avoid evil and do good is the basic similarity among the three Holy Books. This can be found in books of other religions as well, such as Buddhism. Another aspect is that all three are associated with a messenger of God: The Torah with Moses, the Gospel with Jesus, and the Koran with Muhammad.

Other important similarities among the three books are that they all call for belief in the Last Day, the Resurrection, and Heaven and Hell. Also, the Bible mentions that Jesus will return, as does the Koran. Above all, they enforce the concept of God's supremacy and eternity.

Christians, Jews, and Muslims have religious celebrations of their own. For example, the Christians have Christmas and Easter, the Jewish have Rosh Hashanah and Yom Kippur, and the Muslims have two: Eid Al Fitr, which immediately follows Ramadan, and Eid Al Adha.

Differences Between Koran and Others

The differences between the Koran and Torah lie mostly in the rituals, worship, traditions, and attitudes that they preach. The difference between the Koran and the Gospel runs deeper. Both Muslims and Jewish people believe in one God, but Christians see it slightly otherwise. Christians believe in one God with three parts. They say that God's ghost descended to impregnate Mary. As it was the seed of God, Jesus was consequently named His son. At the same time, Jesus was believed to be God on Earth.

Thus, the concept of the Trinity was born: God, the Son, and the Holy Ghost—three parts, but who are simultaneously one and the same. They also believe Jesus was crucified to wash away the original sin of Adam and save humanity from Hell. The Koran provides ample comments on Christian beliefs. Firstly, it denies the original sin of Adam because he repented, and Allah accepted his repentance and cleared his record (see Chapter 12). Second, Allah says that He created Jesus in his mother's womb out of nothing and simply by willing him into existence—just as Adam was created without a mother or father: "Lo! The Likeness of Jesus for Allah is as the likeness of Adam. He created him of dust, then He said unto Him: Be! And he is" (3:59).

Third, the Koran repeatedly confirms that the miracles of Jesus were performed by Allah's will (and not because Jesus is God), just like other prophets performed their miracles. Fourth, it states that Jesus did not die on the cross, but was raised to the Heavens, as the honor of a prophet is not to be wasted. And fifth, it directly denies the Trinity throughout. An elaborate display against the Trinity is found in the following verse: "And when Allah said: O Jesus, son of Mary! Did you say unto mankind: Take me and my mother for two gods beside Allah? He said: Be glorified! It was not mine to utter that to which I had no right. If I had ever said it, then You would have known it" (5:116).

In the Koran, Allah says that He sent Jesus to preach what Moses and all previous prophets had preached, which is belief in the one God. Accordingly, Judaism and Christianity ought to be identical, but they aren't. Muslims believe this is an indication that the Gospel and Torah have been altered by people's interference.

The Koran Calls for Belief in Allah

Muslims call themselves slaves of Allah—a term that sometimes causes others to frown. The Koran explains that Christian and Jewish people prefer a more affectionate description of themselves, such as "God's children" or "God's loved ones," but questions their use of these terms: "The Jews and Christians say: We are sons of Allah and His loved ones. Say, why then does He chastise you for your sins? No, you are but mortals of His creating. He forgives whom He will, and chastises whom He will" (5:18).

According to the Koran, every person, regardless of religion, will be judged and sent to either Heaven or Hell, depending on his or her deeds and beliefs. However, the Koran accuses Christians and Jews of claiming that Heaven is reserved for them alone:

> *And they say: None enters Paradise unless he be a Jew or a Christian. These are their own desires. Say: Bring your proof (of what you state) if you are truthful. Nay, but whosoever surrenders his purpose to Allah while doing good, his reward is with his Lord; and there shall no fear come upon them neither shall they grieve. (2:111—112)*

The key to Heaven is belief, which the Koran summarizes: "Lo! Those who believe (in that which is revealed unto you, Muhammad), and those who are Jews, and Christians, and Sabaeans whoever believes in Allah and the Last Day and does right surely their reward is with their Lord, and there shall no fear come upon them neither shall they grieve" (2:62).

Allah reminds His people that they should follow their religion the way it was revealed, and not the altered versions: "[F]ollow not the vain desires of folk who erred of old and led many astray, and erred from a plain road" (5:77). The Koran, from cover to cover, preaches the message that Allah is one, has no family, is the Supreme Being. It says that those who believe in Him will be rewarded, but punishment will come to those who don't.

Appendix A

Glossary

A

ablution:
Required washing of the arms, face, head, and feet prior to praying, reading the Koran, or engaging in other acts of worship.

Adam:
The first man, created by Allah out of clay. Known as the father of humankind and the first prophet.

Adhan:
The call for prayer announced by a mosque.

Allah:
The sole Creator of the universe, and eternal Supreme Being.

Al Barzakh:
The realm in which the souls of the dead live. Literally the "partition"; that is, the time between death and the resurrection.

Al Mahdi:
A caliph who is prophesied to appear in the future and lead gruesome battles near the end of time.

Al Massih Al Dajjal:
An evil creature that will appear in the time of Al Mahdi and claim he is God. He is one of the major signs of the Last Day.

angel:
A creature of light made to obediently serve Allah.

Angel Azrael:
The Angel of Death, who captures the souls of the deceased.

Angel Gabriel:
The angel who brought down revelations to Allah's messengers, and the one holding the highest position among the angels.

Arabic:
An ancient language that is still in use today among Arabs. It is the language of the Koran.

awra:
Part of the body that must be covered, i.e., from navel to knee for a man.

aya (or ayah):
Koranic verse.

B, D

Buraq:
The creature that carried Muhammad to the Heavens and back on Isra Wal Miraj.

Dabba:
A creature that Allah will release just shortly before the Last Day. It will speak to people and mark believers from nonbelievers.

Declaration of Faith:
An oath declaring belief in Allah as the only God, and in Muhammad as His slave and messenger.

E

Eden:
One of the elite Heavens.

Eid:
Muslim celebration. They are two: Eid Al Fitr, and Eid Al Adha.

Eve:
Adam's wife, created from his body.

F

fard:
Compulsory act or practice, such as fasting Ramadan.

fasting:
Refraining from food, water, and foul behavior from the dawn prayer to the sunset prayer.

G

Gospel:
The Holy Book revealed to Jesus.

H

Hadith:
Quotes of Prophet Muhammad.

halal:
Permitted act or practice.

Hajj:
Pilgrimage to the Kaaba in Mecca, performed at a certain time every year. Required at least once in a Muslim's lifetime unless too difficult for health or financial reasons.

haram:
Unlawful.

Hasana:
Good deed.

I

Iblis:

A creature of the jinn who was banished from the Heavens and cursed until the Last Day for refusing to obey Allah's command. Also known as Satan.

Iftar:

The meal that breaks the fast of a fasting person at sunset.

Ihram:

A pilgrim's costume, composed only of a white terrycloth, and his state of purity.

iman:

Faith.

Imam:

In mainstream Islam, an Imam is an elite Muslim scholar and the person who leads Muslims in group prayers. Shia's Imam is a Muslim supreme guide from Allah.

Islam:

The religion of the Koran, built on belief in the Six Pillars of Faith as well as prayer, fasting, pilgrimage, declaration of faith, and spending toward charity.

Isra Wal Miraj (Night Journey):

Prophet Muhammad's journey to the Heavens and back.

J, K, M

Jannah:
Heaven.

Jesus:
The prophet to whom the Gospel was revealed. Believed in Islam to be created out of nothing inside his virgin mother Mary. He was able to cure the blind and raise the dead by Allah's will. He ascended to the Heavens alive and did not die on the cross according to Islamic teachings.

Jihad:
Exerting an effort for Allah's cause.

jinn:
Creatures that were created out of fire. Among them are demons and decent Muslim jinn. They can see humans but humans can't detect them.

Kaaba:
The cube-shaped structure built by Prophet Abraham in Mecca believed to be directly aligned with Allah's throne in the Heavens.

Koran:
The Holy Book revealed to Prophet Muhammad. Believed to be 100 percent the word of Allah.

mahr:
A gift a groom offers his bride.

makrooh:
Undesirable act or behavior.

Mecca:
City in Saudi Arabia where the Kaaba is located. It is the birthplace of Prophet Muhammad, and the primary place of worship for Muslims.

Medina:
City in Saudi Arabia to which Prophet Muhammad migrated to escape the brutality of the Quraish.

Muhammad:
The last of all the prophets, to whom the Koran was revealed.

mubaah:
Permitted.

Munkar:
One of the two angels who interrogate a soul in the grave. (See also Nakir.)

Mujahid (plural, Mujahideen):
Person who strives in the cause of Allah.

Muslim:
Person who believes in the Six Pillars of Faith and practices the Five Pillars of Islam. He or she believes in Allah as the only God.

mustahab:
Desirable act or behavior.

N

Nakir:
One of the two angels who interrogate the soul in the grave. (See also Munkar.)

Night of Power:
One of the last ten nights of the month of Ramadan, in which the Koran descended onto the Preserved Tablet.

P

Preserved Tablet:
A board on which the past, present, and future of everything is recorded. It also contains the Holy Koran. It is located in the Heavens where no creature can reach it.

prophet:
A messenger appointed by Allah to invite a community to believe in Him.

Q

qadar:
Fate.

qibla:
The direction of the Kaaba, which Muslims face in prayer.

Quraish:
Prophet Muhammad's tribe.

R

Rakaa:
A portion of a Muslim prayer. The shortest prayer is made up of two Rakaas.

rassool (also rasul):
Prophet.

Ramadan:
A month in the Islamic calendar during which Muslims fast.

S

salaat:
Prayer.

shariah:
Islamic jurisprudence.

shaitan (or shaytan); plural, shayateen:
An evil jinn; a devil or demon.

Shia:
A sector of Muslims with a slightly different approach from mainstream Islam. Also known as Shiites.

Suhoor:
The meal taken just before the dawn prayer during Ramadan. Charges the body with a supply of energy to help it last a day of fasting.

Sunni:
Person who follows the teachings of Prophet Muhammad.

Sunnah:
The tradition, chronicles, habits, and quotes of Prophet Muhammad. Together with the Koran, it makes up Islam.

Surah (also Sura):
A chapter in the Koran.

T, Z

Torah:
The Holy Book revealed to Prophet Moses of Judaism.

Zakat:
Obligatory charity and part of the Five Pillars of Islam.

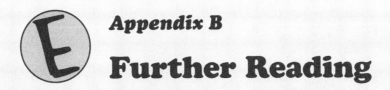

Appendix B

Further Reading

Abu El Fadl, Khaled. *The Place of Tolerance in Islam*. Boston: Beacon Press, 2002.

Al-Ashqar, Umar S. *The World of Jinn and Devils*. Boulder, CO: Al-Basheer Publications and Translations, 1998.

Ali, Muhammad. *A Manual of Hadith*. Lahore: Ahmadiyya Anjuman Ishaat Islam, 1992.

Ali, Muhammad. *History of the Prophets: As Narrated in the Holy Qur'an Compared with the Bible*. Lahore: Ahmadiyya Anjuman Ishaat Islam, 1992.

Anway, Carol L. *Daughters of Another Path: Experiences of American Women Choosing Islam*. Lee's Summit, MO: Yawna Publications, 1996.

Asad, Muhammad. *The Road to Mecca*. Chicago, IL: Kazi Publications, 1997.

Bayman, Henry. *The Secret of Islam: Love and Law in the Religion of Ethics*. Berkeley, CA: North Atlantic Books, 2003.

Bucaille, Maurice. *The Bible, the Quran and Science: The Holy Scriptures Examined in Light of Modern Knowledge*. New York: Tahrike Tarsile Qur'an, 2003.

Cleary, Thomas F. *The Wisdom of the Prophet: The Sayings of Muhammad*. Boston: Shambhala Publications, 2001.

Deedat, Ahmad. *Was Jesus Crucified*. Chicago, IL: Kazi Publications, 1992.

Esposito, John L. *Islam: The Straight Path*. New York: Oxford University Press, 1998.

Fernea, Elizabeth Warnock. *In Search of Islamic Feminism: One Woman's Global Journey*. New York: Anchor Books, 1998.

Khalidi, Tarif. *The Muslim Jesus: Sayings and Stories in Islamic Literature*. Cambridge, MA: Harvard University Press, 2001.

Lawrence, Bruce B. *Shattering The Myth*. Princeton, NJ: Princeton University Press, 2000.

Lewis, Bernard. *The Crisis of Islam: Holy War and Unholy Terror*. New York: Modern Library, 2003.

Lings, Martin. *Muhammad: His Life Based on the Earliest Sources*. Rochester, VT: Inner Traditions International, Ltd., 1987.

Madigan, Daniel A. *The Qur'an's Self-Image: Writing and Authenticity in Islam's Scripture*. Princeton, NJ: Princeton University Press, 2001.

Mitchell, Richard P. *The Society of the Muslim Brothers*. New York: Oxford University Press, 1993.

Nasr, Seyyed Hossein. *The Heart of Islam: Enduring Values for Humanity*. New York: HarperCollins, 2002.

Peters, F. E. *The Hajj*. Princeton, NJ: Princeton University Press, 1995.

Qutb, Sayyid. *Social Justice in Islam*. New York: Islam Publications International, 2000.

Renard, John. *Seven Doors to Islam: Spirituality and the Religious Life of Muslims*. Berkeley, CA: University of California Press, 1996.

Said, Edward W. *Covering Islam: How the Media and the Experts Determine How We See the Rest of the World*. New York: Vintage Books, 1997.

Sells, Michael. *Approaching the Qur'an: The Early Revelations*. Ashland, OR: White Cloud Press, 1999.

Appendix C

Selected Bibliography

Abdel-Ali, Hamudah. "The Economic Life of Islam." *Islam101. www. islam101.com/economy/economicLife.htm* (10 October 2003)

Abi Abdullah, Shamsuddin. *Ar-ruh: The Soul's Journey After Death*. New Delhi: Islamic Book Service, 2001.

Al-Asbahi, Malik Bin Anas. *A Synopsis of Worship in Islam*. Dubai: Al-Bayan Press.

Al-Awayishah, Husayn. *The Grave: Punishments and Blessings*. Riyadh: International Islamic Publishing House, 1998.

Al-Deen, Ameen Mohammad Jamal. *The Age of the Islamic Nation* (Arabic). Cairo: Al-Tawfeeqiya Library, 1996.

Ali, M. Amir. "Jihad Explained." *The Modern Religion. www.themodern religion.com/jihad.jihad-explained.html* (13 November 2003)

Al-Khazraji, Mohammad Bin Hasan. *Islamic Character and Manners*. New Delhi: Idara Ishaat-e-Diniyat, 1984.

Aniff, Mohammad. "Islamic Banking." *Asian-Pacific Economic Literature*, Vol. 2, No. 2 (September 1998): 46–62.

Armstrong, Karen. *Islam: A Short History*. New York: Modern Library, 2002.

Ataur-Rahim, Muhammad. *Jesus: A Prophet of Islam*. New Delhi: Islamic Book Service, 2002.

Azimabadi, Badr. *Three Hundred Authenticated Miracles of Muhammad*. Delhi: Adam Publishers and Distributors, 2000.

Bin Humaid, Abdullah Bin Mohammad. *Jihad in the Qur'an and Sunnah*. Riyadh: Dar-al-Salam Publishers and Distributors.

Browne, Edward G. *Islamic Medicine*. New Delhi: Goodword Books, 2001.

Bucaille, Maurice. "The Quran and Modern Science." *The Modern Religion. www.themodernreligion.com/science/science_bucaille.htm* (20 September 2003)

Cowen, Ron. "Galaxy Hunters: The search for cosmic dawn." *National Geographic*, February 2003, 2–29.

Esposito, John L. *The Oxford History of Islam*. New York: Oxford University Press, 1999.

Girardet, Edward. "A New Day in Kabul." *National Geographic*, December 2002, 90–103.

Gore, Rick. "The Rise of Mammals." *National Geographic*, April 2003, 2–37.

Hall, Mimi. "Typical Inmate: Abused, Abuser, Repeater." *USA Today*, 20 May 1993, p. 8A.

"Human Rights and Justice in Islam." *Islam Guide. www.islam-quide.com/ch3-12.htm* (19 October 2003)

"Jihad – A Misunderstood Concept from Islam." *The Modern Religion. www.themodernreligion.com/jihad/jihad-misunderstood.html* (21 October 2003)

"Jinn According to Quran and Sunnah." *Muttaqun Online. http://muttaqun.com/jinn.html* (10 October 2003)

Khan, Maulana Wahiduddin. *Islam and Peace.* New Delhi: Goodword Books, 2000.

Khan, Maulana Wahiduddin. *Woman in Islamic Shari'ah.* New Delhi: Goodword Books, 2000.

Kidawi, A. R. "Translating the Untranslatable: A Survey of English Translations of the Quran." *The Muslim World Book Review*, Vol. 7, No. 4 (1987). *Available:* Islam101.com; *www.islam101.com* (20 September 2003)

Nasr, Seyyed Hossein. *Islam: Religion, History, and Civilization.* New York: Harper San Francisco, 2003.

Philips, Bilal, and Jameelah Jones. *Polygamy in Islam.* Riyadh: International Islamic Publishing House, 1998.

Philips, Bilal. "Fortunetelling." *Islaam.com. www.islaam.com* (20 September 2003)

Pickthall, Mohammed Marmaduke. *The Meaning of the Glorious Quran.* Kuala Lumpur: Islamic Book Service, 2001.

"Prophet Adam." *The Sabr Foundation. www.islam101.com/history/people/prophets/adam.htm* (20 September 2003)

"Quranic Verses and Modern Scientific Discoveries." *The Modern Religion.* *www.themodernreligion.com/verses_sci.htm* (13 November 2003)

Sakr, Ahmad H. *Al-Jinn.* New Delhi: Islamic Book Service, 2001.

Salopek, Paul. "Shattered Sudan." *National Geographic*, February 2003, 30–67.

"Science and Islam: The Twin Sisters." *The Modern Religion. www.the modernreligion.com/science/science2.htm* (13 November 2003)

Seda, Pete. *Islam Is: An Introduction to Islam and its Principles.* Ashland, Oregon: Al Hamarain Islamic Foundation, 2002.

Shaheen, Jack G. *Reel Bad Arabs: How Hollywood Vilifies a People.* Northampton, MA: Interlink Publishing, 2001.

Uthaymeen, Shaykh Ibn. "The Islamic Verdict on Suicide Bombings." *The True Religion.org. http://thetruereligion.org/suicidebomb.htm* (10 October 2003)

Viviano, Frank. "Saudi Arabia on Edge." *National Geographic*, October 2003, 2–41.

Von Denffer, Ahmad. *Ulum Al-Qur'an: An Introduction to the Sciences of the Koran.* London: The Islamic Foundation, 1989.

Weeramantry, C. G. *Islamic Jurisprudence: An International Perspective.* Kuala Lumpur: The Other Press, 2001.

Yahya, Harun. *Allah is Known Through Reason.* New Delhi: Goodword Books, 2000.

Yahya, Harun. *Islam Denounces Terrorism.* Bristol: Amal Press, 2002.

Yahya, Harun. *Justice and Tolerance in the Quran.* Singapore: Nickledeon Books, 2003.

Yahya, Harun. *Miracles of the Koran.* Toronto: Al-Attique Publishers, 2001.

Yahya, Harun. *Terrorism: The Ritual of the Devil.* New Delhi: Islamic Book Service, 2002.

"Zina (Fornication)." *The Modern Religion. www.themodernreligion.com/ msc/hh/zina.html* (12 October 2003)

Index

A

Ablution, 4–5, 118–19, 264
Abortion, 64
Abraham, 48
Abu Bakr, 21, 26, 39
Abu Jahl, 20–21
Adam, 36, 70, 264
    Allah forgiving, 151
    angels bowing to, 146–47
    creation of, 144, 145–46
    Satan tempting, 150–51
    See also Creation
Addictions, 94–96
    alcohol, 94–95, 111–12
    drugs, 95–96
    smoking, 96
Adhan, 54, 264
Adoption, 67–68
Adultery, punishment for, 107–8
Afterlife
    belief in, 44, 50–51
    See also Last Day
Aisha, 22, 91
Al, defined, 33
Al Baqara (The Cow), 35–36
Al Barzakh, 179, 264
Al Dajjal (Imposter), 158–59, 264
Al Fatiha (The Opener), 32–33, 34–35, 182–83
Al Kurssi (The Throne), 34
Al Mahdi, 158, 264
Al Massih Al Dajjal, 158–59, 264
Alcohol use, 94–95, 111–12
Allah
    belief in, 44, 46–47, 183–84, 261–62
    creating man, 144–47
    declaring faith in, 45, 51–52

defined, 264
depiction of, 24
fear of, 120
invoking, before prayers, 49
meeting, in Heaven, 190
names of God and, 3
as primary Koran purpose, 3
remembering, 23, 121–22
Angel Azrael, 48, 164, 264
Angel Gabriel, 7, 265
    aiding in Koran preservation, 38
    death of, 164
    first revelation of, 7–9, 17–19
    number of visits by, 19, 34
    visiting other prophets, 18, 19
    See also Revelation, of Koran
Angel Israfil, 160–61, 164, 265
Angel of Death. *See* Angel Azreal
Angels
    appearing to people, 48
    attending deaths, 172–73
    belief in, 44, 47–48
    bowing to Adam, 146–47
    defined, 264
    dispute over creation, 144–45
    logging good/bad deeds, 118
Animals
    carcasses of, 99–100
    creation of, 147–48
    as miracles, 232–33
    slaughtering, 101
    treatment of, 126–27
Antonyms, occurrence of, 237
Apostasy, punishment for, 111
Aqsa Mosque, 25
Arabic
    alphabet make-up, 8
    consistency of, 9

defined, 265
English vs., 9
formal vs. dialects, 9
Armageddon, 156–58
    aftermath of, 157–58
    war of, 157
    word origin, 157
Astrologers, 128
Atmosphere, 242–44
Attitudes/virtues
    patience/tranquility, 122–23
    selflessness/generosity, 124
    truthfulness, 123–24
    See also Goodness

B

Banking, 115
Beasts of prey, 100
Behavior toward others, 125–26
    friends, relatives and, 126
    neighborly duties, 125–26
    protecting orphans, 125
Belief
    in Allah, 44, 46–47, 183–84, 261–62
    in angels, 44, 47–48
    in destiny, 44, 50
    in Gospel, 48, 252
    in Holy Books, 44, 45–46, 48–49, 252
    in Jesus, 49, 254
    as key to Heaven, 183–84
    in Koran, 44, 45–46
    in Last Day/afterlife, 44, 50–51
    in Moses, 49
    in Prophets, 44, 49
Beliefs, Holy Books comparison, 259–61

THE EVERYTHING SERIES!

BUSINESS

Everything® Business Planning Book
Everything® Coaching and Mentoring Book
Everything® Fundraising Book
Everything® Home-Based Business Book
Everything® Landlording Book
Everything® Leadership Book
Everything® Managing People Book
Everything® Negotiating Book
Everything® Online Business Book
Everything® Project Management Book
Everything® Robert's Rules Book, $7.95
Everything® Selling Book
Everything® Start Your Own Business Book
Everything® Time Management Book

COMPUTERS

Everything® Computer Book

COOKBOOKS

Everything® Barbecue Cookbook
Everything® Bartender's Book, $9.95
Everything® Chinese Cookbook
Everything® Chocolate Cookbook
Everything® Cookbook
Everything® Dessert Cookbook
Everything® Diabetes Cookbook
Everything® Fondue Cookbook
Everything® Grilling Cookbook
Everything® Holiday Cookbook
Everything® Indian Cookbook
Everything® Low-Carb Cookbook
Everything® Low-Fat High-Flavor Cookbook
Everything® Low-Salt Cookbook
Everything® Mediterranean Cookbook
Everything® Mexican Cookbook
Everything® One-Pot Cookbook
Everything® Pasta Cookbook
Everything® Quick Meals Cookbook
Everything® Slow Cooker Cookbook
Everything® Soup Cookbook

Everything® Thai Cookbook
Everything® Vegetarian Cookbook
Everything® Wine Book

HEALTH

Everything® Alzheimer's Book
Everything® Anti-Aging Book
Everything® Diabetes Book
Everything® Dieting Book
Everything® Hypnosis Book
Everything® Low Cholesterol Book
Everything® Massage Book
Everything® Menopause Book
Everything® Nutrition Book
Everything® Reflexology Book
Everything® Reiki Book
Everything® Stress Management Book
Everything® Vitamins, Minerals, and
           Nutritional Supplements Book

HISTORY

Everything® American Government Book
Everything® American History Book
Everything® Civil War Book
Everything® Irish History & Heritage Book
Everything® Mafia Book
Everything® Middle East Book

HOBBIES & GAMES

Everything® Bridge Book
Everything® Candlemaking Book
Everything® Card Games Book
Everything® Cartooning Book
Everything® Casino Gambling Book, 2nd Ed.
Everything® Chess Basics Book
Everything® Crossword and Puzzle Book
Everything® Crossword Challenge Book
Everything® Drawing Book
Everything® Digital Photography Book
Everything® Easy Crosswords Book
Everything® Family Tree Book

Everything® Games Book
Everything® Knitting Book
Everything® Magic Book
Everything® Motorcycle Book
Everything® Online Genealogy Book
Everything® Photography Book
Everything® Poker Strategy Book
Everything® Pool & Billiards Book
Everything® Quilting Book
Everything® Scrapbooking Book
Everything® Sewing Book
Everything® Soapmaking Book

HOME IMPROVEMENT

Everything® Feng Shui Book
Everything® Feng Shui Decluttering Book, $9.95
Everything® Fix-It Book
Everything® Homebuilding Book
Everything® Home Decorating Book
Everything® Landscaping Book
Everything® Lawn Care Book
Everything® Organize Your Home Book

EVERYTHING® KIDS' BOOKS

All titles are $6.95

Everything® Kids' Baseball Book, 3rd Ed.
Everything® Kids' Bible Trivia Book
Everything® Kids' Bugs Book
Everything® Kids' Christmas Puzzle
    & Activity Book
Everything® Kids' Cookbook
Everything® Kids' Halloween Puzzle
    & Activity Book
Everything® Kids' Hidden Pictures Book
    Everything® Kids' Joke Book
Everything® Kids' Knock Knock Book
Everything® Kids' Math Puzzles Book
Everything® Kids' Mazes Book
Everything® Kids' Money Book

All Everything® books are priced at $12.95 or $14.95, unless otherwise stated. Prices subject to change without notice.

Everything® Kids' Monsters Book
Everything® Kids' Nature Book
Everything® Kids' Puzzle Book
Everything® Kids' Riddles & Brain Teasers Book
Everything® Kids' Science Experiments Book
Everything® Kids' Soccer Book
Everything® Kids' Travel Activity Book

KIDS' STORY BOOKS

Everything® Bedtime Story Book
Everything® Bible Stories Book
Everything® Fairy Tales Book

LANGUAGE

Everything® Conversational Japanese Book
    (with CD), $19.95
Everything® Inglés Book
Everything® French Phrase Book, $9.95
Everything® Learning French Book
Everything® Learning German Book
Everything® Learning Italian Book
Everything® Learning Latin Book
Everything® Learning Spanish Book
Everything® Sign Language Book
Everything® Spanish Phrase Book, $9.95
Everything® Spanish Verb Book, $9.95

MUSIC

Everything® Drums Book (with CD), $19.95
Everything® Guitar Book
Everything® Home Recording Book
Everything® Playing Piano and Keyboards Book
Everything® Rock & Blues Guitar Book
    (with CD), $19.95
Everything® Songwriting Book

NEW AGE

Everything® Astrology Book
Everything® Dreams Book
Everything® Ghost Book
Everything® Love Signs Book, $9.95
Everything® Meditation Book
Everything® Numerology Book
Everything® Paganism Book
Everything® Palmistry Book
Everything® Psychic Book
Everything® Spells & Charms Book
Everything® Tarot Book
Everything® Wicca and Witchcraft Book

PARENTING

Everything® Baby Names Book
Everything® Baby Shower Book
Everything® Baby's First Food Book
Everything® Baby's First Year Book
Everything® Birthing Book
Everything® Breastfeeding Book
Everything® Father-to-Be Book
Everything® Get Ready for Baby Book
Everything® Getting Pregnant Book
Everything® Homeschooling Book
Everything® Parent's Guide to Children
    with Asperger's Syndrome
Everything® Parent's Guide to Children
    with Autism
Everything® Parent's Guide to Children
    with Dyslexia
Everything® Parent's Guide to Positive Discipline
Everything® Parent's Guide to Raising a
    Successful Child
Everything® Parenting a Teenager Book
Everything® Potty Training Book, $9.95
Everything® Pregnancy Book, 2nd Ed.
Everything® Pregnancy Fitness Book
Everything® Pregnancy Nutrition Book
Everything® Pregnancy Organizer, $15.00
Everything® Toddler Book
Everything® Tween Book

PERSONAL FINANCE

Everything® Budgeting Book
Everything® Get Out of Debt Book
Everything® Homebuying Book, 2nd Ed.
Everything® Homeselling Book
Everything® Investing Book
Everything® Online Business Book
Everything® Personal Finance Book
Everything® Personal Finance in Your
    20s & 30s Book
Everything® Real Estate Investing Book
Everything® Wills & Estate Planning Book

PETS

Everything® Cat Book
Everything® Dog Book
Everything® Dog Training and Tricks Book
Everything® Golden Retriever Book
Everything® Horse Book
Everything® Labrador Retriever Book
Everything® Poodle Book

Everything® Puppy Book
Everything® Rottweiler Book
Everything® Tropical Fish Book

REFERENCE

Everything® Car Care Book
Everything® Classical Mythology Book
Everything® Einstein Book
Everything® Etiquette Book
Everything® Great Thinkers Book
Everything® Philosophy Book
Everything® Psychology Book
Everything® Shakespeare Book
Everything® Toasts Book

RELIGION

Everything® Angels Book
Everything® Bible Book
Everything® Buddhism Book
Everything® Catholicism Book
Everything® Christianity Book
Everything® Jewish History & Heritage Book
Everything® Judaism Book
Everything® Koran Book
Everything® Prayer Book
Everything® Saints Book
Everything® Understanding Islam Book
Everything® World's Religions Book
Everything® Zen Book

SCHOOL & CAREERS

Everything® After College Book
Everything® Alternative Careers Book
Everything® College Survival Book
Everything® Cover Letter Book
Everything® Get-a-Job Book
Everything® Job Interview Book
Everything® New Teacher Book
Everything® Online Job Search Book
Everything® Personal Finance Book
Everything® Practice Interview Book
Everything® Resume Book, 2nd Ed.
Everything® Study Book

SELF-HELP/ RELATIONSHIPS

Everything® Dating Book
Everything® Divorce Book
Everything® Great Sex Book

All Everything® books are priced at $12.95 or $14.95, unless otherwise stated. Prices subject to change without notice.

Everything® Kama Sutra Book
Everything® Self-Esteem Book

SPORTS & FITNESS

Everything® Body Shaping Book
Everything® Fishing Book
Everything® Fly-Fishing Book
Everything® Golf Book
Everything® Golf Instruction Book
Everything® Knots Book
Everything® Pilates Book
Everything® Running Book
Everything® T'ai Chi and QiGong Book
Everything® Total Fitness Book
Everything® Weight Training Book
Everything® Yoga Book

TRAVEL

Everything® Family Guide to Hawaii
Everything® Family Guide to New York City,
  2nd Ed.

Everything® Family Guide to Washington D.C.,
  2nd Ed.
Everything® Family Guide to the Walt Disney
  World Resort®, Universal Studios®,
  and Greater Orlando, 4th Ed.
Everything® Guide to Las Vegas
Everything® Guide to New England
Everything® Travel Guide to the Disneyland
  Resort®, California Adventure®,
  Universal Studios®, and the
  Anaheim Area

WEDDINGS

Everything® Bachelorette Party Book, $9.95
Everything® Bridesmaid Book, $9.95
Everything® Creative Wedding Ideas Book
Everything® Elopement Book, $9.95
Everything® Father of the Bride Book, $9.95
Everything® Groom Book, $9.95
Everything® Jewish Wedding Book
Everything® Mother of the Bride Book, $9.95
Everything® Wedding Book, 3rd Ed.

Everything® Wedding Checklist, $7.95
Everything® Wedding Etiquette Book, $7.95
Everything® Wedding Organizer, $15.00
Everything® Wedding Shower Book, $7.95
Everything® Wedding Vows Book, $7.95
Everything® Weddings on a Budget Book, $9.95

WRITING

Everything® Creative Writing Book
Everything® Get Published Book
Everything® Grammar and Style Book
Everything® Grant Writing Book
Everything® Guide to Writing a Novel
Everything® Guide to Writing Children's Books
Everything® Screenwriting Book
Everything® Writing Well Book